Horary Astrology
Rediscovered

Horary Astrology Rediscovered

A Study in Classical Astrology

Olivia Barclay, Q.H.P.

A division of Schiffer Publishing, Ltd.
1469 Morstein Road
West Chester, Pennsylvania 19380 USA

Horary Astrology Rediscovered
by Olivia Barclay

Library of Congress Card Number: 89-051779
International Standard Book Number: 0-914918-99-0

Manufactured in the United States of America

Published by Schiffer Publishing, Ltd.
1469 Morstein Road
West Chester, Pennsylvania 19380
Please write for a free catalog.
This book may be purchased from the publisher.
Please include $2.00 postage.
Try your bookstore first.

Dedication

Dedicated to Jupiter
through whom, under God,
much goodness reaches us

"The heavens declare the Glory of God; and the firmament showeth his handywork."

--Psalm 19:1

"Heaven is the instrument of the Most High God whereby he acts upon and Governs Inferior Things."

--The Tenth Aphorism of Cardan

"Nothing is as old as the truth and nothing is as new as the truth."

--Hazrat Inayat Khan, *The Guyan*

List of Contents
and Main Diagrams

Acknowledgment

I would like to acknowledge my debt to William Lilly and all the astrologers before his time. Also to those who assisted me in a practical way, Jane Ardizonne, Esther Arendell Q.H.P., Sue Ward Q.H.P. and Honor Kupicha.

Foreword

Robert Hand

Inanimate nature may be subject to immutable laws but the techniques of consciousness expansion are human arts and statements about the essence of a culture and its people. Cultures and peoples change. Therefore a change in an art of consciousness is an indication that the art is truly relevant to human needs. It is not an indication of inherent flaws or weakness. Astrology has undergone change in the twentieth century, and as with all such changes, there is much that is good and much that is not so good.

The greatest change within astrology has been the movement of astrology from a primarily predictive tool to a tool for the exploration of human consciousness; the Humanistic Astrology movement, led by the late Dane Rudhyar and the late Marc Edmund Jones. These two and their many disciples saw that the old astrology was no longer appropriate for modern humanity. We needed something more than an astrology that saw life as the working out of blind fate in the lives of individuals. Most modern humans do not perceive life purely as the result of fate. We feel a strong sense of our responsibility for the creation of our own lives. Even in those moments in which we feel most victimized by conditions seemingly beyond our control we try to glimpse energies flowing from within us that help to create the circumstances in which we live. We needed an astrology that would help make us more aware of our own energies, to help us take responsibility for them and acknowledge our own creativity within our own destiny.

This new astrology saw the planets and other symbols of astrology as signs of our own unfolding and of our creative potential, of what we could be as well as what we would be. We saw the older astrology representing us as victims of whimsical fortune leaving us with little to do but await the inevitable. It was rejected as "fatalistic." For the most part, the new Humanistic Astrology was an evolution, a step forward.

But some change may have been simply for the sake of change. Some change is simply wandering off track. And whenever this happens, further change is needed to bring us back on track. As we gained a new perspective of ourselves and our relationship to destiny, we also nearly lost much that was of value in the old astrology, which we need to reclaim. Much of this is embodied in horary astrology, the art of answering questions by means of astrology.

Horary Astrology has held an ambiguous place in the transformation of twentieth century astrology. It seemed to many of the practitioners of the "new" astrology to be a kind of atavistic survival, a fortune-telling technique in a time of the quest for self-development. Yet it has been practiced by many of the best and brightest of modern astrologers, the late Barbara Watters for example. One member of the Humanistic Astrological movement even attempted to bring horary in line with the ideology of that movement in a book on humanistic horary astrology. But despite the vitality of horary in modern times, it has reminded many of Kepler's description of all of astrology in the early seventeenth century. He described astrology as the "foolish daughter" of her old mother, astronomy, who nevertheless justified herself by earning the money needed to keep her old mother well. It seemed to many that there was conflict between what horary astrology had to show us and the program of Humanistic Astrology.

More recently in the 1980s a new movement has begun in astrology. At first look it seems to be a kind of counterrevolution, an attempt to go back to the "old-fashioned," fortune-telling astrology of the Middle Ages and Renaissance. It consists of a reaction to excessive modernism and a return to the study of the classics of Western Astrology from ancient times through the Renaissance. But it was much more than a mere reaction, a turning back. A major effort was under way to recapture and hold on to what was being lost by the humanistic school.

Different astrologers will give somewhat different accounts of exactly what was at stake and what follows is simply this astrologer's effort at describing what seemed to be the limitations of the humanistic school.

Modern astrology as a whole, not merely the Humanistic school, has broken with the past on much more than the fortune-telling issue. And simple ignorance of what the old traditions really said was as much of factor as was a conscious effort to improve. Granting that many of the older authorities simply parroted astrologers that had come before them without critical review, many moderns went to the opposite extreme and began promulgating teachings that completely contradicted tradition without being themselves any more thoroughly thought out. Everyone felt free to innovate on their own. While this was not all bad, the various opinions of the various authors began to muddy the waters of astrology to the extent where one could not see anything clearly. We have run the risk of restructuring the symbols so that everything in astrology always and at any time can mean anything.

Typical of this trend is the current work on the symbolism of the planetoid (now known to be a comet), Chiron. Chiron is obviously important to modern astrology, but a reading of the literature on the subject leads one to believe that Chiron has rulership over everything. Symbolic rigor is lacking here. And the work on Chiron is not significantly more defective than the work being carried on in other areas of symbolism as well. Is the Ego symbolized by the Sun, the Moon, the M.C., the Ascendant or Saturn. In modern literature we find all of the above. Nor do we usually find a definition of the term *Ego*.

We have other sources of muddiness as well. Pollyanna is rampant! In modern astrology nothing is bad, nothing is necessarily good, any aspect can be wonderful and all is love and light! This, despite the fact that even in the best of lives there is considerable pain and almost every astrologer, at least in private moments, will acknowledge that, while nothing is necessarily evil, there are many symbols that usually designate discomfort.

What modern astrology often overlooks is that if everything means everything then nothing means anything. It lacks any kind of symbolic rigor. The goals which modern astrology seeks to serve are worthy, but they are not clearly thought out. But horary astrology is a practical astrology. Questions demand answers. Answers demand rigorous and logical interpretation of symbols. Horary can serve to bring us back to symbolic rigor. Symbolic rigor can help us build a truly solid and therefore useful astrology. We should all realize as well that symbolic rigor only improves the communication that the symbols have to offer us. It does not in any way make our view of life more fatalistic. It makes the many alternatives clearer.

A second point is related to this first one. Modern astrology tends to be very abstract. We have seen the literature of modern depth psychology, especially the work of C.G. Jung, and it is good. It provides a language that modern humans can relate to. It promises to bring astrology back into the mainstream out of the backwater of strangeness and disrepute. But it has also brought into being a language that is none too precise in its meaning and which is often divorced from everyday experience.

I do not reject the discriminating use of modern psychological vocabulary and concepts in astrology. It would be arrogant as well as wrongheaded to assume that the astrological tradition knows all and has nothing to gain from mixing with other traditions, but we must be careful about how we do this. Depth psychology might describe an individual as an introverted, sensation type. Astrology might describe another individual as headstrong, rash, easy to anger with a tendency to take foolish risks. Language and human nature being what they are, neither description is completely precise in the way that physics might be in describing the path of a projectile. But the second description, a description that an astrologer might give of an Aries or angular Mars type, is much more readily intelligible to most people. Astrology is capable as a language of giving very clear and definite descriptions of human personalities. We must be careful not to lose this strength with a new language that sounds academic but may be meaningless.

But the older astrology was even more concrete than that. Saturn was not merely an aspect of the human ego. It was also anything old, rejected, solid but lacking in glamour, bones, teeth, and rocks. It was low places on the earth. In the vision of the old astrology everything bore the signature of the astrological symbols. We were not dealing only with a device for human potential but with a language that gave insight into all aspects of the workings of the world, a world in which ourselves and our consciousnesses were integral parts. All of the symbols were immediate and at the same time showed a spiritual dimension of existence that would speak to us constantly if we would but listen.

Divination is a word that has not been wholly respectable in recent years. Yet what does it mean? It means knowing what the Divine is doing, what the state of the spiritual underpinning of reality is. It is prophecy in the original sense of the word, not the prediction of the future, but the explanation of the present.

If one truly understands the word *mysticism*, astrology is applied mysticism. Materialists should be banned forever from using the word. To them mysticism is simply mystification, a source of confusion and of an irrational understanding of the nature of things. Mysticism is much higher than that. It is the understanding that beneath the apparent diversity of the universe and despite the seeming alienation of all beings from each other and nature, it is all One. Our inner and outer worlds are one. We are all one with each other, despite our barriers. The old astrology showed us a world in which Venus was within ourselves as well as in our gardens, that Saturn was an old bone dug up from the earth as well as our inner sense of order and strength. By showing us that the same symbols exist in the outer world as exist within our psyche, it showed us that we and It are one. Astrology is the day to day experience that the universe is one. In such a universe it is not necessary to ask how astrology could work. How could it not?

This immediateness of symbols is the main thing that horary can show us. A practical art with practical methods and objectives, it seems at times to be mundane and without spiritual depth as it pursues its ends, yet it reveals the working of spirit in the most seemingly ordinary of human activity. It is therefore an art to be used with care and discretion. One should not bother Spirit needlessly with trivial questions. But yet even when one asks a question that seems to be purely of interest for personal gain, the answer reveals that the spirit is working within nature. Horary in the hands of the skilled practitioner is capable of waking up the blind and materialistic to what really lies within the world.

In this book Olivia Barclay shows that very dimension of horary. Even the lost pet cat precedes in a universe where the symbolism declares the nature of the cat's essence, a universe where at some level the cat matters. She reveals that nature and ourselves are bound together by a network of living metaphors. And she does so completely within the tradition of Western horary. Her astrology is scholarly without being stuffy and academic. She has read the classics as well as the best of the moderns and she uses what they teach in her practical art. The practical and the spiritual become one. Horary at its best is truly living astrology and this is that kind of horary.

Orleans, Massachusetts
April 1989

Preface

In studying astrology one needs to forget the ego with its tiresome introspection and look deeply and uncompromisingly for the truth, for astrology is a Divine subject.

There is a belief that each of us is comprised of many bodies: besides our physical body we have emotional, psychic, and thinking bodies, as well as our Inner Spirit. It seems that not only does the Inner seek to know the unity of existence, but the thinking body too, can search for it, and the nearest it can get is through astrology. Astrology demonstrates the Oneness of life. Thought, through the brain can only grapple with the idea, but the Inner Spirit, which exists without conscious thought, finds unity by inner experience according to the Path you choose. This has nothing to do with astrology, for in the Spirit there is no thought. Certainly you can have astrological theory about intangible matters, but that is no nearer the Spirit than any other mental occupation, and usually consists of many words about not very much.

When the ancient Egyptians said, "Man, know thyself" they did not mean "psychoanalyze your ego." They more probably meant "meet your Inner Spirit", surely a far greater experience. This misunderstanding has practically lead to the deification of psychoanalysis.

With the knowledge of planetary and star positions our thinking selves can work out the quality of the moment extant, and if we are following traditional astrology we can prove we are correct by the sequence of events that follow. We can translate the planetary positions into the meaning of mundane events, and even thought forms, so that if the question arises in the mind at a particular moment the likely outcome can be calculated. This is horary.

In trying to understand why ancient astrology is more effective than ours I have concluded that centuries ago powers of observation were highly developed. We can see this by our ancestors' paintings and sculpture. The structure of society was different, enabling people to practice their arts, and their ability for creative thought appears to have been greater than ours. They did not have the slogan, "Time is Money." Their environment was more conducive to astrology.

In our own society we do not have time for deep thought, we are concerned with the business of life. I contend that it is from the ruminations of an unhurried mind that creative thought emerges, whether in music, sculpture, or astrology. If we could forget our present conditioning, remove ourselves from the press and shove of our times, fix our minds on the miraculous reality of our existence and that of the earth and sky, forget the cleaning and shopping and gardening, then in that time we contact a greater understanding.

Liz Greene writes that prediction was possible in the concrete medieval world, but that universal consciousness has shifted and so it is no longer possible. But it is rather the astrological method that has changed, not the consciousness. *If You Use The Ancient Methods You Will Achieve The Ancient Results.* It is only that nobody will pause to learn how to do it. If you clear away most of the clutter of modern innovation it is still possible to make a likely prediction.

There is a very interesting book called the *Hermetica,* the ancient Greek and Latin religious and philosophic teachings ascribed to Hermes Trismegistus in which you can read of the Creation with astrology included. It describes the theory of planetary energy present, molding us, penetrating, seated in our very nerves and sinews. "For at the time when each of us is born and made alive, the daemons [planetary energies] who are at that moment on duty as ministers of birth take charge of us."[1]

This is obviously a different idiom from our own, yet what it boils down to is that planetary energy is present at the time of birth, which molds us, and that is the unlikely theory behind our very study!

Astrology in no way contradicts Christianity, and many Popes and Cardinals have practiced it. Here are the words of Saint Augustine, "and so if anyone use judicial astrology for studying...those things which are dependent on natural causes and the heavenly bodies, it is plainly not a sin."

The sentence in the *Hermetica* I personally appreciated was: "The Ruler of Heaven is Zeus, (Hypatos) for life is given to all beings by Zeus through the Medium of heaven." There is Zeus Neatus "responsible for life in air" and Zeus Chthonios "responsible for the fruits of the earth."[2] It has always seemed to me that our present society is in the grip of a Saturnine science (at least since the industrial revolution and reliance on coal), and that it is working to destroy Zeus and his plentiful fruits of the Earth by the systematic destruction of our environment. Jupiter--Zeus--is under-estimated in our thinking and in our chart interpretations.

It is through the agency of Jupiter, under God, that great good reaches this world, for are there not principalities and powers?

Introduction

As we hurtle through space on this ball of rock we call Earth, we look out at the Universe to see where we are. It has always been so. Since pre-history, in the very first century of man's existence, or in the twentieth century A.D., the relationship between Earth and the Universe is the same, the laws the same.

Astrology is the comparison of the position of the heavens with events on Earth. If we can calculate where the stars will be, we can also conjecture the trend of events which will take place here on Earth. The prediction of these events is not necessarily the purpose of our watching, however; that is just an incidental bonus and the living proof that the comparison exists--that life is one, that as it is Above so it is Below, and the Inner is as the Outer, and there is one Life and one Law. I see no reason for saying any branch of astrology is divination, whether it is the analysis of the moment of birth of a human being or of a question.

I read that my viewpoint has been expressed before in a book called the *Speculum Astronomiae*, by Roger Bacon or Albert Magnus. "If births are natural things then interrogations [horaries] are natural things."[1]

The motivation that eventually brings us to a deep and serious study of astrology is the compulsion to penetrate the reality behind manifestation. Now we see as through a glass darkly, captive within our senses, but if our thoughts search undeviatingly for the truth, we arrive in the end at astrology. It is undeniably the design in which all life participates; it is, in the words of Cardan, "The Instrument of the Most High God, whereby He acts upon, and Governs Inferior things."

For horary astrologers it is a language to learn and think in, a language of symbols discovered and revered thousands of years ago. It would be foolish to ignore or repudiate it.

Horary is the part of that ancient tradition least tampered with by present day writers. It is also, perhaps, the part of astrology that is most difficult for our present society to believe, because the premise upon which it is based is not materialistic or tangible any more than life itself, yet it is observable.

Our classical Western predictive tradition, which is probably even older than the Indian tradition, [2] is the obvious complement to the use of astrology in psychology with which we have all become so familiar. The earliest chart fragments and interpretations that I have seen are in a book called Greek Horoscopes [3] by Neugebauer and van Hoesen. This covers a period between the time of Darius in 406 B.C., and including the lifetime of Vettius Valens, until the fifth century A.D. Here we see the succession of astrology from Egypt to Greece as we read the words of Antigonus studying the methods of the Egyptians before him. (It is interesting that these early chart fragments are circular.)

We have the testimony, too, of Manilius, who lived at the time of Christ, and who wrote a beautiful poem called the Astronomica.[4] We also have the testimony of Ptolemy's Tetrabiblos in the second century, and The Mathesis of Firmicus Maternus in the fourth century. (These books are now translated and available.) After astrology was so persecuted that it was driven from Europe, it was preserved and enriched by the

Arabs, and we benefit from the contributions of such men as Al Biruni, Albu Mashar, and many others. In the twelfth century Bonatus and then Cardan in Italy added their knowledge to our art.

But it was not until the seventeenth century that this knowledge was translated into English by our greatest predictive astrologer, William Lilly, in his eight-hundred-page masterpiece, *Christian Astrology*. It remains the definitive work on horary astrology, and its information is as true today as when it was written. Lilly explains carefully and laboriously exactly how he reached his conclusions, for his Sun was in Taurus. Yet the book is not easy to understand, being in the language and idiom of his times. I hope my small book will be a useful adjunct to those struggling to absorb what Lilly teaches, and will bring a contemporary outlook and new impetus to horary astrology. I hope it will make clear to beginners that astrology is not a form of entertainment, and to those experienced in our art that prediction can as probably be derived from the tropical zodiac as from the sidereal. Proficiency in this art takes many years and is not as simple as it looks. Its rewards, however, are very great.

I am indebted to William Lilly for nearly all I write--and so are most English-speaking astrologers, whether they know it or not.

Many of the rulers and rulerships are different in horary astrology from those natal astrologers have been taught. Bear with this. Do not let it anger you. You will find these rulerships work for horary.

Part One: How to Do It

Chapter 1
The Moment
and the Question

A moment of time has its qualities, whether that moment is of an event, or a birth, or the crystallization of a problem, as in horary. The analysis and interpretation of that moment is our art, and shows the inter-relatedness and Oneness of the Universe. The acknowledgment by a horary astrologer of the importance of thought form is not materialistic, though the problems dealt with may be very practical.

At the outset there is the question. I would like to express my personal feelings about it, and you may not agree with my opinion. For me, the moment of the question is a moment of contact with a greater intelligence. To that extent it is divine. The planetary and fixed star positions then extant are an expression of that greater intelligence, a writing that our pea-sized brains can decipher, once we understand the code. From that pattern, that state of the Universe, we understand to the best of our ability the outcome of the moment.

Consider the breathtaking significance of this. We are probing for the truth, we are not playing a parlour game. Someone religious could pray for assistance at such a time. An astrologer may joke in public, but at work he is in earnest. If not, you may know that individual for a charlatan. This does not mean you cannot ask about the winner of the Grand National if you do so with sincerity and in accord with that particular time. But if you ask a question at the wrong time you will get no reply. It is wonderful that your earnest curiosity for a reply will come at the right moment. William Lilly said it depends on our nearness to God, though others might use a different terminology.

Being able to recognize the moment when your question is ripe is not easy, but it is very important. It is a moment of deep and sincere thought, and should be written down when you are quite sure of the wording. Include the exact time; this way you will not change a word of it. The time of judgment is when the astrologer *understands* the question, *not* when the querent first thinks of it. Indeed, the question may have been in the querent's mind for several years!

If it is something you should not ask, the chart will show that it is invalid. Perhaps it would be wiser not to enquire. The chart also will be invalid if some other worry is in the forefront of your mind, and concern with it is confusing the response, or if you have already asked the question before, by horary, or by the I Ching, Tarot, or some clairvoyant. *There is only one time for each question so you cannot ask twice.* Half the secret of horary is knowing the moment when your question comes to a head.

The enquirer, or *querent*, is symbolized by the Ascendant and its ruler, and usually by the Moon. These are called the *querent's significators*.

The person or matter being enquired about is called the *quesited*, and is symbolised by the planet ruling the sign on the cusp of the house that pertains to the question. This is referred to as the *quesited's significator* or symbol.

When the question has been understood by the astrologer and the chart drawn up there is the judgment. In this the whole chart is evaluated and considered. This process has nothing to do with psychic ability or hazy impressions. Just as in a court of law you abide by the law of the land, so in astrology you judge by the universal laws of astrology. First you must learn to read and understand these laws; nothing is invented and hopefully nothing important is omitted. The facts are before you and you read and interpret them. You decipher the code, and if you are clever enough, you sum up the situation shown by the heavenly positions. It is not your responsibility, you are only the interpreter, but you must be sure you understand the code, the language of the stars. The heavenly bodies will show you what to say; they will indicate what has happened and what will happen. You can rely on that.

I have come to the conclusion that the horary chart is much like a photograph. It describes a situation, its environment, and the main characters involved. Like a photograph, if it is well focussed the imagery should be crisp and clearly defined.

For many years I used the astrologer's location to calculate the chart for the question, but now I have concluded that, like a photograph, the "picture" can be taken from more than one position. This is especially so if the question is asked by telephone and the astrologer fully understands it while it is being asked. In these circumstances, provided the chart gives a clear description of the situation and the chart is in no way invalid, I would use the querent's location rather than the astrologer's, but otherwise I use my location. The criterion is that calculations must be based on the time the astrologer understands the question.

The Ascendant and its ruler should describe the querent; to the extent to which the querent is implicated in the question. The Moon will show what he or she is thinking. Slowly one learns to recognize an apt chart. But if you use the location of the querent, be wary of using the time the person started to think of the problem. The time must always be when the question is clearly formed and expressed and the astrologer understands fully with the intention of analyzing it by horary astrology. When the question occupies the querent's mind to the obliteration of all else, it is then that it will be truly in focus.

A horary question will not tell you about a psychological condition, nor will it make any moral judgment, nor help you counsel anyone. It *will* tell you the facts. For example, if you ask whether you should buy a specific house, the chart will tell you if the price is too high. If you ask whether you would be better off without your husband, it might tell you that he is a short distance away, having an affair with a large lady who drinks a lot. If you have lost your diamond ring, it can tell you where it is.

The answers to these questions can be tested for the truth. However, if you have not used the correct ruler of a house, if, for instance, you have preferred Pluto as ruler of Scorpio instead of Mars, you will look for your ring in the wrong place. This is useful for checking your astrology. Horary astrology appears to work best with the traditional planetary rulerships.

To the general public of the twentieth century prediction is an amusing idea. Most people do not in their hearts believe it. To someone learning astrology, its reality begins to dawn, and some may think it wiser to ignore impending difficult aspects looming in their progressions. It may seem better to live happily and hopefully.

However, specific problems can and do arise for which I, for one, appreciate help. In fact, this seems the only excuse for inquiring into the future: the need for help with a problem. These problems are the realm of horary. It is much simpler to ask a direct question and work out a direct answer, than to wrest it from a natal chart with progressions, transits, and ambiguities. You need never ask what you do not want to know.

Chapter 2
The Planets

During this century the great emphasis on psychology, and the adaption of astrology for psychological purposes has almost smothered knowledge of traditional predictive methods, or altered them beyond recognition.

Many of the attributes which our ancestors associated with the planets have been annexed, in modern natal astro-psychology, by the signs, so that it is hard to know whether a quality belongs to the one or the other. Does red belong to Mars or Aries, does freedom belong to Jupiter or Sagittarius? Very often it seems to belong to both. Nevertheless, there are some qualities which the sign has, that the planet ruling it does not. Aries, for instance, is eastern; Mars is not. The modern tendency has been, as I say, to take the values away from the planets, but the planets were there first, where it all started. They were the physical bodies in the sky that early astrologers watched; they were the symbols of the matters about which our ancestors asked. They were the chess pieces and the sky was the chessboard.

Books from which "astrology" is now taught give lists of adjectives connected with the planets. For horary, these need to be changed into nouns. Venus, for example, is natural ruler of rings and money. Jupiter is the natural ruler of horses. The Sun is the natural ruler of men, and the Moon the natural ruler of women.

In horary there are two ways of determining the significator for which you are searching. One is to take the ruler of the house concerned, that is, the planet ruling the sign on the house cusp. The other way is to consider the planet that is the natural ruler of the matter. These frequently identify. Suppose you are looking for your car keys. First, you would look at the second house cusp, because the second house signifies your possessions. Perhaps you find the sign Aries is there. You then look at Mars, its ruler. Look at its house position, its sign, and its dispositor. But you would also look at Mercury, the natural ruler of keys. You need to know the sort of things connected with each planet.

The evaluation of the planet's position is extremely important. Its strength can be assessed and a score given if you are in doubt. For example, if the ruler of the illness was stronger than the ruler of health (sixth house ruler or first house ruler) astrologer-doctors knew that the patient might not easily recover. But their rules were full of further complications. If you want to arrive at the truth you often have to evaluate the planets. There is a Table of Fortitudes, handed on to us from Ptolemy, by which we can assess these "dignities" of the planets, and which I will discuss later.

Meanwhile, following is a list of the planetary rulerships. I include some of the information from the seventeenth century book of Lilly's, *Christian Astrology*.

The Sun

The Sun well-placed is equivalent to a benefic planet. It is more temperate than Mars. Yet a planet within 8 degrees of the Sun is unfortunate and weakened, (except Mars) and is called *combust*, so long as it is in the same sign as the Sun.

The Sun is the natural ruler or symbol of gold, the heart,

men, gentlemen, royalty, magistrates.

In a daytime chart it represents the father, the person in charge, the king of the castle, workers in gold, minters of money. It symbolizes someone who will keep a promise, who is trustworthy, judges well, behaves humanely and royally, who has favorites like a king, who walks or drives in the middle of the road. Such a one speaks deliberately with few words, loves luxury, (does not want to be entertained in the kitchen). No sordid thought can enter his heart! If the Sun is not well placed, of course, it symbolizes a less admirable man, one purblind in judgment, arrogant, domineering, tiresome, extravagant, a snob, one who hangs onto someone else's generosity, and thinks the world owes him a living.

Illnesses of the Sun are connected with the heart, mouth, or eyes. The Sun's colors are gold, yellow, scarlet, and purple.

Plants associated with the Sun are those that smell pleasantly, grow majestically, and love the Sun, usually being red or yellow. These plants were once believed to strengthen the heart and provide comfort, to clear the eyes, and help one resist the effects of poison.

The places related to the Sun are grand buildings, such as theatres and palaces.

The Sun rules not only gold, but also rubies.

The Sun rules the sign Leo.

Leo is eastern, animal, fiery, barren, masculine, commanding, and creative. (This may seem an incongruous list to natal astrologers, but if you are looking for a house, eastern may be the very word you require!)

It rules the back, ribs, and sides of the body, and all diseases, pains, and weaknesses of them. The eyes are also in its domain.

The places it rules are wild and rocky, barren and inaccessible, as well as forests and woods. It rules buildings that are eminent, castles, theatres, palaces. When considering the interior of a house, associate fireplaces and the areas in the vicinity of fireplaces with Leo.

Old descriptions of a person's physical appearance must surely be modified with the present mixtures of races. However, large eyes and head (goggle eyes), upturning curly hair which springs upward from the forehead, and uneven teeth are a signature of Leo.

Leonine countries include Italy and France. Rome and Bristol are Leonine cities.

The Moon

As the Queen is the strongest piece in chess, so is the Moon the strongest planet in horary. If the Moon makes no aspect in the chart, it is called *void of course*, which means nothing can be done about the situation.

The Moon is like a verb; it is of interest when deciding timing, and its speed should be taken into account. It shows what the querent is thinking about.

The Moon is feminine, nocturnal. It signifies a soft, tender creature, who searches after novelties, with a natural propensity to move her home, who is changeable in all things, timid, easily frightened, peace-loving, who wants to be irresponsible. It also shows a person who knows something of many trades.

If badly placed, it signifies someone who dislikes work, who drinks too much and is idle, not really caring about the conditions in which she lives, especially if at the same time Saturn is badly placed and is in aspect to the Moon.

The Moon can symbolize women, and those whose work is connected with the sea, with breweries, water, and liquids. In Mundane astrology it symbolisms the general public.

When related to physical appearances, the Moon shows faces that are pale, circular and Moon-like or Moon-shaped. When it is in watery signs, it indicates freckles.

The Moon is connected with illnesses of the stomach, women's complaints, rheum of the eyes, rheumatism, the bladder, measles, coughs, and what used to be called "rotten coughs."

The Moon's colours are pale, but especially the colour and metal silver. Mother-of-pearl, pearls, and anything that reflects are also in the Moon's domain.

It rules plants that do not have much flavour, such as unripe fruits. The Moon's plants have thick, soft, juicy round leaves. Mushrooms also are associated with the Moon.

Animals that live in water, like frogs and all shellfish, as well as the night owl are Moon-ruled.

The Moon's places are wet, such as rivers, fish ponds, boggy places, and baths.

It rules stones like crystal.

The Moon rules the sign Cancer.

Cancer is a northern, feminine, movable, fruitful, watery, mute sign, home-loving, and sentimental.

It rules the stomach and breasts, and all illnesses and diseases connected with them. Dropsy, too, is associated with Cancer.

The places it rules are watery: the seaside, estuaries, rivers, springs, wells, navigable waters, marshes, ditches with rushes, damp basements in houses, wash-houses, and cisterns.

The people signified by Cancer usually have Moon-shaped faces, small eyes, and are heavier in the upper body than in the lower. Saturn in this sign, however, greatly changes the appearance and makes it much bonier. The nose, instead of turning up, then has a high bridge.

The average Cancerian person can be recognised by his or her interest in food and cooking.

Cancer countries include China and the United States.

Mercury

Mercury can be either masculine or feminine, being strongly influenced by any connected planet, either by its dispositor or by aspect. It changes sex or attitude accordingly.

Mercury represents any sort of communication, letters, papers, the tongue, words, travelling short distances here and there, cars, talking.

It is the natural significator of the arms, hands and shoulders.

Mercury is also the significator of subtlety, tricks, cunning, and perjury.

It symbolises someone who is clever, intellectual, good at discussion, logical, eloquent, a researcher, witty, interested in learning, enjoys travel, interested in divination. If the person is in the trades, he or she is very inventive and clever. Mercurial people are tall and thin with high foreheads, and long arms and fingers. Mercury when connected with Saturn is heavy, with Jupiter temperate, with Mars rash, with Venus jesting.

Mercury symbolises mathematics (as well as statisticians and computers), tradespeople, office workers, secretaries, writers, poets, advocates, printers, accountants, solicitors, tailors and dressmakers. The illnesses it rules are connected with the head and those parts related to communication. Diseases of the brain, headaches, stammering, imperfections of the tongue, delusions, defective memory, hoarseness, dry cough, all snufflings in the head and nose, too much spittle, dumbness are related to Mercury.

Its colors are grey and mixtures, and its metal is quicksilver. Multi-colored stones are Mercury-ruled.

Mercury's plants are multi-colored and grow in sandy, barren places. They are said to help the tongue, brain and memory. They include some of the grasses.

The places associated with Mercury are shops, markets, fairs, schools, bowling alleys, and tennis courts.

In Mundane astrology it would represent the press.

Mercury rules the sign Gemini.

Gemini is a western, human, airy, nervous, intellectual, double-bodied sign. It is masculine.

It rules the arms, hands, shoulders, and veins, and any infirmities connected with them. Problems with the nerves, breathing, and delusions also come under this sign.

Its places are high and airy, hills and mountains. Upstairs rooms, as well as rooms where we play, write, or read are ruled by Gemini. High places, and chests and boxes are associated with this sign.

Mercury describes a body that is tall and straight. In centuries past, it would show a person with eyes that were piercing and hazel, (but now, of course, we are a mixture of races, so this may be tempered) and of good sight, who possessed excellent understanding, and astuteness in worldly matters. Notice that Geminians gesticulate frantically in order to communicate even more fully. They also seem to like the colour emerald green.

One country with a probable Gemini Ascendant is the U.S.A.

Mercury also rules the sign Virgo.

Virgo is southern, earthy, feminine, barren, dry. It rules the intestines and any illness connected with them.

Its places include those associated with grain or groceries. Outdoors this includes haystacks and corn fields. Rooms where work is carried out, such as offices or studies, where books are kept, cupboards, and store rooms of merchandise are Virgo's domain. It also suggests things at floor level or low down.

The body is not as tall as that associated with Gemini. People who limp, or nearly limp, or who walk with their feet pointed inward often belong to this sign. They are sometimes studious and interested in history. Virgos seem to like small brown patterns.

I find Virgos look downward and often find lost articles on the ground, especially metal ones.

One country ruled by Virgo is Switzerland.

Venus

Venus is called a Benefic. It is fortunate and rules such matters as affection, love, good deeds, money, victory, enjoyment, and amusement.

It is a feminine planet. Venus symbolises a quiet person, not likely to quarrel, who is pleasant, affable, enjoys food and wine and lovemaking, who is always having love affairs, is musical, sociable, enjoys baths, and is not very interested in hard work.

When badly placed it makes one extravagant, riotous, careless, and lazy, without credit or repute, and inclined to bed where one should not, who spends time drinking with loose companions.

Physical attributes are good looks and full lips. Women, in particular, are pretty with "eyes full of amorous enticement." The true sign of Venusian influence is a dimpled face. Venus does not bring height, but roundness.

It symbolises jewellers, painters, drapers, musicians, songs, (though now Neptune also seems to be connected with music), wives, mothers, young women, upholsterers, perfumers, decorators. It also is associated with everything for female adornment and beauty, as well as purses and cash.

Venus signifies those illnesses connected with the back and belly, and with sex. It also signifies hernias.

Its colors are light, such as sky blue, and its smells are delectable.

Venusian plants include sweet apples and white roses (surely all roses?), peaches and apricots, lilies and lily of the valley.

Copper belongs to Venus, as do lapis lazuli, coral, alabaster, cornelian, and blue sapphire.

Venusian places are gardens, fountains, bedrooms, beds, wardrobes, cushions, dancing schools, places connected with beauty and art.

Venus rules the sign Taurus.

Taurus is a southern sign, earthy, feminine, animal, fixed, domesticated, obstinate. It is a strong sign, slow to move, signifying one who loves beauty and slow-beat music.

It rules the throat and all illnesses and diseases connected with it. Its rulership of the throat produces fine singing voices.

The places associated with Taurus are low houses, farm buildings for animals, pasture and agricultural land, lightly wooded places, the countryside. It rules low-ceilinged rooms and cellars.

The Taurean body is short and strong with a large chest and shoulders. Women are Junoesque.

Taureans often like the colour of green grass.

Countries connected with Taurus include Ireland and Cyprus.

In his book on metals and astrology, Nick Kollerstrom tells us that women have more copper in their bodies than men, *1 and Venus has always ruled both copper and women!

Venus also rules the sign Libra.

Libra is a western, moveable, airy, masculine, humane sign.

It rules the kidneys, loins, and haunches, and all illnesses and diseases of them. It also is connected with corruption of the blood.

Libra's places are high and windy, hillsides and mountains, also outhouses, and places where wood is cut. Inside houses, it represents the upstairs rooms, attics, one room within another, also bookshelves, and high places.

In Libran people, thought rather than emotion predominates, and words flow easily. They are straight-bodied, with attractive and well-proportioned faces; their necks are sometimes short. They have soft voices, enjoy pleasant surroundings and melodious music. They seem to like the color sky blue, and always prefer harmonious colours.

Japan belongs to Libra, and so does the city of Lisbon.

Mars

Mars is masculine, fiery. It is considered the lesser Infortune, the starter of quarrels, the planet of strife and anger, an initiator of action, and a help when it is ascending in a combat chart.

Mars well positioned denotes someone who is courageous, war-like, bold, and confident. It also signifies a person who is immovable, without reason, contentious, challenging, who enjoys war, peril, and everything to do with it. This sort of person obeys nobody, submits to nobody.

If Mars is badly placed it signifies someone who loves slaughter, quarrels, murder, thievery, who is a promoter of riots, fights and commotion. It indicates a traitor, perjurer, or one who is obscene, rash, inhuman, fearing nothing, un-thankful, treacherous, furious, violent, and boasting.

Mars gives a physical body that is strong, with big bones, and rather lean. The Martian Anglo-Saxon has a reddish face, often red and sandy hair, and sharp eyes. Mars represents an active and fearless man. If Mars is on the eastern half of the chart, the man's body is hairy. A strong Mars shows a scar on the face.

Mars rules soldiers of all sorts, generals, captains, ser-geants, gunners. It also rules butchers, surgeons, and every-one who uses knives and firearms, or works with metal, such as watchmakers, barbers, cutlers, and carpenters. It indi-cates all who rule by oppression, all who mock and scorn.

It signifies high fevers, migraines, shingles, all wounds and cuts. If Mars is in a fire sign, it often shows burns. All frenzies, all hurts from iron, all illnesses that result from too much anger are Martian in nature. It rules the left ear.

Mars rules the colours red, yellow, and orange, and tastes that are bitter.

Its plants have sharp, pointed leaves and taste hot. They grow in dry places. Nettles, thistles, radish, and prickly thorn trees are Martian plants. Mars rules iron, nettles contain even more iron than spinach. Nick Kollerstrom in his book on astrology and metals tells us it has been discovered that men have more iron in their blood than women. And we know that Mars rules both iron and men.

Mars rules the sign Aries.

Aries is eastern, masculine, moveable, cardinal, fiery, angry, animal, intemperate, and violent.

It rules the head and face, and all pimples and disfigurements thereon. Ringworm, headaches, baldness, as well as some mental troubles are associated with Aries.

The places connected with Aries are those where animals such as sheep are kept, hiding places (suitable for thieves), isolated places, newly-ploughed land. In houses, the roofs, ceilings, and plastering are Arien.

Aries describes a person with a lean body with large bones, a longish face and chin. I distinguish Arien individuals by their love of competitive sport, which includes every sort of ball game. They often like the colour bright blood red. If you want to find them, look at the front of the queue. Their red cars, too, are usually in the fast lane. I find they start out energetically, but never finish.

Aries countries include England and Germany.

Mars also rules the sign Scorpio.

Scorpio is northern, feminine, fixed, watery, fertile, subtle, mute, secretive, deeply emotional, passionate, and jealous.

It rules the sex organs and all illnesses connected with them.

Its places are those where insects and beetles proliferate, especially poisonous ones. Scorpio is the natural ruler of reptiles, thus, it rules ruins, bogs, stinking places, lakes, gardens, orchards, moors, and muddy places. In houses, the kitchen or rooms with water in them, as well as anywhere damp would be associated with Scorpio.

Scorpionic people are frequently slightly bow-legged. Their eyes are close under the brows. The energy of Mars here is brought under control. These people do not start quickly, like Aries, but sustain their energy and finish their work with thoroughness. Although they do not respond to reason, only to emotion, their expressions remain dead pan and controlled, so you would never know. Their conversation may stray to the subjects of death, sex, or plumbing. They make wonderful detectives, and forget nothing. We all know what passionate lovers they are.

The blood red enjoyed by Aries, because of the delayed action of Scorpio, now has turned a deeper colour, to maroon, and mixes with the colors of the deep sea, dark green, for Scorpions have great depth.

One country associated with Scorpio is Morocco. I noticed there was an earthquake in Turkey the day Uranus entered into this sign. Liverpool is a Scorpio city. The Liverpool beat sound of the Beatles coincided with the transit of Neptune into Scorpio. Note the word "Beetle" in my paragraph above regarding places ruled by Scorpio.

Jupiter

Jupiter is known as the Greater Benefic. It is masculine, temperate, fair-minded, protective, happy, content, lucky and large.

People ruled by Jupiter are magnanimous, faithful, grateful, and aspiring in thought. They have integrity and deal fairly with others. Whatever gods they have, Jupiterians love them. These people are charitable to needy causes and dislike anything sordid. They are large in body, thought, and deed.

If Jupiter is badly placed these people may be wasteful, hypocritical, wanting everyone to make a fuss over them. They also can be stiffly conventional.

The Jupiter-ruled body is upright and tall, and the teeth wide, with the front ones uneven. The face is oval (like Elvis Presley's), and the men often have black beards. They have strong thighs, and hence love walking. The feet are the most unattractive part of the body.

Jupiter rules judges, senators, councillors, ecclesiastics, clergy, lawyers, woollen drapers, foreigners, and middle-aged men.

Illnesses of Jupiter concern the liver, lungs, palpitations, pains in the back, and illnesses caused by too much good living.

Jupiter also rules sweet scents, large gentle animals, always horses, and whales.

Its plants include figs, linden trees, mulberry, and acanthus (which apparently still grow larger on the Temple of Jupiter in Rome than anywhere else!).

Jupiter's places are courts of justice, altars, important public places, and foreign places.

Its metal is tin, its stones amethyst, topaz, emerald, marble, and surely sujelite.

Another side of Jupiter symbolises gambling, luck, horse racing jockeys, the winner in any matter. There seems to be some affinity with advertising, no doubt because it is enlarging, for Jupiter enlarges all it touches.

Jupiter placed in the tenth house of your natal chart will put your name in a newspaper.

Its colours seem to be royal blue, and colours containing indigo, such as purple and navy blue.

In the ancient world it was considered that Jupiter produced Nature, it is the planet of birth and plenty.

Jupiter rules the sign Sagittarius.

Sagittarius is an eastern, fiery, masculine, part animal (the last part), double-bodied, freedom-loving, optimistic sign. It is the sign and joy of Jupiter.

It rules the thighs and backside and any diseases or illness concerning them, as well as falls from horses and hurts in sport.

The places it rules are open and high, where one can see into the distance: hills and fields, open sea and high mountains. It also is connected with places where large animals live. In houses, Sagittarius represents upstairs near the fireplace.

Sagittarian people are inclined to tallness and have large front teeth. They enjoy outdoor life, and are especially fond of walking with long strides. They also drive fast. All Sagittarians love nature, whether they preserve it, or (if Mars is strong) hunt it. Nature is where they feel at home. They often wear tweeds with large checks and navy fisherman's jerseys.

Spain is a Sagittarian country;Toledo one of its cities.

The flippancy of Sagittarians often covers deep thought.

Jupiter also rules the sign Pisces.

Neptune certainly has an affinity here.

Pisces is a northern, watery, feminine, fruitful, mute, dreamy, bi-corporeal, indecisive, self-effacing sign. It represents lack of action.

It rules the feet and infirmities of them, yet limping seems to manifest more often in the opposite sign Virgo. Pisces also rules what old books call "moist diseases."

The ground it denotes is full of water: places where there are water fowl, springs, wells and pumps, and rivers--especially when full of fish. Places of meditation, buildings such as churches, hospitals, and prisons are Pisces-ruled. Inside houses, floors and floor coverings, places where shoes are kept, and places near standing water are connected with Pisces.

Piscean people have fine hair, which women sometimes wear long, like mermaids. They do not have strong, straight backbones, and have difficulty finding comfortable shoes. These people enjoy the sea and usually like eating fish. They often have short legs. A country belonging to this sign is Portugal.

Saturn

Saturn is the greater Infortune, or Malefic. It is cold, melancholy, pessimistic, limiting, solitary.

It represents a man who is severe, austere, reserved, speaking little, patient, someone who will acquire the goods of this world by slow and steady stages. If Saturn is badly placed it represents someone envious, covetous, mistrustful, timid, who condemns women, and is never content.

It signifies a body of medium height, pale complexion and black eyes. It relates to those who work with the earth, farm laborers, miners, plumbers (who work with lead), old men, and in a night chart, fathers. Monks and solitary religious people, and beggars also are represented by Saturn.

It rules the back teeth. Deafness, illnesses caused by cold or melancholy, rheums, fears and nightmares are Saturn-related, and if in Leo or Scorpio it causes ruptures. It is the natural significator of lead and could indicate lead poisoning.

Places ruled by the planet are deserts, pine woods, places near yew trees, obscure valleys, churchyards, wells, eaves, holes, ruins, graves, dirty or dark places. In houses, doors or thresholds (because Saturn rules boundaries and limits) are connected with Saturn.

Its tastes are bitter and sharp.

Besides lead, Saturn rules diamonds and all hard black stones, also ordinary stones that are grey.

Its colour is black.

Nick Kollerstrom tells us in *Astrochemistry* that the bones of old people contain more lead than those of young people, and both the old and lead share one symbol.

Saturn rules the sign Capricorn.

Capricorn is a southern, moveable, earthy, feminine, melancholy, animal, cardinal, ambitious, depressed, hard-working sign.

It governs the knees and all diseases connected with them;

also those of the skin or bone.

The places it rules are farm sheds where animals are kept, especially goats, or where farm implements or wood is stored, sheep pens, barren fields, dung heaps in fields, bushy or thorny land, and mountain paths. In houses it is associated with places near the floor or threshold.

Saturnine people are hard-working and efficient, the men often bearded, and the women's hair often thin. They have narrow chins. Their houses frequently contain a goatskin rug. Usually they like goats. They also like ladders.

Capricorn countries include India and the Orkneys.

Saturn also rules the sign Aquarius.

Aquarius is western, airy, fixed, masculine, rational, humane. The old books say it is the principal house of Saturn, "the house wherein he most rejoiceth," (they often used the word house instead of sign).

Aquarius governs the legs and ankles, and all illnesses of them. It also rules defects of the blood circulation.

The places it rules are hilly and uneven, newly dug, quarries, places where minerals have been discovered, vineyards, and places near a little spring or conduit. In houses roofs and upstairs rooms are related to Aquarius, as are places off the floor or near windows.

Aquarian people like waves of any sort, be they waves of the sea, sound waves, or statistics illustrated in waves. They are interested in photography. They seem to like the colour yellow.

Countries belonging to this sign include Russia.

Uranus

Uranus is thought by some to have affinities with Aquarius. In horary the outer planets usually only add information to what is indicated by the traditional ones. I mean that the "yes" or "no" answer to a question, the "headlines," can usually be judged without them. Mrs. Watters tells us how they can add some "special conditions existing in the social world beyond the control of the querent." [2]

Uranus, as every astrologer knows, rules unexpected matters like earthquakes, electricity, revolutions, as well as aircraft and airfields. It certainly seems to be a natural indicator of divorce in horary charts, and also of telephone calls.

It represents eccentric and unusual people.

It probably is related to the circulation of the blood, and in my opinion rules the colour prussian blue.

It obviously rules uranium.

Neptune

Neptune represents whatever dissolves. It is vague and nebulous. Drugs, alcohol, poison, weakening illnesses, sleep, and fraud are Neptunian. Visions and visionaries, in whatever form they express themselves, are ruled by Neptune. So are occupations of the ocean, such as sailing and fishing.

I always think poppies belong to Neptune--especially the mauve ones. The colours of seaweed, misty colours, the colour where the sea becomes almost purple, relate to Neptune.

I doubt if it rules any metal, but perhaps it rules all gasses. Certainly the Bhopal disaster occurred with the entrance of Neptune into Capricorn (the sign which rules India).

Pluto

Pluto, for me, equates with the word "ejection," also, "bringing to light." I hear that in the U.S.A. it is sometimes connected with plutocracy--a lot of money. This is interesting because Manilius called the second house the Gate of Hades, and the Portal of Pluto. Firmicus called it the Gate of Hell, and it reminds one of the Bible story of the rich man for whom it was difficult to reach heaven. (Remember the second house rules riches.)

Obviously, it is connected with plutonium.

Pluto also seems to be associated with death.

Benefics and Malefics

The natural benefics are Jupiter and Venus. These are called Fortunes. The natural malefics are Saturn and Mars. They are called Infortunes.

The natural beneficity or maleficity of planets is tempered by house position, contact with other planets and the Nodes, by speed of motion, and by whether they have what is known as "essential dignity." Essential dignity means a planet is in its own sign, exaltation, triplicity, term, or face (which will be explained in a later chapter).

As mentioned above, Saturn and Mars are naturally malefic; however, they may not always be so. It depends on the question and on the houses they rule. If, for example, they rule the fourth, sixth, eighth, or twelfth houses in a chart they are often considered unfortunate. But if either of those planets symbolises the querent or quesited they may not be malefic at all. Lilly, for instance, shows a chart of the reunion of two brothers. One is symbolized by Venus and the other by Saturn retrograde. The trine between the two planets shows the hoped for meeting of the two, "who did agree lovingly together." Saturn represented a saturnine man.

Conversely, Jupiter and Venus are benefic naturally, yet if they rule unfortunate houses in a chart they could be unfortunate.

The Moon is function, the action, the verb. We can see from its contacts what has happened and what will happen. The aspects made by the Moon include any made from the sign in which it is placed. This is a peculiarity of horary. Once the Moon has left the sign it is in, matters are beyond the scope of the question asked. If it makes no aspect between its present position and the end of the sign it is in, it is called void of course, and nothing can be done; the matter is not achieved. Only major aspects are considered at first.

The Moon going to an aspect of Jupiter, ruler of the unfortunate twelfth house, could mean imprisonment. The Moon going to an aspect of Saturn, ruler of the eleventh, a fortunate house, could mean the fulfillment of some earnest hope.

Every horary astrologer, unlike natal astrologers, must be aware of the relative speeds of planets. This concept pervades all chart interpretation, and beginners must think of our solar system and how our planets move--but more of that later.

Chapter 3

The Houses

Without a clear knowledge of the matters ruled by each house it is useless to attempt to understand horary astrology. Every action, every event, every thing, and every person in this life belongs to one of the houses. You have to understand your question and its implications, then look for the house that is involved.

This rulership is not a matter of opinion, but of facts tried and tested by generation after generation of astrologers for thousands of years. The rules are fixed as in a chess game. You cannot change them half-way through.

William Lilly wrote in *Christian Astrology*, "he that shall learn the nature of the Planets and Signs without exact judgment of the Houses, is like an improvident man, that furnisheth himself with a variety of household stuffe, having no place wherein to bestow them."[1]

In horary, partnership belongs to the seventh house, whether it is a business or marriage partnership. Dreams belong to the ninth, ambition and hope to the eleventh, cars to the third, and so on. Having decided the department with which you are dealing, (and this may involve some soul searching), look at the ruler of the sign on the cusp of that house. If you are considering an issue of profession, for instance, look at the tenth house cusp, and if the sign on it is Sagittarius look at Jupiter, weigh up its position, its strength and weakness, its connections. Jupiter, then, would be the symbol of the profession. It simplifies matters if whoever wants to know the answer asks the question, then at least you are sure of the houses involved.

A question asked with naive simplicity is better than a carefully contrived one. If your question is indirect, so will the answer be. Sometimes it may take a while to understand your own motive in asking a question. We live in an age of euphemisms, when directness and forthright honesty--so necessary in asking questions in horary--is a strangely rare and unpracticed art. Some people are incapable of an honest approach, saying "Is this a good moment to start a new venture?" and hoping you will think they mean a business en-terprise, when in reality they mean, "Will I have a love affair with so-and-so?" The astrologer must know the *real* question because judgment depends on understanding it, and under-standing depends on the house selected.

The most frequent questions seem to be "Shall I leave my husband?" and "Where is the cat?" The most valuable ques-tions are the verifiable ones, because then we know our astrology is on the right track.

The First House

The first house rules the querent, the first person, the physical body. If you ask a horary question for yourself, the sign ascending is often your own natal Ascendant, Sun sign or Moon sign--espe-cially with the first chart you try. The first house represents "myself," ourselves, the vehicle in which we travel.[2] For example, if you ask about a ship in which you travel, you want to look at this cusp.[3] (Cars, though, belong to the third house because it is concerned with short journeys.) The first house will describe the shape of the physical body, as the vehicle in which the soul travels; the Ascendant ruler signifies the *person* rather than just the physical body.

The first house symbolisms the head and face in particular. Saturn, Mars, or the South Node positioned here, badly placed, will indicate a blemish on the face, or on the part of the body symbolized by the sign on the cusp. If few degrees of the sign ascend, the blemish will be higher up; if many degrees ascend it will be lower.

Because this house has a connection with the colour white, a planet placed here makes one paler.[4] It will tell you (if you should ask and if a significator is here) that the colour of clothing or animals involved in the question is a pale one.

If the symbol of a lost article appears in this house, the article is at home, with the owner, in the house of the querent.

Because of its connection with the head, Mercury positioned here, which denotes the tongue, shows a good speaker, or someone good with words, with a good memory and imagination. In antiquity the first house was known as Stilbon, which meant Mercury, and it was called the temple of Mercury by Manilius.[5] Already, you can see that the houses are by no means identical to the signs!

The first house is the east angle. It is a masculine house. At the Spring Equinox or major conjunction of the planets, the first house represents the people, or general state of the country where the chart is drawn. This is its use in Mundane astrology.

The Second House

The second house is considered if your question is about personal possessions which are movable or portable, or about the acquisition of wealth. It rules all money, wealth, salary, profit and gain, loss, income, your bank account--everything that is yours. In fact, every succedent house shows the resources of the preceding angular house.

Jupiter placed here increases wealth, but the Sun or Mars shows dispersion of it.

If you have lost something, note the sign on the second cusp, consider its ruler and locate its house position. For example, if the ruler of the sign is in the twelfth house, the lost object is probably in the bedroom. (If the article is mislaid around the house, the rule is different, and you may have to look at the fourth cusp.)

The second house is related to the colour green.

At an eclipse, or major conjunction, it would be used in Mundane astrology to indicate the resources of the nation.

The Third House

The third house signifies brothers and sisters, relatives and neighbours. It also is connected with short journeys, cars, all forms of communications, including messengers, rumours, lies, newspapers, reporters, writing, letters, post offices, and telephone calls.

It rules the shoulders, arms, and hands.

Red, yellow, and light brown are its colours.

The Moon in this house means much moving about. Mars placed here is not so unfortunate as elsewhere. In antiquity, the third was called the House of Brothers and was ruled by the Moon. Before that it was called Goddess [6] because it is opposite the ninth, the House of God.

The Fourth House

The fourth house is concerned with our beginning, our base, our ancestry, the father, the soil, real estate. It also is associated with towns, castles, buildings, fields, gardens, orchards, the quality and nature of the ground one buys (wooded, stony, barren, etc.). The fourth is also the end of anything and rules treasures hidden in the ground.

When Lilly says "inheritance" in connection with this house, he means ancestry, the family house, one's native country. He is not referring to wills--that is an eighth house matter.

When looking for an article lost indoors, a significator in this house shows the lost item is in a room in the center of the house or where the most elderly person likes to be. For since antiquity this house has been ruled by Saturn, which also rules fathers and the fate of the old.[7]

When an article is mislaid in the house it can be found by the ruler of the fourth house, as if the building itself has power over the article.

A significator here can denote drowning, if that is relevant to the question. The house used to be called the Angle of the Earth.

It is a feminine house.

The Fifth House

The fifth house represents pregnancy and one's children. Saturn and Mars in this house show disobedient children.

It also is connected with enjoyment and entertainment, games, gambling, theatre, banquets, and, as old books say "Ale houses and Taverns," which I suppose must be pubs. Speculation and the stock market, ambassadors, the arts, the Muses, and amusement are all ruled by this house. Mr. Lilly says it is the house "of pleasure, delight and merriment."

But note well: it does not rule love affairs, as some modern books say. These belong to the seventh house, though the fifth may rule affairs of pleasure.

Its colours are black, white, and honey.

The Sixth House

The sixth house rules such matters as service and work. It is connected with employment, work, toil, and as such, was considered an unfortunate house in antiquity, for people did not want to work and would have been surprised to learn that we today do not want unemployment!

This house concerns trade and merchandise, especially grain. It rules employees, office or factory workers, farm workers, lodgers, tenants, accountants, and secretaries.

Also associated with healing, the sixth house shows the illness from which a patient suffers, whereas the first house rules health. If a patient takes to bed because of illness, the ruler of the sixth cusp will identify the illness. Healers and dentists belong to this house. Mars and Venus positioned here show a good doctor.

Culpeper has very interesting things to say about this house in *Astrological Judgment of Diseases* which consists of extracts from Culpeper's *The Decumbiture of the Sick*. [8] The sixth rules small animals up to the size of sheep and goats.

It is a feminine house.

In mundane astrology, the sixth house would indicate the Civil Service or government workers.

The Seventh House

The seventh house concerns partnerships of marriage, business or love. It gives judgment on all kinds of love questions. The first house shows "the self," the person asking the question, while the seventh indicates "the other" and describes the person about whom the querent is asking. It is the house of open enemies, whether in divorce, lawsuits, contracts, or war. It also is the house of thieves and kidnappers, banishment and runaways.

The seventh rules the colour black. (I have come to the conclusion that pale colours belong to the left side of the chart and dark ones to the right, and that when old books say "black" they mean very dark. The seventh house, however, is allocated "dark black.")

Mars and Saturn positioned here show an unfortunate marriage. The Moon in the seventh house suggests a change of partnership or ownership.

This is the angle of the west, and it is a masculine house.

The Eighth House

The eighth house used to be called the House of Death, but now it is more often called the house of other people's money. In horary, it will never show the death of the querent. In certain cases it will refer to the death of a person, but one needs a great deal of additional evidence to determine this. It will show, for instance, the sinking of a ship. It also describes the sort of death. *It is unwise to predict death and this leads to trouble for astrologers.*

The eighth house is associated with the deceased's estate, wills, legacies, and dowry. It also rules undertakers.

Like all succedent houses, the eighth indicates the resources of the preceding angular house, the resources of the other, the partner's money, and in lawsuits, those assisting the opponent.

It rules tax collectors.

In the body it signifies the sex organs, the bladder, and is connected with piles, stones, and strangury. It is also the house of surgery and cutting, because in surgery a part is often cut away, and dies.

It is a feminine house and associated with the colour black, (or dark colour).

In Mundane astrology, this house reflects the resources of the enemy.

The Ninth House

The ninth house rules distant travel, whether in mind or body. Overseas travel and foreign countries, voyages, foreign trade, explorers, world assemblies all are the province of the ninth.

It is associated with deep thought, religion, clergy, the Church, bishops, learning, education beyond elementary levels, ceremonies, insurance, and publishers. It also rules dreams and visions.

The ninth house rules the hips and thighs. Its colours are green and white.

Jupiter placed in this house indicates a religious person.

Since antiquity the ninth house has been called "God" and associated with the Sun. Firmicus said, the Sun God. [9]

The Tenth House

The tenth house signifies royalty, kings, queens, princes, dukes, as well as those held in esteem in the world. It also is the house of judges, magistrates, anyone in command, presidents, commanders, captains, prime ministers.

This house is associated with one's profession or trade. The position of the ruler of this house plus the Sun will show the profession.

The tenth is connected with the abstract values of honor, authority, and dignity of office. Lilly includes lawyers in this house, but more modern writers say lawyers belong to the ninth. Perhaps the role of lawyers has changed.

In its capacity of seventh from the fourth, this house signifies mothers.

It rules the knees and calves, and is related to the colours red and white.

The tenth is the south angle, the M.C. It is a feminine house.

In antiquity this house was ruled by, and was the joy of Venus. It was called the House of Glory.[10] The Sun or Jupiter positioned here is considered fortunate, but Saturn or the South Node denies honor in the eyes of the world, and not much luck with trade or profession.

The Eleventh House

The eleventh house was called the house of the Good Daemon and was the most fortunate of all. It was ruled by Jupiter. Wishes particularly belong to this house. If someone asks about a wish but does not disclose it, the outcome can be judged from the planet ruling the sign on the eleventh house cusp.

Like all succedent houses, it denotes the resources of the preceding house. Thus, it shows the ambition, hope, confidence, and friends needed for career or success, their help and praises. It denotes societies and their members.

The eleventh rules yellow and saffron. The body parts associated with it are the legs and ankles. It is a masculine house.

The Twelfth House

The twelfth house shows secret enemies, hidden matters, family scandals, sorrow and undoing, witches and informers, affliction.

It rules large institutions such as hospitals and prisons, and, therefore, jailers. Solitude, mysticism, monks, nuns, and sleep are also in the domain of the twelfth.

Large animals such as horses and elephants are ruled by this house. The colour green and the feet are also connected with the twelfth house.

William Lilly said, "Saturn does much joy in this house, for Saturn is the author of mischief."

If you have lost something indoors and it is shown by the twelfth house, the lost object could be in the bedroom.

To sum up we can say the first house represents the person of the querent, the second house his possessions, the third his brother or sister, the fourth his father or real estate, the fifth his children, the sixth his work or sickness, the seventh his partner, the eighth concerns death or the partner's money, the ninth his travel or deep thought, the tenth his standing in the world, the eleventh his friends or hopes, the twelfth his secret enemies.

Turning the Chart

When the question one asks is on behalf of, for example, the man next door, then the chart is turned. The third house becomes the first house of the neighbour and represents his body. Now the fourth would be the man's second, and represent his possessions, the fifth would be the man's third and represent his near relations, the sixth would be his fourth and show his father, the seventh would be his fifth, and indicate his children, the eighth would be his sixth and show his work, and so on right around the chart.

It can be seen that there is little identification of houses with signs, except perhaps with the parts of the body and even then there are exceptions. (This point is made clear in Manilius' *Astronomica*), Loeb edition, pages 147 to 159.) You can see that the history and derivation of the houses and the signs were quite separate. The houses were considered more important than the signs, which merely lent their flavour as they passed through in their rotation. In a later chapter we will examine this history more carefully.

There is only one book that provides enough detail to give a good horary judgment and that is William Lilly's *Christian Astrology*. It is suggested that a student of astrology wishing to understand houses should buy that book and learn the broad categories of house meaning given therein, without reference to "house rulership books." It is the principles behind the meanings that matter; understand those and you will know your house.

The Axes: A Further Discussion of Houses

The First/Seventh Axis

The most important places in the heavens astrologically are the angles. Ptolemy gave pride of place to the Midheaven and Lilly to the Ascendant. This means that any planet positioned here has great strength. The nearer the planet is to the angle, the stronger. If a planet is in an angular house but in the sign adjacent to the one on the cusp, the effect is weakened. The first house is called the *House of Life*. Firmicus called it *Vita* and Ptolemy called it the *Horoscope*. The first house particularly describes the head, but also the body's shape, colour, and the complexion of a querent. It is the vehicle we move in, the ship in which we sail, we ourselves, the home team. It is the vehicle of the soul.

When reading books from former times one gets the feeling that there was a greater awareness of the dichotomy between ourselves and our bodies. People did not identify quite so closely with their bodies. Al Biruni speaks of the first quadrant as representing body without soul.

Anatomically, the first house represents the head and face, and in that context it corresponds with the first sign of the zodiac: Aries. Some ancient astrologers reasoned therefore that it also corresponded with Saturn, the (to them) first planet. Previous authorities, however, had called the first house the Temple of Mercury, or Stilbon, the Glistener. Throughout the centuries it has retained this connection with Mercury, being named its "joy," because Mercury rules the memory and certain kinds of thought, as well as the tongue, thus showing its kinship with the head. Through Mercury the gods gave us the knowledge of astrology, according to Manetho. Mars on the contrary, ruler of Aries, has little in common with the thinking processes, and tends rather to rash, un-thought out action. In a horary, Mars ascending can show anger, or someone who is out of his mind. Or it can show aggression and initiative, a good fight fought, or else cutting of the body. But Mercury placed here shows a good brain, and even the dispositor of Mercury in the first house indicates intelligence. In mundane charts the house represents one's own nation and the condition of it.

There are many ways that a horary astrologer must study the first house. First of all, if fewer than 3 degrees or more than 27 degrees ascend, the chart is invalidated--unless in the former instance the querent has a natal planet exactly at the horary chart's ascending degree, in which case that planet becomes important in the judgment, or in the latter case if the querent is the same age as the degree ascending. [11]

The Ascendant and its ruler must describe the querent to an extent, and often they reflect the Sun sign, Moon sign or Ascendant of the querent's nativity. Lilly could derive physical and behavioral descriptions in a way that we have lost. In traditional natal and horary astrology it was from the Ascendant and its ruler that our ancestors mainly derived information about the body and characteristic behavior, whether a person was of sanguine, melancholic, choleric, or phlegmatic humour. Other factors also contributed, such as the Moon and those planets aspecting her, the lord of the chart, (which wasn't always the lord of the Ascendant), and also the Sun sign, and fixed stars.

The four humours were named after the four liquids of the body, on which it was thought the appearance and manners (behavior), depended. Implicit in this is the understanding that from appearance one can judge manners, or, as Bernard Shaw said, "He is a fool who cannot judge by appearance." Sanguine (blood) made a person courageous, optimistic, ruddy; melancholic (blackbile, whatever that is) was connected with Saturn and caused prudence, severity, and caution; cholerick (bile) caused ambition and impetuousness; and phlegmatic (of the phlegm) made one apathetic because of an overabundance of phlegm in the body. Before you laugh your heads off at such an idea, wait till you are getting a cold and your body has too much phlegm, then consider how you feel. Is this classification any sillier than the twelve Sun-sign types? The factors deciding it were less simple; you had to consider the planets that had most dignities in the ascending sign and the sign intercepted in the first house, any planets in the first and their dispositors, and if these were fortunate or weak or strong. If they were infortunes there was "ever a tincture of poison;" if many planets were placed in the first there would be a variety of behavior. (I do not really think we shall return to the definitions of the humours unless the herbalists lead us there should they find them appropriate for their particular kind of medicine.)

So we learn that planets near the Ascendant show behavior. If the planet is Mercury, judge by any planet it conjuncts, and if it is not in conjunction, Mercury assumes the nature of its dispositor and planets it aspects. (I have found this to be true in my experience of nativities). Judge behavior also, we are told from the planets aspecting the Moon, for Mercury and the Moon are the reflectors. If no planet aspects them, judge by the Lord of the Ascendant. But most important of all is to judge by any fixed star on the Ascendant. (Lilly lists very few in this context.)

Because we no longer have the ability to give accurate physical descriptions from these indicators, as Lilly could, I shall illustrate this with a chart from *Christian Astrology* which shows some of Lilly's long lost methods of delineating physical appearances from a horary chart.

Before going on to the chart, however, I will say a little about the seventh house, which being opposite the first always describes "the other," whether in love or marriage or war. It gives judgment on all manner of love questions, and describes sweethearts, husbands, wives, and partners, their shapes and conditions. It is the house of open enemies rather than unknown ones (which are shown by the twelfth). In questions of marriage it is unfortunate to find Mars or Saturn here. In questions of theft or crime the banished party appears here, and a peregrine planet placed in the seventh or as the seventh ruler can be a thief.

When the astrologer is not the querent, the seventh shows the astrologer. For that reason we are warned that if Saturn is in the seventh or is ruler of its cusp, afflicted, the astrologer's judgment may not be good, and for the astrologer's protection it may be wiser to say nothing. This does not apply to questions concerning the seventh house, for we must be able to read a negative to questions about partnerships.

Lilly tells us that in an Annual Ingress chart the seventh shows whether war or peace may be expected.

At the time of death there is often a planet on the seventh cusp afflicting the first, the House of Life, by opposition. Perhaps that is the reason Manilius associated the house with death, calling it the "portal of Pluto," the Temple that buries the Sun. Ptolemy called it Occident and moved the House of Death to the eighth. Notice how, in the horary chart for the Herald of Free Enterprise (in chapter 20, Figure 20.7), Saturn is here afflicting, and sinking the boat.

In medicine the seventh represents the doctor (the sixth and its ruler show the disease, the tenth, the cure, the first, life). In Bonatus' *Anima Astrologiae* you may notice in the 68th Consideration what I believe is a translator's error. Here the word Medicine has been used instead of Medic. That the seventh is the doctor and not the medicine can be seen from the context of the sentence and from Lilly's first four aphorisms on page 282 of *Christian Astrology*.

The chart and interpretation following are from *Christian Astrology*.

Figure 3.1: If she should marry the man desired

If she should marry the man desired?

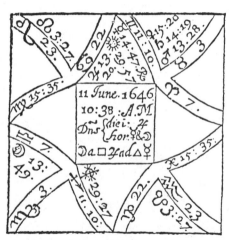

The querent was tall, ruddy complexioned, quiet, discreet and well spoken, the quesited was very tall, slender, thin, with a long face, and black hair. His tallness Lilly attributed to Jupiter, being in the terms of Mercury and the seventh cusp also being in the terms of Mercury (any significator in the terms of a planet makes variation, and colours the description according to its dignity). The dullness of his hair Lilly conceived to be from Jupiter's aspect to Saturn, and the square of the Moon to Saturn, the Moon being subterranean. Mercury, symbol of the querent, is retrograde and under the Sunbeams, showing she was upset and afraid he would not have her, not without reason because Jupiter was exalted and near sextile Venus; indicating his self estimation and that he had been interested in another (Venus). But the semi-sextile (the only mention of this aspect in the horary volume) and the translation of light by the Moon from Jupiter to Mercury, the main significators--especially with Mercury angular and received willingly by retrogradation towards the Moon--showed a fortunate outcome, and produced a marriage.

Notice the absence of psychology from these splendid descriptions. You may think physical description trivial. I say it is much harder to deduce. It can be proved, unlike vague characteristics. Emulate it if you can.

In the Bible Christ told a man his sins were forgiven and He was doubted; so then He told the man to pick up his bed and walk because his body was cured. This was tangible evidence, and it convinced His challengers that He really knew what He was talking about.

Astrology certainly needs some tangible statements at present. We are like people saying "Your sins are forgiven" and unable to say "Take up your bed and walk."

Tenth/Fourth Axis: Parents

The tenth house rules authority, those in command, success, and glory; but I would like to discuss this axis specifically in regard to parents. In the ancient body of knowledge that comprises Western astrology the Moon rules the mother. Some astrologer said the Moon always does so; [12] others, like Ptolemy, that the Moon does so by night that Venus does so by day, and that the House of the Mother is the tenth. [13] (That is what you need to know as horary astrologers).

The Moon also rules the sign Cancer. The sign Cancer does not rule mothers, the Moon does.

Lilly's definition for Natal astrologers is as follows: "The Mother's significators are; first, the tenth house; secondly, the Lord therefore, thirdly, Venus in a diurnal nativity, Moon in a nocturnal; fourthly a Planet or Planets in the tenth house." [14]

Consider this. You do not just look at the sign on the tenth and say, "That's not like my mother." Not at all. Your mother may be described by the Moon, or by the tenth ruler in a particular sign. Because these laws were discovered long ago does not mean they are stultified. We have much more to discover, many areas to which we can apply our ingenuity and creative thought. Why in one chart is the mother shown by the Moon and in another by the ruler of the tenth? Is it because of the difference in male and female maps or because of the relative evaluation of the planets involved? Already we find hints that a day and night nativity are dealt with differently, and I have often wondered about male and female charts. (If you have read Nick Kollerstrom's book *Astrochemistry* you may notice the female body contains more copper and a male more iron. May not a feminine chart respond more strongly to Venus? This is conjecture, not statement.) It is probably only in this century that so many female charts have come under consideration.

I am unconvinced that the statement by Firmicus and Al Biruni that the fourth rules parents, [15] in any way contradicts the above. In a question about both parents together I would certainly look at the fourth, because the fourth is the House of Fathers, our forebears, our heritage, our basis, our origin, our source. In such a question as, "Will my parents come to stay?" I would consider the fourth. But in a question such as, "Will my mother come to stay?" I would look at the tenth. It seems to me that this is what Lilly means when he says of the tenth that "it peculiarly denotes the Mother." [16]

Just as you yourself are shown by the first and your partner is shown by the opposite, so if the father is shown by the fourth the mother--his partner--is shown by the opposite. Look at the chart on page 455 of *Christian Astrology* where King Charles is shown by the tenth and the Queen by the house opposite, (incidentally demonstrating the uselessness of books on house rulership).

There has been some confusion about fourth/tenth house rulerships. People have been accustomed to thinking that signs rule, whereas in traditional astrology the planets rule. Astrological thought has been turned upside down. This is because of the overriding influence of psychology, for people will pay to hear themselves talked about and the signs will describe them *ad infinitum*. The signs are like adjectives, the planets like nouns.

Let us read about the sign Cancer in *Christian Astrology*. "The only house of the Moon...of the watry Triplicity...Watry, Cold, Moyst...Movable mute and slow of voice...Fruitful." (A list of illnesses follows, then the description continues). "The Sea, great Rivers, Navigable Waters...Rivers, Brooks, Springs...Sellars in Houses, Wash-houses, Marsh grounds, Ditches..." Then he gives the adjectives that describe those whose significators are found in the sign: short, upper part of the body bigger than the lower, round pale face and small eyes. Finally, there are countries and towns such as "York and Amsterdam." [17]

There is no word of mother. True, it is a fruitful sign, and in a question about pregnancy you would take that into account. All the water signs are fruitful. [18] In such a question, consider the nature of the signs in which the Planets are placed..."the quality of these Signs is to be mixed and conferred with the nature of the Planets." [19]

But that does not infer that the sign Cancer rules the Mother, nor does it infer that because Cancer is the fourth sign, the fourth house exercises the role of the Moon. However, there is a correlation between the signs and the houses anatomically. Culpeper mentions this in his chapter on illnesses, and Lilly, in his first definition of the fourth house, says it has as its co-significators the sign Cancer. [20] (NOT the Moon.) Lilly must have been referring to this anatomical correlation, of which there is no doubt. In fact, all the houses and signs correlate in this particular.

They do not, however, relate in other particulars, and I am sure Lilly would be horrified that his one phrase--that the fourth house has as co-significator the sign Cancer--has lead us so far astray. Culpeper foresaw the difficulty when he wrote "some authors hold an opinion that the signs carry the same significance as the houses of heaven do." [21]

The signs describe place, person, direction, and illnesses in horary charts. The planets symbolise (in events and questions) people and things. Their sign positions describe them.

The sign Cancer signifies the sea, so that in comparing Cancer with the Moon it might be apt to remember the Moon rules the tides, but the sea is not responsible for the phases of the Moon.

In traditional Western astrology the fourth house rules fathers. [22] (This is what you need to know in horary charts.) But remember that generally so does the Sun in a day time chart, and Saturn in a nighttime chart. The Sun also rules Leo, but Leo does not rule fathers in a day chart, the Sun does. Saturn rules Capricorn and Aquarius, but Capricorn and Aquarius do not rule fathers, Saturn does.

The fourth house is the domain of Saturn. Lilly mentions that the Sun is co-significator there, [23] which is because of this connection of the Sun with fathers, I assume. Again, this does not mean you necessarily recognize the characteristics of your father from the sign on the fourth.

Lilly's definition for natal charts is: "The significators of the Father in every Geniture are, First, the fourth house, secondly, the Lord thereof; thirdly, the Sun in a diurnal Geniture, Saturn in a nocturnal; fourthly the Planet or Planets in the fourth are considerable." [24]

The psychologist's suggestion that the dominant parent is symbolized by the tenth house is inappropriate. There is very little psychology in traditional Western astrology. Things are where they are because God, (and under God, the gods) put them there. It is as useful to ask why Africa is where it is, or Australia. Manilius came as near to an explanation as any I have heard when he said, the fourth, at the base of the chart controls the foundation of things, [25] so one looks there not only for fathers and the old, [26] but for wealth from the Earth and mining. [27] And, of course, the fourth house is at the bottom of the chart, supporting it.

In oversimplified books you may read that the agreement of the parents depends on the aspects of Sun and Moon. But if you follow our art more deeply, you may realize that in a nocturnal chart, one should look at the aspects between Saturn and the Moon.

The name given to the fourth house by the Greeks was Daemonium. [28] Seasonally the fourth coincides with midwinter. The Ascendant is seen as Spring, the M.C. as midsummer, the Descendant as Autumn, and the I.C. as mid-winter. Its title reminds me of Pandemonium, and the "heathen" festival of misrule in midwinter. This is only conjecture, but it brings to mind the possible connection between Saturn and Pan.

In its capacity as ruler of the soil, the fourth is the house to look at when searching for hidden treasure. This was a common question for horary astrologers before the days of banks. Samuel Pepys tells of having to bury thousands of pounds and how his family buried it in broad daylight on a Sunday when people going to church could have seen, and it made him mad! Gadbury tells an amusing story of a friend who dug so diligently that he broke into a cesspit, or earth closet, called then a "jakes" in slang. Benefics in the fourth of a horary chart would indicate treasure in the ground, and of course, you would note the sign on the fourth cusp and take direction from it.

This is not entirely a thing of the past. I had a friend who is extremely wealthy and she gave her son an eighteen-piece silvergilt canteen of cutlery, worth about £ 12,000. She then regretted her generosity.

One day the canteen of cutlery was stolen and she wept bitterly because her wicked son and daughter-in-law thought she might have stolen it back and were asking the police to search her house!

Months passed and it had not been found. Then one day she came to me in tears again, but the story was different this time. "I did steal back the cutlery," she said. "While you were away I buried it in your garden and now I can't find it." At the time I thought it funny, but now realize how much I could have been implicated! I must admit that I borrowed a metal detector and found it for her, and did not use astrology, for I did not see how astrology could pinpoint the exact place. She gave it back to her son.

There are areas where fourth house rulership overlaps with that of the eighth house, for it has been associated with our forefathers and spirits of the departed, with graveyards, sextons, etc. Legacies and wills remain the domain of the eighth, yet heritage--our heritage, our land, what is ours from our family--is associated with the fourth. The fourth is more in the nature of what is fixedly ours than of those things recently, or about to, become ours by a current will, those things which recently belonged to someone else, which are eighth house matters.

The fourth house rules the beginning and the end of the matter.

The Eleventh/Fifth Axis

This axis was originally thought to be ruled by the Benefics. The eleventh house was (and still is in my opinion) Agathos Daimon, [29] Fortuna Felix, the most fortunate of all, for it derived its characteristics from the Greater Benefic Jupiter, [30] that is, it is the House of Friendship, [31] comfort, and relief. It is the house of reassurance, hopes, and wishes, from which you can only be carried upward, whereas in the tenth, the House of Glory, you could only fall.

If the querent will not tell you what he or she is hoping for from the horary, you can judge success from this house and its ruler.

As the tenth rules whoever is in authority, the eleventh, being succedant from it, rules the resources of the tenth. If the tenth is the government, the eleventh is its treasury; if the tenth is your sovereign, the eleventh is the wealth of the sovereign; if the tenth is your employer, the eleventh is the finances of the firm. (But your own finances, including salary, are always a second house matter.)

The eleventh shows attributes we require for our place in the world, hope, ambition, trust.

It is associated with the colour yellow.

When you are considering parts of the body, the eleventh reflects Aquarius and ankles. Yet this kinship with Aquarius by no means puts the house under the domination of Saturn, whose characteristics are entirely foreign to its qualities. Even more foreign are the characteristics of Uranus. Uranus certainly gives no comfort and relief.

In antiquity, Jupiter placed in this house signified the greatest good, and I suggest it still does.

The fifth was called the House of Luck, [32] chance, ruling games of chance and pregnancy (presumably pregnancy has been a game of chance for many generations), pleasure, and amusement. Who is to say if an affair is an amusement or love? (If it is love it will be shown by the seventh house, not the fifth.) From pregnancy it follows this is the house of children. Saturn and Neptune here do not bode well for having children. The Sun here shows distress to the parent through the child, (as if the house were combust). Jupiter placed in this house is a strong and an undeniable indication of pregnancy no matter what else is there, for all proliferation comes from Jupiter.

It is Venus who has given her characteristics to the fifth house, its amusements and the Muses, too, the arts, theatre, music, sculpture, painting, beauty. Surely flowers and honey belong to the fifth. If sex is a pleasure, then I think it belongs here. Perhaps it is not a pleasure to those who allocate it to the eighth, for no reason other than that the eighth sign is Scorpio.

Derek Appleby has studied a lot of contest charts and concludes that the fifth is important to the campaigners, indicating their luck more than the eleventh does.

Anatomically, the fifth rules the heart, stomach, liver, sides, and back, and in this reflects something of Cancer and Leo.

The colours it rules are black, white, and honey-colour. It also rules ambassadors and messengers, though I can't work out why.

The Ninth/Third Axis

This axis was once said to be ruled by the Luminaries.

The ninth house is called masculine and cadent. It has always been known as the House of God [33] and in the pre-Christian era as the House of the Sun God. There was a time when the word for God and Sun were one. In some early Greek horoscopes the Sun in the chart was referred to simply as god. [34]

In practice the ninth house deals with those matters appertaining to religion, the church, and clergy. Once it would have been obvious that learning should be in the same bracket, but at present that is not quite as obvious.

The ninth rules deep thought, visions, and dreams. It affects the brain by ranging thought, and the body by ranging travel, two facets of the same thing; thus, we allocate voyages to this house.

I have heard a Native American Indian called Beautiful Painted Arrow say, "do you know we create by thinking...by thinking you create form, God was the first dreamer and out of the first dream...the vision...and out of the vision came us...and we do the Sun dance in July to honour that very beautiful moment...because that moment is right now...we medicine people have visions about creation...and out of that came religion...folk tales...it is all very real."

In that paragraph is the essence of the ninth house--even the dance is in July when the Sun is strong in the northern hemisphere.

It is the joy of the Sun, (the time when we all sit in the Sun if we can, after lunch) Jupiter is very well placed in the ninth showing a devout individual, unlike the South Node, Saturn, or Mars which when placed here signify the opposite. There is doubtless a very strong connection of Jupiter to this house, for both are associated with publishing, ceremony, and law.

Anatomically the ninth equates with the hips and thighs. Its colours are green and white.

Gauquelin discovered that successful athletes often have

Mars in this house, and I have stated elsewhere that this seems to reinforce the ancient belief in the strength of the Sun in this house. My reasoning is that Mars is of the same nature as the Sun--hot and dry--and is not hurt by combustion. Its aggression is a help in combat charts when it rises, it manifests not as a malefic but as a strong fighter. This quality in the Sun's house strengthens the athlete's ability to shine. Mohammed Ali has Mars here; he is known for his athletic ability and physical energy, but he is also a man of God.

Astro-psychologists have associated the twelfth with dreams, but actually the twelfth is a place of retirement, not of mental activity--least of all mental activity of a divine source.

Remember when you look at the ninth to look at the planet ruling the sign on its cusp and planets positioned in it, not just at the sign.

From the ninth house you should be able to decide questions relating to countries, like "Shall I go to Australia?," which I show later.

Every country has its charter, but we are sure about only a few, and a great deal more research is needed in this area. In America there recently has been an enormous and combined effort to analyze 649 historic maps to ascertain the time of the signing of Independence, comparing events with precision. This was chiefly the work of Susan Manuel, and the final conclusion arrived at was 3:02 A.M. L.M.T., July 4, 1776 with 20° 11' Gemini ascending, and 26° Aquarius on the M.C. [35] This vast enquiry coincides with the publication of a book by Laurie Efrin called *Commonsense*, on the same subject. In it Efrin examines similar evidence and reaches the conclusion that the Ascendant in the U.S. chart is 17° 38' Gemini. Following B. Watters I have always used 7° Gemini. (It has always puzzled me that a country where nobody walks could be ascribed to Sagittarius, as some astrologers have suggested.)

So if someone asks, "Where shall I emigrate" and you see Gemini on the ninth cusp of the horary chart, it might suggest to you the States.

The third house was once called Goddess,*[36] after the Moon, for the qualities of the third in many ways resemble the qualities of the Moon: inconstancy and fluctuation, short journeys and restlessness, brief communications, telephone calls, letters, and early education; quick flights as opposed to long voyages. The Moon personifies change through its waxing and waning, and the Moon positioned in the third house shows many short journeys.

The third is also called Brothers. This seems to include neighbours and anyone who lives a short distance away, as well as cousins and kindred.

Because of its anatomical connection with Gemini, the third rules the arms, hands, and fingers.

In closing, I would like to draw attention to something that has puzzled me ever since I started to learn astrology, so much so that I once wrote to the *Quarterly* asking about it. The mystery that perplexed me is that Cancerian women who usually like to camouflage themselves in neutral or sandy-coloured clothes occasionally wear a bright red jersey. (These women, if they do not have Saturn strong in their charts, usually have large busts.) Why do they do this, when it contradicts their very nature? The answer lies, I suggest, in the rulership of the third house by the Moon and the affinity of that house with the colour red.

The Second/Eighth Axis

We are unsure of the original rulers of this axis, as both houses were named the Portal of Pluto and Abode of Typhon.

The second house rules all one's possessions that are movable, including money in the bank. From it can be judged the wealth of the querent. The Moon positioned here usually shows that the querent is thinking of his money no matter how the question is phrased. The second house signifies the neck and in that way is reminiscent of Taurus, as is its rulership of the colour grass green. Yet I have noticed that a malefic on the second cusp often indicates tragedy or death as much as it does on the eighth cusp. An example is the Bhopal disaster, (see Chapter 21).

The eighth house is the House of Death, although nowadays people prefer to call it the house of other people's money. It shows your partner's wealth and resources, or whatever belongs to someone else, such as money to be borrowed or tax to be paid, or the library book. It also shows money you inherit by wills. Formerly it was associated with war and violence.

It does not show the querent's own death. It is unwise and overbold to foretell death of people, and in history whenever astrologers have done this our art has been banned. It will do us no good. This spreads fear of astrology and works against us; better we should be considered entertainers. These rulerships show that we cannot tidy up astrology, anymore than we can tidy up nature. We might as well dictate to the sea what size waves it should have.

The Sixth/Twelfth Axis

These houses, being inconjunct the Ascendant and cadent, are ruled by the infortunes and considered unfortunate in horary. They were described as falling from the angles. Their misfortune depends on the context of the question, of course. As the ruler of small animals, the sixth house is no more unfortunate than fortunate, and similarly with the twelfth, which rules large animals.

The sixth was called the house of labour, Laboris, Valetudo, [37] and derives its qualities from the lesser infortune, Mars, who joys in this house. Labour was not originally counted among the advantages available to the human race--that is a fabrication of our present times.

The sixth also rules illness. The first rules health, and the sixth illness. These words are confused in our present society. It is against the law in Britain and many other nations for an astrologer to diagnose illness, and for that reason I have not concerned myself with this facet of astrology. But recently some doctors and herbalists have interested themselves in astrology again, and it is vitally important that they understand the original meanings of planets and houses, because to try to diagnose illness from the wafflings of some astropsychology would surely be disastrous.

The art of understanding a Decumbiture is a long study in itself, and it is to be noted that the chart is not turned for a decumbiture, but stands in its own right, because it is an Event.

Culpeper's original herbal called the *English Physician Enlarged* contained a chart showing his method of diagnosis. It has been omitted from modern books, but I include it in a later chapter. All his herbals give the planetary rulerships of plants. This should be bought and valued by anyone interested in medical astrology or horary, before a money-minded trader wants the rulerships changed to Sun signs!

It seems apparent that some medicines cure some people and harm others, and that we should be treated according to our kind, as in homeopathy. This was evidently the conclusion of previous generations when at least an attempt was made to categorize physical type, even to the days of the Egyptians and their Iomathematical medicine.

It was believed that the shape of plants described their medical use. For instance, those with heart-shaped leaves might be good for the heart, or the roots of the lesser celandine, which look like haemorrhoids, could heal them. This was called the "Doctrine of Signatures." There were also proper hours to pick herbs and hours to treat with medicines. This was not merely a rural belief; the abbeys, churches, and cathedrals had extensive herb gardens, and not for culinary purposes. Who is to say what energies are contained in living things? (The downs near Canterbury, now called Harbledown, were once called Herbaldown). I believe the essential oils used in aromatherapy to be full of virtue. (I am told by my herbalist friends that the chemically manufactured medicines purporting to be comprised of the same ingredients as those made from plants do not have the virtues of the plants.)

There is a story of a Native American who observed deer eating a particular moss. If a deer was debilitated it ate the moss more, and then recovered. So when the Indian was ill he too ate the moss and recovered. Then a large manufacturing firm heard of it, and asked the Indian to point out the moss so that they could manufacture a medicine that cured people who were ill. They offered him large sums of money, but he would not tell them. Eventually he gave in and told them, and received the money. The medicine was made from the moss, but proved to be ineffectual. They reproached the Indian with this. He insisted it did work; "But," he said, "you must enter into the spirit of the deer first!"

We may not all have the ability to enter into such a spirit, but perhaps our own essence blends with the essence of some plants more than others. It is very impressive in Kirlian photography to see the energy of the body, and I am sure the plants have similar energy. I wonder if the pattern of energy has an astrological pattern.

But I digress. The colour associated with the sixth house is black, not "dark black," but some dark colour. The part of the body especially indicated by the sixth is the lower section of the belly and guts, and in this way it is associated with Virgo.

In a horary, an illness is discerned from the sign on the sixth cusp and from planets in the sixth. The illness also is described by the sign in which the ruler of the sixth is positioned, for example, if the ruler of the sixth is in Aries it affects the face or head. The sign on the sixth cusp indicates if the illness will be of long (fixed); short (cardinal); or medium (mutable) duration. Late degrees show the illness is near its end. When the ruler of the sixth is stronger than the ruler of the first, (health), a long and difficult disease is indicated. This sounds antiquated, but try it out. Remember, a Decumbiture does not start until the patient takes to their bed; the time of just feeling ill is not considered.

A word, too, about the sixth as the house of work. This does not mean your professional job, your standing in the world, which is a matter of the tenth house. The work of the sixth is usually manual work, or else healing work.

The twelfth house of unknown enemies was called Bad Spirit, Malus Daemon. [38] It was considered to be the abode of Saturn and worked against the querent in unknown ways. I notice in assassination and murder cases the symbol of the ambushing villain lurks here.

If the same sign is on the twelfth cusp as is on the Ascendant the querent is his own enemy. If the significator of the querent or the planet ruling the twelfth cusp is in the twelfth it signifies that the querent is imprisoned or confined. The twelfth seems to rule all places and forms of confinement, whether prison or hospital, as well as places of retirement and isolation from the world.

The colour of the twelfth house is green. I don't know if there is still the superstition that wearing green is unlucky, meaning particularly bottle green, the dark Saturnine green.

Large animals are ruled by this house simply because they are the opposite to small ones. Some modern astrologers are trying to invent that the sixth rules all animals, but fortunately Lilly has left us a good example of a lost horse that shows incontrovertibly that we must consider the twelfth to signify large animals.

It is connected with the feet, thereby its association with the sign Pisces. Indeed, many Pisceans have trouble with their feet and shoes. This in no way brings the rulership of the house to Jupiter, however, and less still to Neptune, whose characteristics are in no way shown by the house.

Chapter 4
The Satellite

Before we go on to discuss aspects and some of the techniques of horary, I would like to demonstrate an example chart, which you will come to understand better as you read on. This was predicted with witnesses before the event.

This is a chart about the satellite that was encircling the Earth in January 1983. As you can see by the planetary positions, the chart was drawn on the evening of 20 January 1983. We had just been told by the television news that nobody knew where it would fall. The Belgians were sitting in concrete bunkers in anticipation.

My question was, "Where and when will it (the satellite) come down?" (See Figure 4.1 on the following page.)

The Ascendant represents the querent--ourselves--asking about the satellite. It also represents the vehicle we travel in, our Earth (our ship in space). Pisces on the seventh cusp in the chart appropriately signifies "the other": boundless space.

Mercury, ruler of the Virgo Ascendant, signifies what is of the Earth--in this instance, the satellite. Note that Mercury is retrograding, which shows that the satellite is *returning*, to

Earth (Mercury is positioned in the fourth house of "the end").

To what part of the Earth will it return? Lilly writes that the quality of the place or ground...must be judged from the sign where the significator is. [1] Mercury is in the sign of Capricorn, and India is ruled by Capricorn.

Figure 4.1: "When and where will it (the satellite) come down?"

Regiomontanus House System

20 January 1983
8:50 P.M. G.M.T.
Deal, England
51° 13' N 1° 20' E

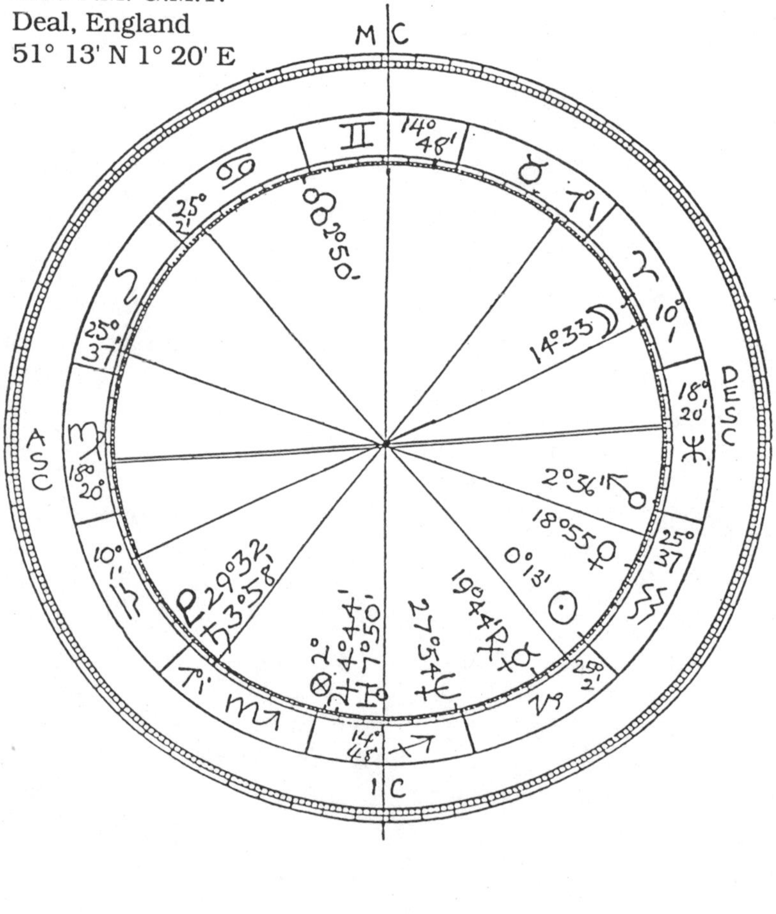

Four planets are in fire signs and three in air, so it was assumed that the satellite would mostly burn up on entry. Some of it, however, would return, for Mercury was retrograding (retrogradation signifies returning). I decided that it would not fall on ground, for only one planet is in an earth sign. For the following reasons it seems likely to fall into the ocean:

Mars is important as the ruler of the eighth house, the house of death, and the projectile is falling to its end.

Mars is in Pisces trine Saturn in Scorpio, both signs of the ocean.

The very fact that the main significator (Mercury) is in the fourth house is a likely sign of drowning. Saturn, too, is a significator of falling and or drowning (Mercury is in Capricorn, ruled by Saturn). Neptune in the fourth adds confirmation of drowning.

Therefore, the evidence points to both India and the ocean: the Indian Ocean.

The Moon is particularly important in deciding direction and it is always considered in connection with fugitives. It is in Aries, an easterly sign, and the main significator, Mercury, is in Capricorn, a southerly sign. This again confirms a southeast position, judging from my location in England.

All the planets are in the northern hemisphere of the chart, with the exception of the Moon, showing the northern hemisphere of the Earth.

The Moon moves from the trine of the Jupiter-Uranus conjunction in the third house, signifying the travelling satellite's communicative journey, to the square of Mercury retrograde--the fall. This aspect is intercepted by the Moon sextile Venus.

Venus at 19° Aquarius is conjunct Uranus of the natal map of Russia. In any case, Aquarius here seems to symbolise Russia, for the Sun is positioned here, and it is all a Russian matter. This interception of Venus shows a helpful, good intervention from Russia (diverting the satellite to a more fortunate fall). This is aided by the strength of Jupiter's placement in Sagittarius.

Ivy Goldstein Jacobson considers that the planet the Moon last passed over and the one she will pass over next are relevant. Here the Moon last passed over Mars in Pisces and will next pass over Pluto in Libra. Lilly tells us that the ancients equated Pisces with the oars of a ship, [2] and we all know Pisces rules the feet. I concluded, therefore, that a means of propulsion--the engine--went wrong; perhaps it burnt out (Mars) and after wandering (the Moon is peregrine), the Moon finally opposes Pluto in Libra and the satellite is ejected from the air.

At a later date I realized that the satellite fell at 25° S 84°E on the TROPIC OF CAPRICORN!

The satellite actually fell on 24 January 1983. I had judged it would fall in five days because there were five degrees between the Moon and Mercury, both in cardinal signs. It took only four days, no doubt because Mercury was retrograde and went to meet the Moon's aspect more quickly, but also the Moon was moving fast.

The remaining section burnt out on re-entry sixteen days after the question was asked. There are fifteen degrees between the Moon and Pluto, and I had expected it would take fifteen days, but the Moon's motion by then was slower.

A few things to remember:

1. Retrogradation indicates a returning. When something is lost it means you will find it again. If Mercury is retrograde it means you will alter your mind.
2. There is a detailed explanation of retrogradation in the text following.
3. Peregrine means a planet without dignity. A detailed explanation follows later.

Chapter 5
Terminology and Aspects

In horary we are usually concerned with events: "Will an event happen?" or "Has an event happened already?" The sequence of events is mainly indicated by the aspects the Moon makes while in its present sign.

As I explained earlier, the Moon is function, the action, the verb. From its contacts we can see what has happened and what will happen. Those planets which the Moon has already contacted symbolize what is past, and those with which the Moon next makes contact symbolize what is yet to happen. This can be judged by using only the major aspects: the square, trine, opposition, sextile and conjunction.

The aspects made by the Moon include any made from the sign in which it is placed. Once the Moon has left the sign it is in, matters are beyond the scope of the question asked. The situation has begun a new chapter. If the Moon makes no aspect between its present position and the end of the sign it is in, it is called *void of course*, meaning there is nothing you can do about it.

Natal astrologers are not used to this. They have been

concerned in nativities with characteristics that last a life-time. A past aspect has meant very much the same as an applying one.

A good way to discern past events from future ones is to arrange the planets in order of their degrees, on squared (graph) paper. I have used for this example the Satellite chart. (See Figure 5.1.)

Figure 5.1: Discerning Past and Future Events

	Past, From														Future, To															
	0	1	2	3	4	5	6	7	8	9	10	11	12	13	14	15	16	17	18	19	20	21	22	23	24	25	26	27	28	29
	☉		☊	♄	♃			♅							☽				♀	☿								♆		♇
	0°		2°	3°	4°			7°							14°				18°	19°								27°		29°
	13'		50'	58'	44'			50'							33'				55'	44'								54'		32'
	♒		♋	♏	♐			♐							♈				♒	♑								♐		♎
		♂																		℞										
		2°																												
		36'																												
		♓																												
		⊗																												
		2°																												
		♐																												

The above diagram can be written as ☽ from △ ♃ ♅ to ⚹ ♀, □ ☿ ℞, △ ♆ ☍ ♇. ♂ to △ ♄. We can note ♂ in the degree of the ☋ ☊.

You can see clearly here that the Moon is at 14 degrees, and separates from a Jupiter-Uranus conjunction in Sagittarius. That was past. The conjunction is in the third house, showing all the communications the satellite had been making successfully. Now the Moon moves on to contact sextile Venus and square Mercury, retrograde. Venus shows the Russian action which made the satellite (Mercury) fall back to Earth where it did.

From this chart, too, we can see the closely applying aspect of Mars trine Saturn.

It is a good idea to include the Ascendant and M.C. on your

diagram if they are relevant to your question.

By stating that the judgment of a question can be made from the major aspects only I do not mean to imply that the other aspects do not exist. Of course they do, and after the major aspects have been given due consideration, the minor ones will describe many contributory factors to elucidate your answer. In her book *Horary Astrology and the Judgment of Events*, Mrs. Watters frequently mentions quincunx aspects to midpoints. However, with a horary, your answer should be derived primarily from the main significators and the Moon and the major aspects. If it is not clear enough for this to be possible, wait, as Lilly says, "until another question better inform you." (No, not the *same* question again.)

The final aspect made by the Moon can be important in some questions as it may show the final outcome, provided it is not prevented or frustrated before then. (Also, if the next aspect made by the Moon supplies the quesited, there is no need to look further.)

If the Moon is void of course the chart can be judged, but no action can be taken; for if nothing happens to the Moon, nothing happens to the event. Usually I find *there is nothing you can do about the situation*. Any planet not making an aspect before it leaves the sign can be void of course.

When planets draw together to make an aspect this is called **application**. A faster-moving planet always applies to a slower one, (unless one of them is retrograde, when, of course, they apply to each other). A car approaches a garage, a garage does not approach a car. If the meeting is rather like a head-on collision because one of the planets is retrograde, the effect in interpretation is to make the event occur more suddenly and unexpectedly, but if they are *both* retrograde everything will be delayed.

Another meaning of a retrograde planet is that a lost person, animal, or object will return. It can also weaken the planet.

If an aspect is made in the order of the signs, as from Aries to Leo, the aspect is called **sinister**. If it is made against the order of the signs, as from Leo to Aries, it is called **dexter**. A dexter aspect is stronger. The aspect is made by the faster of the two planets. In our example chart the Moon's application to Venus and Mercury is dexter, but its application to Pluto is sinister.

As soon as the aspect is completed it starts to separate. This is called simply **separation** and it begins from 6 minutes after exactitude. The event has occurred. However, the two planets are not entirely separated until beyond half the sum of their joint orbs. As soon as they separate we would no longer say they are in aspect, but rather that they are separating from aspect.

Orbs are considered according to the planet rather than to the aspect. An orb is like an aura around a planet. Opinion varies about the exact orb. The Sun has a large orb, 15 degrees to 17 degrees, but this only means 7 degrees to 8 degrees on each side of the Sun. Such a half-measure of the whole orb is called the **moiety** of the orb. Any planet within an orb of 8 degrees of the Sun and *in the same sign* is called **combust**. Its strength is sapped by the Sun--unless the planet involved is Mars. The Moon is particularly debilitated when combust. On the other hand, it is interesting to note that any planet at the very heart of the Sun, within 17 minutes of its centre, is called **cazimi** and is considered most fortunate.

So it is to the planets that **orbs** belong, for an orb is circular and shines round a planet like the halo 'round the early saints. So powerful is the orb of the Sun that other planets give up their strength in combustion of such power--other planets except Mars, that is. Mars is of the same hot and dry nature as the Sun, and de Vore's *Encyclopedia of Astrology* tells us Mars' power is increased there. [1] Lilly does not mention this, although it sounds reasonable. The Sun is so strong that not only is a planet debilitated by being combust, it is also slightly weakened by being within 17 degrees of it. It is then said to be **under the Sun-Beams**. I am not sure if, as in combustion, the planet must be in the same sign. The effect is slight. (See Figure 5.2 on the following page.)

Figure 5.2: Orbs of the Planets

Saturn 9° or 10°	(moiety 4 1/2° -- 5°)
Jupiter 9° to 12 °	(moiety 4 1/2° -- 6°)
Mars 7 1/2° or 7°	(moiety 3 1/2° -- 3 1/4°)
Sun 17° or 15°	(moiety 8 1/2° -- 7 1/2°)
Venus 8° or 7°	(moiety 4° -- 3 1/2°)
Mercury 7°	(moiety 3 1/2°)
Moon 12 1/2° or 12°	(moiety 6 1/4° -- 6°)

Years of experience will eventually reveal the orbs of the outer planets to us. In actuality, the moieties are very much the kind of orb we would allow nowadays in nativities.

Discussing separation, Lilly gives us this example: "admit two Planets significators in Marriage at the time of the question, are lately separated but a few minutes; I would then judge there had been but few dayes before great probability of effecting a Marriage, but now it hung in suspense, and there seemed some dislike or rupture in it, and as the significators doe more separate, so will the matter of affection of the partners more alienate and vary,"[2] and when the faster planet is beyond the orb of the aspect that was between them, then the partnership will be broken off. He adds that if the significators are in cardinal signs and angular houses, and if the daily motion of the planets is fast, this hastens the time period involved. But if they are in fixed signs and cadent houses, and their movement slow, this slows down the time. Timing is complicated and might be a life-study for someone.

Old books say that two planets "behold" each other, which implies an approaching aspect or a perfect aspect. But as soon as the planets are separating they are no longer beholding. It is over--they cannot see out of the backs of their necks.

If two planets are applying to an aspect, but before the aspect can be completed another planet intercepts, this is called **prohibition**. Prohibition affects and usually prevents the completion of the action. Such a prohibition can occur by conjunction or aspect. For example, Venus may be at 5 degrees and moving towards Jupiter at 10 °, but before she can reach him, Mercury, who was lurking at 4 °, passes Venus and reaches Jupiter first. This is *bodily prohibition*, or prohibition by conjunction. However, the same can be effected by other aspects. Mercury could complete its trine aspect to Jupiter, for instance, before Venus attains 10 °, the place of Jupiter.

Another kind of prohibition is called **refranation**. Here one planet is travelling towards another, but it goes retrograde before reaching it. Or, the pursued planet slips into the next sign before it can be caught, and therefore, it is out of reach.

Translation occurs when a swifter planet leaves a heavier one and then catches up with another heavier planet. The swift one then translates, or passes on, the light from one to another. The two heavier bodies can be separating from aspect, or approaching an aspect. [3]

The translating planet should be received by the first planet in some of its dignities, thereby showing its sympathy. For instance, let us say we have a chart with Mars in 4 ° Taurus, Mercury in 7° Cancer, Venus in 8° Aries. Mercury translates from dexter sextile Mars to dexter square Venus, and is received by them both being in the triplicity of Mars and the face of Venus. If there is no sympathy, a planet might not be inclined to translate. Mars might not *want* to translate from Saturn because they are unfriendly planets.

Think of their symbolism in the question. Translation is something done by a friend, to help. Being received in translation is not quite the same as mutual reception where planets are in each other's places and degrees. Being received merely means one planet is disposited by another planet in any of their essential dignities.

Another example of translation might be Saturn at 2° Sagittarius and Moon at 3° Libra and Jupiter at 15° Aquarius. The Moon separates from sextile Saturn and carries its light to trine Jupiter and is received by Saturn in its exaltation. This can be done by conjunction or by aspect. The trouble is that if it is an infortune to which the light is carried, and it is badly placed, it could destroy the question.

However, assuming the planets in our example to be well-placed, such a configuration might be interpreted as the querent, Saturn, wishing to contact Jupiter, the quesited. He seeks a means to do this and might give a message or letter to a Moon-like person, or a person represented by the house that had Cancer on the cusp, to be conveyed to Jupiter. If Cancer was on the third cusp, the Moon would be a brother or sister; if Cancer was on the ninth, it would be a foreigner, etc. There is a good example of translation in Part Two, Chapter 19 in "Where are my spectacles?".

Frustration means that a faster planet is travelling towards a slower one, but before the conjunction can take place the slow one joins up with some other planet. You might have Venus at 5° Capricorn trying to reach Mars at 12° Capricorn, but before she can do so Mars comes up to Jupiter at 14° Capricorn. It is very frustrating for her! The traditional implication of frustration was of "corporeal aspect." (I mention this to help you when you read old books.)

Collection occurs when two significators are not in aspect, but both aspect *towards* another planet that is weightier than themselves. This weightier planet then collects the light of them both. If it is a good, well-placed planet, it will accomplish the event, but if it is an infortune, badly placed, the matter could be destroyed. In interpretation one might have Venus, representing the querent, aspecting towards Jupiter, representing the uncle, yet desiring to meet Mars, representing the young man. Venus and Mars are not in aspect, but both aspect Jupiter (both know him) and he, the third party, arranges the desired event. However, if it was Saturn poorly placed that they both aspected the outcome could be unsatisfactory. Strictly speaking, the collecting planet should be received by the faster planets in some of their dignities, showing sympathy. Natal astrologers find collection hard to understand and readers are referred to Chapter 10 where "The Comet" shows a good example.

The old word for an exact aspect is *partill*.

The word for an inexact aspect is *platick*. Here the planets are within the moiety of both their orbs.

The *dispositor* of a planet has a great effect on that planet, especially reflective planets such as the Moon and Mercury. For instance, the dispositor of Mercury positioned in the first house gives intelligence.

The importance of dispositors seems to be neglected in natal astrology today. William Lilly provides us with an example of a man who asked "Will I be rich?" In this case, the second cusp (possessions) is ruled by Scorpio, so the man's riches depended on the placement of Mars, ruler of Scorpio. Mars ascended in Libra, and one might be tempted to think that a malefic rising would portend misfortune, but not at all. Lilly judged that question by the state of Venus, the dispositor of Mars, which was strong, angular and in a fixed sign (unwavering). The querent would have his riches.

One begins to see that not only do the signs belong to the planets, but all the disposited planets do, too. They are disposited by sign to a greater extent, and disposited by other dignities to a certain extent. In ancient Greece, the dispositors were said to rule the planets disposited.

Our ancestors also considered it important whether a planet was *oriental*. There is one sense in which this means "on the eastern side of the chart" in the oriental quadrant, and there is another sense in which it means to rise before the Sun.

Occidental can mean "on the western side of the chart," or it can mean that a planet rises after the Sun. The inferior planets were considered more fortunate when occidental, and the superior more fortunate oriental. I do not know enough about this to advise you, but it is a field of research. [4]

A planet *besieged* is unfortunate. It is between Mars and Saturn, trapped. In Lilly's day the planet would be in the same sign as the two infortunes, but today a planet is counted as besieged if several signs intervene between them.

Aspects: A Clarification for Newcomers

If the Moon is at 6° Leo and Mercury at 7° Libra, the Moon moves to a sinister sextile of Mercury. They aspect, or behold one another.

If the Moon is at 7° Leo and Mercury at 7° Libra, they are in partill sinister sextile aspect.

If the Moon is at 8° Leo and Mercury at 7° Libra, the Moon separates from a sinister sextile. They no longer behold one another. They are not in aspect, they separate from aspect.

If the Moon is at 6° Leo and Mercury at 7° Gemini, the Moon moves to a dexter sextile of Mercury. They aspect, or behold one another.

If the Moon is at 7° Leo and Mercury at 7° Gemini, they are in perfect dexter sextile aspect. This is a partill aspect.

If the Moon is at 8° Leo and Mercury at 7° Gemini, they are separating from dexter sextile. The aspect is over, and they no longer behold one another. They are not in aspect.

If the Moon is at 6° Aries and Mercury at 7° Aquarius, the Moon aspects Mercury with a dexter sextile aspect. Note: The relationship of direction is the same as from Leo to Gemini--against the order of the signs.

"Behold" implies being in aspect or going towards being in aspect.

Make your major decision, your headline answer from the major Ptolemaic aspects. The semi-sextile and quincunx, not being major aspects, are not considered until after the major ones. After the decision is made they can add details.

At first use only major aspects to derive your answer.

Planetary Movement

One consequence of astrology having been adapted to psychology during this century is the loss of an understanding of time passing in the chart, and with that of course, an inability to make predictions.

Past events are known by aspects that have passed, and future events are known by aspects that will be made. The main indicator is the Moon, because of its speed of motion, but the same also may be seen in planets that are significators.

When two planets go towards an aspect it is like two people going to meet each other, (the planets then behold each other). When the aspect is exact it is as if the two people are meeting, (the planets still behold each other). As soon as the planets separate by only minutes it is as if the meeting is over and the two people separate. (The planets are then no longer beholding each other. They are, in fact, no longer in aspect.)

Figure 5.3: Planets and Their Speed of Motion

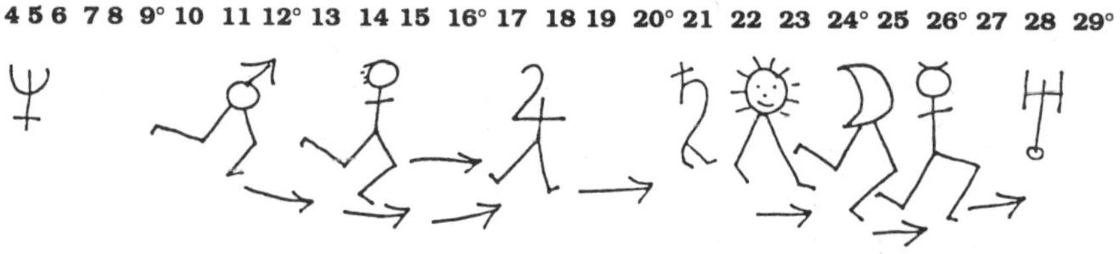

4 5 6 7 8 9° 10 11 12° 13 14 15 16° 17 18 19 20° 21 22 23 24° 25 26° 27 28 29°

In this diagram Venus has passed Mars (she runs faster so will not contact him). However, he is running to Jupiter and so is she. Jupiter will collect the light from them both, especially if he is friendly, which can be emphasized by the sign(s) in which they are placed, and thereby Jupiter affects a contact between them. The collecting planet must be in a higher degree than the other two or it will not be able to help. Notice that Jupiter here at 16° could not help Mercury, because Mercury runs fast and has escaped. Jupiter will contact Saturn, for he is walking in that direction. Saturn might turn round and go back to meet him (go retrograde), which would make their meeting more sudden.

The Sun, who moves faster than Saturn, has left him. Saturn cannot catch up with the Sun, so they cannot meet again for the Sun never retrogrades.

Perhaps the Sun wants to reach Mercury, and would be unable to because Mercury runs faster. Fortunately, the Moon, fastest by far, leaves the Sun and takes the Sun's message to Mercury, whom she catches before the end of the sign. That is, the Moon translates the light of the Sun to Mercury. Will she catch him before he joins up with Uranus?

Of course, all of them have left Neptune far behind.

These drawings show the planets in order of their speed of motion. The Moon is fastest, hence her long legs. Mercury, as you recall, was referred to as the "winged one." If the planets were in the degrees indicated in the diagram below, from aspecting signs, much would happen as the Moon ran into each planet in turn.

Figure 5.4: Much Happens

0 1 2 3 4 5 6 7 8 9 10 11 12 13 14 15 16 17 18 19 20 21 22 23

But if the planets were in the degrees indicated below, nothing would happen at all. Each planet escapes from the one before it and cannot catch the one in front.

Figure 5.5: Nothing Happens

0 1 2 3 4 5 6 7 8 9 10 11 12 13 14 15 16 17 18 19 20 21 22

Stations

A retrograde planet or one that is stationary and about to
retrograde can be unfortunate, and can show delay, dissolu-
tion, and destruction. But a stationary planet that is about to
go direct shows an aptness and renewing of strength, [5] rather
like a cat waiting to pounce.

It is important not to have builders start working on your
house when a planet is in its station, about to retrograde. I had
read this advice in *Bonatus Guide*, however, builders do not
always come when they should, but rather when it pleases
them. My builder, for instance, decided to turn up on the day
Mercury was at its first station. I had waited several months
for him, so I could not tell him to go away. The work he did was
unsatisfactory and, as Bonatus said, "Any work or building
then begun, it will not be finished."[6] Things went from bad to
worse. I did not look to see if Mercury was "under the earth,"
because then, says Bonatus, "It will take thirty years." What
the builder started remains poorly completed and unsatisfactory still.

The second station, when the planet is going to direct,
shows accomplishment, but slowly, intricately, with pains
and trouble; however, it eventually will be done. I began
teaching this course in horary astrology at such a time.
Astrology needed reviving from its tragic lethargy, which I
hope is past and over. As Al Biruni says, "the second station
shows delivery is near at hand."[7]

More On Sinister And Dexter

I repeat, a sinister aspect is made by the faster of two planets in the direction of the flow of the signs. A dexter aspect is against the flow of the signs. Aries to Gemini is a sinister sextile; Aries to Aquarius is a dexter sextile and so is Aquarius to Sagittarius.

Here I should mention Edward W. Whitman, whose book *Astro-kinetics* reverses the names of these aspects. Alone among notable astrologers, Whitman has written, "A dexter aspect is one which is made forward in the zodiac whilst a sinister aspect is one made backward in the zodiac. [8] This is a pity because it must have confused many astrologers. It does not detract from the excellent interpretations made by Whitman, who examines the differences between the two categories of aspect, and surpasses any other explanations I have come across. I recommend them to natal and horary astrologers alike. But for my own sanity and clarity of mind, I went through his book crossing out "sinister" and writing in "dexter," in pencil, and vice versa. Luckily, by page 60, Mr. Whitman, who by then may have noticed that he used the opposite word from everyone else, changes to saying "aspects made backwards." Whitman's book was compiled and published posthumously, and may explain why he never altered those words.

There is a good deal of difference between the meaning of dexter and sinister. Nowadays they seem unpopular, perhaps because a dexter aspect implies that the thing happens to you, rather than you make it happen; there is more force of circumstance, it is more of a fatality. Whitman gives pages of examples of the differences between dexter and sinister in particular cases; I will give one random example (with my pencil alteration). In telling us of Jupiter square Fortuna Whitman says, "an unwise adherence to the factor of luck interferes with the application of practical remedies for solving difficulties...the sinister square will bring disappointment through misplaced personal efforts, the dexter square through being let down by other people."[9] [These are the words of Mr. Whitman except I have altered his word "dexter" to "sinister" and sinister to dexter.]

Chapter 6

The Dignities
and Evaluations
of the Planets

Figure 6.1 (on the following page) shows Ptolemy's Table of Essential Dignities and Debilities of the Planets. The first vertical
column lists the signs. The second column names the planets
that rule those signs. Beside the glyph for the planet you see
a D. or an N. This is because fire and air signs were considered
positive, masculine and of the day (D); earth and water signs
were considered receptive, feminine and of the night (N).

In the traditional rulerships, you will notice that each
planet rules a masculine and a feminine sign, for each has a
masculine and a feminine way in which to express itself. Mars
is expressed more positively in Aries and more subtly in
Scorpio. Aries was, therefore, referred to as the day house of
Mars ("house" in this context means "sign"). The rulership of
signs by planets has an exact pattern, as shown in Figure 6.2
(on page 95).

You will notice the arrangement is alternately masculine
and feminine, so that each planet has one sign of each. Read
up the right-hand column and down the next and you see the
order is fire, earth, air, water.

In Figure 6.3 (page 95) it is shown more clearly. Here you

Figure 6.1: Ptolemy's Table of Essential Dignities

PTOLEMY'S TABLE OF THE ESSENTIAL DIGNITIES AND DEBILITIES OF THE PLANETS

	SIGNS		EXALT-ATION	TRIP. DAY	TRIP. NIGHT	TERMS					FACES			DETRI-MENT	FALL
E	♈	♂ D.	☉ 19	☉	♃	♃ 6	♀ 14	☿ 21	♂ 26	♄ 30	♂ 10	☉ 20	♀ 30	♀	♄
S	♉	♀ N.	☽ 3	♀	☽	♀ 8	☿ 15	♃ 22	♄ 26	♂ 30	☿ 10	☽ 20	♄ 30	♂	
W	♊	☿ D.		♄	☿	☿ 7	♃ 14	♀ 21	♄ 25	♂ 30	♃ 10	♂ 20	☉ 30	♃	
N	♋	☽ D. N.	♃ 15	♂	♂	♂ 6	♃ 13	☿ 20	♀ 27	♄ 30	♀ 10	☿ 20	☽ 30	♄	♂
E	♌	☉ D. N.		☉	♃	♄ 6	☿ 13	♀ 19	♃ 25	♂ 30	♄ 10	♃ 20	♂ 30	♄	
S	♍	☿ N.	☿ 15	♀	☽	☿ 7	♀ 13	♃ 18	♄ 24	♂ 30	☉ 10	♀ 20	☿ 30	♃	♀
W	♎	♀ D.	♄ 21	♄	☿	♄ 6	♀ 11	♃ 19	☿ 24	♂ 30	☽ 10	♄ 20	♃ 30	♂	☉
N	♏	♂ N.		♂	♂	♂ 6	♃ 14	♀ 21	☿ 27	♄ 30	♂ 10	☉ 20	♀ 30	♀	☽
E	♐	♃ D.		☉	♃	♃ 8	♀ 14	☿ 19	♄ 25	♂ 30	☿ 10	☽ 20	♄ 30	☿	
S	♑	♄ N.	♂ 28	♀	☽	♀ 6	☿ 12	♃ 19	♂ 25	♄ 30	♃ 10	♂ 20	☉ 30	☽	♃
W	♒	♄ D.		♄	☿	♄ 6	☿ 12	♀ 20	♃ 25	♂ 30	♀ 10	☿ 20	☽ 30	☉	
N	♓	♃ N.	♀ 27	♂	♂	♀ 8	♃ 14	☿ 20	♂ 26	♄ 30	♄ 10	♃ 20	♂ 30	☿	☿

see a six-pointed star of the positive signs, and a similar one could be made of the negative signs. This demonstrates that Saturn is the opposite to the luminaries; Mercury is opposite Jupiter, and Venus opposite Mars. This was important when herbalists cured either by using plants in sympathy to the disease or of the opposite nature.

Figure 6.2: Rulership of Signs

fire masculine Leo	**SUN MOON**	Cancer feminine water
earth feminine Virgo	**MERCURY**	Gemini masculine air
air masculine Libra	**VENUS**	Taurus feminine earth
water feminine Scorpio	**MARS**	Aries masculine fire
fire masculine Sagittarius	**JUPITER**	Pisces feminine water
Earth feminine Capricorn	**SATURN**	Aquarius masculine air

Figure 6.3: Planetary Rulerships

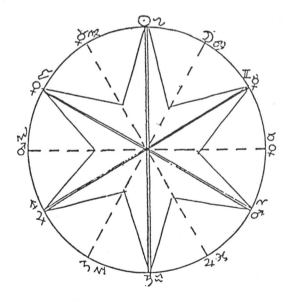

The diagram also explains the detriment of the planets. The Sun is detrimented in the sign opposite it in this star, that is, in Aquarius. The Moon is detrimented in Capricorn.

I conclude that the outer planets do not rule signs, as is commonly accepted among many natal astrologers today. Nor do they rule days of the week or planetary hours. They have no part in this ancient pattern. They do, however, rule specific things--especially modern things like telephones, aircraft, bombs, and electricity.

Referring back again to Ptolemy's Table (Figure 6.1) you will see that the third column is headed "Exaltations". Exaltation applies to the whole sign. The reason the Sun is given 19° Aries in particular must be that from time immemorial that degree seemed to be an especially good one for the Sun. Lilly mentions it in his interpretation about the battle of Alsford, where it greatly helped the Parliamentary side. [1]

John Gadbury tells us about hypothetical charts of the Creation of the World from ancient times. The Egyptians and Arabians, and Josephus, favoured the time of the autumn equinox, and Mercator decided on the summer. Others preferred the spring, and among them, Virgil and Junctinus. It was not, perhaps, that the chart was literally believed, for what coordinates would be taken? And anyway, there wouldn't have been any seasons! Presumably, this was a subject astrologers could waffle about, rather as today's astrologers hope for applause when they write about nothing very much for several pages. However, the springtime map is the one given by Gadbury in *A Collection of Choice Nativities*, [2] and in it all the planets are in their exaltation degrees, except Mercury which could not possibly be so far from the Sun. There may well be a deep, and so far unrealized by me, significance in these positions.

The fourth column, headed Triplicity (Trip.), includes the words DAY and NIGHT. This column refers to the triplicities as we know them: earth, air, fire, and water. Aries, Leo, and Sagittarius are the fire signs, and if you see the Sun in a fire sign in a daytime chart you account it in its own triplicity. If you see it in a nighttime chart this is not so. Jupiter in fire signs in a night chart is in its own triplicity, but not so in a day one. So as you see in the table, Venus rules the earth triplicity in the daytime and the Moon does so at night. Saturn rules the air in the daytime and Mercury does so at night. Mars rules the water triplicity all the time.

You may wonder at this arrangement, and the explanation can be read in Ptolemy's *Tetrabiblos*, 1.7. Here we find the planets divided into two teams, the *sects*: masculine, active, daytime planets on one team, and feminine, passive, night-time planets on the other. The Sun and Jupiter were called masculine, and Venus and the Moon feminine planets. Mercury was neutral and belonged to both sects.

Next the allocation of the malefics was decided. Mars is naturally too hot, and although more akin to the day, he was allocated to the night to break his power. Saturn was so cold he is more akin to the night, so he was allocated to the day to break his power. This does not really contradict the sign rulership of the planets, for there they are given a dual mode of expression, regardless of whether they are male or female. All this decision-making may sound unreasonable, but "reason is an illusion of reality." [3]

The fifth to the ninth columns show the **terms**, boundaries, or termini of planets, a sub-division within signs. Starting with the top line you see that Jupiter rules from the beginning of Aries to 6° Aries. Venus rules from 6° Aries to 14°, then Mercury takes over. We would say, therefore, that Jupiter at 5° Aries is "in his own terms." (Those who ponder this way of reading the table should consult page 510 of *Christian Astrology* where Lilly discusses it further.) A planet in its own terms is said to be "in its dignity."

The terms are quite powerful, much more so than the **faces**, which are shown in columns ten to twelve. Notice the faces are a rulership by planets. A planet in its own face has *some* dignity, but not much. It is poor, but not like a tramp. This ten-degree rulership of planets must be extremely ancient as you will realize when considering the order of the planetary hours. This order of the planets, called the Chaldean order, is the ever-repeated order of the hours which determines the names of the days of the week. Thus, it is as old as the week, and the week is as old as the faces.

Reading the planets across we have in Aries Mars, Sun, Venus; in Taurus Mercury, Moon, Saturn; in Gemini Jupiter, Mars, Sun, Venus, Mercury, etc. This is the order of the hours. It reflects a knowledge of the relative speeds of the planets, for if Earth is substituted for the Sun in the arrangement, we have the order of the planets in our solar system. But reading the planets downward we have the order of the days of the week: Mars (Mardi, Tuesday), Mercury (Mercredi, Wednesday), Jupiter (Thorsday, Thursday), etc. So Ptolemy's Table of Essential Dignities is a very useful and interesting table.

If you find, when examining a chart, any two planets are in each other's dignities, this is called **mutual reception**. The planets can then be read as if back in their own dignity. When this happens, they exchange degrees--not actually, but as if it were by reflection--with the planet with whom they are exchanging places. If the mutual reception is by sign, between the major significators in question, it can give an affirmative answer, even without aspect--so long as there is no contradictory indication. Ptolemy called this technique "exchange of sign." [4] It gives a way out, an escape.

In saying that the two planets exchange places, much as a planet reflects its position in solstice points (antiscia), I do not infer that the new position is so tangible that it could be used to make or receive aspects. This would be outside the pattern of traditional astrology. However it has power in the degree in which it is mutually received.

An example of mutual reception by exaltation would be Venus in Capricorn and Mars in Pisces. This alone is not strong enough to give an affirmative answer.

An example of mutual reception by triplicity in a daytime chart would be Mars in Libra and Saturn in Cancer.

An example of mutual reception by term is Venus in 24° Aries and Mars in 16° Gemini. I quote this example because it is the one given in *Christian Astrology*, (page 112) but mis-printed in the 1647 edition--the one Regulus reprinted--but was corrected in the second edition in 1658. The example is precious for it makes evident the fact that planets must also exchange degrees. Some of my esteemed colleagues in this art deny this.

Mutual reception by exaltation and triplicity, term and face, is not strong enough alone to give an affirmation, but shows a sympathy. Mutual reception by face is very weak--I'd say non-existent. Andrew Bevan has investigated mutual reception by detriment. I have not used this. I do not think our astrology is sufficiently sophisticated to include such refine-ments yet.

If a planet is not in any dignity, that is, if it is not in its own sign, exaltation, triplicity, term, or face, nor can mutually exchange with another planet back into such position, it is called **peregrine**. A planet that is peregrine is like a wanderer, without a home. It is weak. We are told that a planet peregrine could indicate a thief. [5] (Also, when looking for a thief, the ruler of the seventh house can show one.) A planet peregrine can be in aspect to another planet. (There is an idea that it could not!)

When you look at Ptolemy's Table in various books you see there is variation in information. Remember that the original *Tetrabiblos* is no longer extant. Every version you see today is someone's interpretation. Lilly had three versions, according to his list of books, and as he was a hugely successful astrologer who put his information to practical use, I follow his version. It is nearer to Al Biruni than to the Loeb edition of the *Tetrabiblos*, and that, too, has probably been changed over time. Luckily, we have Lilly's original work and know what he advocated.

Al Biruni tells us quite simply that his *Egyptian and Ptolemaic Tables of Terms* are the best and "there is no use in discussing any others," [6] which I found endearing.

In the Satellite chart discussed in Chapter 4 (Figure 4.1), Venus is at 18° 55' Aquarius, and as you see in Ptolemy's Table, from 13° to 20° Aquarius belong to Venus. She is, therefore, in her own terms, and thus, strong. Jupiter is also in his own terms, which encompass from 0° Sagittarius to 7° 59' Sagittarius. [7]

It is useful to make a list beside your chart of the dignities of planetary positions so you can spot mutual receptions. (See Figure 6.4.) In this example, Venus and Jupiter, the benefics, are strong as dispositors. The Sun is in the terms of Saturn, Saturn is in the terms of Mars, and Mars is in the terms of Venus. Therefore, Venus is the dispositor of the Sun, Saturn, and Mars.

On the side of Ptolemy's Tables, I have marked E (for east), S (for south), W (for west), and N (for north) on the extreme left beside each sign. I find it convenient to have this reference with the Table. It is not properly part of the Table, but it is particularly useful in questions about location. If, for instance, you had lost a horse and the significator was in Aquarius, the horse would be in the west. (Lilly gives another list of more specific directions, on page 204 of *Christian Astrology*.)

Figure 6.4: Signs and Directions

♈ East, ♌ East by North, ♐ East by South
♎ West, ♊ West by South, ♒ West by North
♋ North, ♏ North by East, ♓ North by West
♑ South, ♉ South by East, ♍ South by West

The Dignities and Evaluation of the Planets

The nature of the aspect is of less importance than the nature of the planets involved. The Titanic went down during a facile trine of the significator to a malefic Mars conjunct Scheat--it went with ease to its watery grave.

On the other hand, there could be some questions where the nature of the aspect is of primary importance, for instance, if you want to know if two people would be friends. An opposition or square aspect would make me decide that the answer is no, for there is no *ease* shown with these aspects.

I reproduce for you below a table--To Examine the Fortitudes and Debilities of the Planets--by which our ancestors assessed the strength of the planets. (See Figure 6.5.) Perhaps you will be interested to do the same. You will notice that a planet in conjunction with the Nodes was given a high score, yet I find Mrs. Watters rule--that any planet in the degree of the Nodes is *unfortunate* works. She calls it "A degree of fatality." The house in which the North Node appears seems to be fortunate, and the one of the South Node, as Lilly states "prenotes detriment and impediment of such things as are signified by that house." [8]

At least we should know this technique exists, and when it is hard to judge between two planets' strengths, it can be used. Natal astrologers may be surprised to see how it alters natal judgments. (See Figure 6.5 on the following page.)

This brings us to the subject of the outer planets, which cannot be assessed for fortitudes and strengths. Indeed, unless you know better than the authorities on astrology for the last two thousand years, unless you negate the validity of Lilly's work, of Al Biruni's, of generation after generation of astrological work, and unless you personally and by experience know exactly where the dignities of the outer planets are, their exaltations, triplicities, terms, faces, and signs, I do not believe that you can use the outer planets as if they appear in Ptolemy's Table of Essential Dignities, for they do NOT.

It is true that the outer planets naturally rule specific matters--for instance, Uranus rules, it seems, electrical equipment, airplanes, and divorce--and in these contexts we use them. But we do not assign to them sign rulerships, nor do we mutually exchange their places. These planets have their functions, but they are not really family. I have never seen a chart in which their mutual reception is relevant to the interpretation.

In fact, there has been confusion about terms since before Roman times. Some astrologers used Ptolemy's system, others used what are generally called Egyptian Terms. Appar

Figure 6.5: Table to Examine the Fortitudes and Debilities of Planets

ESSENTIAL DIGNITIES	SCORE	DEBILITIES	SCORE
A planet in its own sign, or in mutual reception with another by sign	5	In detriment	-5
		In fall	-4
		Peregrine	-5
In exaltation, or reception by exaltation	4		
In own triplicity	3		
In own term	2		
In own face	1		

ACCIDENTAL FORTITUDES		ACCIDENTAL DEBILITIES	
On M.C. or Asc.	5	In 12th house	-5
In 7th, 4th, or 11th house	4	In 8th or 6th house	-2
In 2nd or 5th house	3	Retrograde	-5
In 9th house	2	Slow in motion	-2
In 3rd house	1	♃ ♄ ♂ occidental	-2
Direct	4	☿ ♀ oriental	-2
Swift in daily motion	2	☽ decreasing in light	-2
♄ ♃ ♂ oriental	2	Combust	-5
☿ ♀ occidental	2	Under the sunbeams	-4
☽ increasing in light or occidental	2	Partill ♂ with ♄ or ♂	-5
Free of combustion and the sunbeams	5	Partill ♂ with ☋	-4
Cazimi	5	Partill ☍ of ♄ or ♂	-4
Partill ♂ with ♃ or ♀	5	Besieged of ♄ or ♂	-5
*Partill ♂ with ☊	4	Partill ☐ of ♄ or ♂	-3
Partill △ with ♃ or ♀	4	Conjunct Algol, or within 5°	-5
Partill ✶ with ♃ or ♀			
♂ with Cor Leonis	6		
♂ Spica	5		

* (My personal opinion is to disagree with this item)

ently, Vettius Valens used a system in which the luminaries were included in the terms. When more works of ancient astrologers have been translated we may have the opportunity to assess the value of their methods, for our present-day experience is inadequate. Meanwhile, we can only do our best to try to rebuild our art and hope that it will not be lost again. At least we know Lilly's methods did work (he judged thousands of charts yearly) and he knew his job. And that because he expected to die of the Plague daily (having lost two servants because of it) as he wrote his great book, [9] his work is remarkably sincere. I have decided, therefore, to try the methods Lilly advocates.

Chapter 7
Planetary Hours

From antiquity there has been a condition upon which the validity of a chart depends, and which I have not so far mentioned, and that is upon planetary hours. Is it stretching the bounds of credibility too far to suggest that not only a moment, but an hour has its quality? Zadkiel omitted planetary hours entirely throughout his book *Introduction to Astrology* which purported to be the work of Lilly. But since Lilly, whose infallibility is second only to Perry Mason's, used them, I shall be at pains to explain them.

Before our present generation the consideration of planetary hours had always been an integral part of astrology. They were used in other ways besides determining the validity of a chart. If, for instance, the ruler of the hour is angular, a person or object looked for is within the house of the querent just as much as if the ruler of the second house is angular. In questions of theft the ruler of the hour can symbolize the thief. Ancient aphorisms tell us about planetary hours. Lilly's first aphorism reads, "See the Question be radical, or fit to be judged, which is when the Lord of the ascendant and hour be of one nature or triplicity." [1] Zadkiel changes this to "See the question be radical and fit to be judged." [2] This is a typical example of the way Zadkiel treats the work of Lilly. Perhaps he was afraid that mention of planetary hours would associate astrology with superstitions that used to be held. In the seventeenth century medicines were given at appropriate hours, and herbs were collected according to the proper hours. Nowadays, surely, astrologers can use them again to help us in our work.

The use of planetary hours is Western. I believe the Hindu system of astrology does not use it.

Everyone associates the days of the week with the planets: Sunday with the Sun, Monday with the Moon, Tuesday with Mars (French *Mardi*, Northern Europe *Tui,*), Wednesday with Mercury (French *Mercredi*, Northern Europe *Woden*, as Wode, the blue-staining plant), Thursday with Thor or Jupiter, Friday with Venus (French *Vendredi*, or Northern Europe *Frigg* or *Freya*), and of course, Saturday with Saturn.

A day was considered to start at daybreak, at sunrise; the hours were of uneven lengths--except at the equinox. The time between daybreak and sunset was divided into twelve equal periods, called hours. Thus, a summer day had long hours and a summer night short hours. A winter day had short hours and a winter night long hours. Each day begins with the hour of the planet after which it is named. For example, the first hour on Monday is the hour of the Moon. Each hour belongs to a planet in a never-ending sequence. Even between one day and the next the sequence is not broken.

Figure 7.1: The Sequence of Planetary Hours

The order of the sequence is: ☉ ♀ ☿ ☽ ♄ ♃ ♂ ☉
So, Sunday's hours are: ☉ ♀ ☿ ☽ ♄ ♃ ♂ ☉ ♀ ☿ ☽ ♄ ♃ ♂ ☉ ♀ ☿ ☽ ♄ ♃ ♂ ☉ ♀ ☿
Continuing on Monday: ☽ ♄ ♃ ♂ ☉ ♀ ☿ ☽ ♄ ♃ ♂ ☉ ♀ ☿ ☽ ♄ ♃ ♂ ☉ ♀ ☿ ☽ ♄ ♃
Continuing on Tuesday: ♂ ☉

Notice that when each day starts it is the turn of the hour of that day! Then refer to Ptolemy's Tables of Dignities and look at the faces of the planets. You will see that the same sequence is repeated here. Look at the faces of Aries (♂ ☉ ♀) then Taurus continues (☿ ☽ ♄) Consider now the antiquity of this arrangement. The sequence is Egyptian. If Earth is substituted in the place of the Sun the sequence looks more familiar.

We are told that a horary chart is not valid unless the planetary hour harmonizes with the Ascendant or ruler of the Ascendant, but I am coming to the conclusion that this means a chart may not be a happy one without the above proviso. This mattered a great deal in the days when an astrologer was thrown over the cliff if his solution was not what an emperor wanted to hear, as in the time of Thrassyllus. Certainly the best charts do have this harmonization. It can be expressed in the following ways.

1. The ruler of the hour should be of the same triplicity as the Ascendant. To discover this, look at Ptolemy's Tables of Dignities, (Figure 6.1). For instance, if Saturn is ruler of the hour and the day chart Ascendant is Gemini, this harmonizes because Saturn rules the air triplicity in the daytime, (a connection many astrologers might overlook!). Or, if the planet of the hour was Mars and the Ascendant a water sign, this is in accord because Mars rules the water triplicity.

2. The ruler of the hour should be the same as the ruler of the ascending sign, as with Sagittarius rising and Jupiter the ruler of the hour.

3. A chart is said to be valid if the hour and the Ascendant are of the same nature. This needs a little explaining. In old astrology books the signs were described as follows. (I always wondered why.)

Figure 7.2: Attributes of the Signs and Planets

♈ hot and dry ♉ cold and dry ♊ hot and moist ♋ cold and moist
♌ hot and dry ♍ cold and dry ♎ hot and moist ♏ cold and moist
♐ hot and dry ♑ cold and dry ♒ hot and moist ♓ cold and moist
The planets, too, were given such attributes
☉ hot and dry ♀ cold and moist ♂ hot and dry ♃ hot and moist
♄ cold and dry ☿ cold and dry ☽ cold and moist

If Leo ascends in a nighttime chart, and the Moon is ruler of the hour, one would consider that Jupiter is ruler of the triplicity, and if the Moon is in trine to Jupiter, that would be considered valid, according to conclusions reached by studying Lilly's example charts.

If you decide to use planetary hours it is a good idea to make a table for reference. This table must suit the vicinity in which you live, because periods of time between sunrise and sunset vary according to locality.

Raphael's Ephemeris gives the times of sunrise and sunset for all Sundays between 60° North and 50° South. This time then is divided into twelve equal periods to give the hours of daylight. In summer they will be long, and in winter short. Next, the time between sunset and sunrise is divided into twelve equal periods, giving the hours of the night. These will be short in summer and long in winter. It is interesting that the last hour of the night rules the night, just as the first hour of the day rules the day. Hence, the violence that is common on Saturday nights, when Mars rules the night. The order of the hour continues, day or night, never varying.

In my example of the Satellite chart, (Figure 4.1) the Moon ruled the hour and the Ascendant, because it was a nighttime chart, and the Moon rules the night triplicity of Virgo.

There is no doubt that charts with the ascending sign and its ruler blending with the planetary hour are more apt, although this is something only a good horary astrologer can recognize. Our natal colleagues may remain cynical, even as the general public is cynical about nativities. But since we know that the quality of one hour differs from that of another, we realize how past generations understood the integration of life with the movement of the inner planets in particular, and the rest of the Universe in general. We must hold fast to these truths before some ludicrous "astrologer", intent on including the outer planets wherever possible, invents Uranusday, Neptuneday, and Plutoday, and puts fifteen hours in a day!

Chapter 8
Divisions
of the Ecliptic

Signs

"It must be kept in mind that each sign always acts according to the nature and Zodiacal state of its Ruler. In so far as it is a Sign, it depends essentially on its Ruler." [1] (For the nature of the signs, therefore, refer to Chapter 2.) Morin.

There is also modification of interpretation of the planets according to the signs in which they are positioned. Today the signs have been over-emphasized to conform to astropsychology, at the expense of the planets and houses. Since everyone knows his or her Sun sign, commercial use also has been made of this.

The signs are the adjectives. A planet is a symbol of a person or thing and the sign it is in will describe that person or thing. Rightly used, the signs supply information in a horary chart in four main ways. First, they describe appearance, condition, and what kind of person the querent or quesited is. Note the sign on the cusp of the house concerned, its planetary ruler, and the sign containing the Moon; from these derive your adjectives. Lilly gives one example to work from: "for if the Signe be humane, aieriall that ascends or descends, and the Lord of that Signe or the Moon in any Sign of the same triplicity or nature, you may judge the Body to be handsome, and the conditions of the party to be sociable, or be very courteous." [2] I wish he had left us more like this.

The second way in which signs are used is to describe illness or disease. Notice the signs on the Ascendant and on the sixth house, which will help describe the illness. Both Lilly and Culpeper give lists of illnesses belonging to signs and to planets. In a general way, fiery signs indicate fevers, earthy ones show longer, tedious illnesses, airy signs are connected with blood impurities, and watery ones are associated with cold and dampness. In telling us about decumbitures (the time a patient takes to his or her bed) both Lilly and Culpeper say the sixth rules the illness and the first the health, for the first is the House of Life. But the diagnosis of diseases depended on more than the knowledge of sign rulership of disease. The importance of the Sun and Moon also was taken into consideration.

Illness was like a battle between the strengths of the planets ruling the sixth and of those ruling the first. Or if the disease was really serious, between the forces of the sixth or the eighth, the House of Death. The time of illness was taken from the decumbiture or when the doctor received the urine, for as the doctor was an astrologer, that time was an *event* and judged as a horary.

Another, third useful attribute of the signs is that they describe parts of the body. In this they connect with the houses (but so far as I can find, it is ONLY in this). Briefly, the correlations are as follows: Aries, the head; Taurus, the neck; Gemini, arms and hands; Cancer, the stomach; Leo, the heart and back; Virgo, the intestines; Libra, the kidneys; Scorpio, the sex organs; Sagittarius, the thighs; Capricorn, the knees; Aquarius, the ankles; Pisces, the feet.

Fourth, each sign indicates direction, as I have already mentioned. Either you can judge *where* something is by the sign in which the chief significator is placed [3] or, if the Moon is stronger, you can judge by the Moon. Judge by the stronger. [4] When judging by the Moon use the quadrant it is in. The signs also rule specific places, such as countries and towns. Much research is needed into this, and our colleagues in mundane astrology are useful here.

Even in Roman times it was known that England was ruled by Aries, and their chief entrance to our country (apart from Cornwall) must have been at Ramsgate--the gate into England. At the crowning of William the Conqueror on Christmas day, 1066, Aries ascends, and in our national chart, though the Sun is in Capricorn, we have always been considered an Arien nation. Unfortunately Ireland, a country of soft greens and cattle, is predominantly Taurean and inconjunct Aries, of England. Many books have lists of sign rulerships of countries which I do not mean to repeat here. Lilly gives several, though some of the countries' names have changed.

Very good work is now being done by those who collect data of recent charters to inaugurate countries. [5] Some older countries have altered their boundaries, or joined with adjacent countries, necessitating new charters. The British 1801 chart seems valid for our political events, but I usually use the crowning chart of 1066. That chart was obviously calculated by a knowing astrologer, and its strength contrasts with the charts of newer countries, despite its cardinality. We invent things, others profit from them. We spend much time on sport--Aries--and politics--Capricorn. We are well described by the 1066 chart.

It has always been a puzzle to me that any astrologer could associate America with Sagittarius, rather than Gemini. Ebenezer Sibley, not a good astrologer, seems to be the originator of such an idea. It is a country of few pedestrians, constant change of communications as on T.V., short journeys by air and by road. They play football with their arms and hands, and demonstrated their solidarity by holding hands across the continent; also, Geminian people love to live high up, (skyscrapers).

Australia, on the other hand, has a Sagittarian feeling. The kangaroo, with its large hips, is a brilliant emblem for the country. Australia is so non-aggressive.

Ptolemy's Book 2.3 is concerned with geographical ruler-ships, and he lists Spain under Sagittarius. (Toledo is a Sagittarian dream.) India is eternally Capricornian. He names Leo as ruler of Italy, which is unchanged, but France is also Leonine now. Portugal is Piscean, and its capital Lisbon is like Venus exalted in Pisces.

Different theories are put forward about Africa. Ptolemy lists it under Cancer. Equatorial Africa, since forests belong to Leo, should surely belong to that sign, and the original inhabitants of that country move with the grace of the lion family. It is the source of gold, a commodity of the Sun. Modern countries arising within the continent have a variety of charters; Africa has been so politically mutilated.

Towns and cities have their sign of rulerships also; for instance, London is Geminian. Wigglesworth's *Astrology of Towns and Cities* is the book to consult on British cities. (For more about the nature of signs, see Chapter 7.)

The signs also are divided into masculine--Aries, Gemini, Leo, Libra, Sagittarius, and Aquarius--and feminine--Taurus, Cancer, Virgo, Scorpio, Capricorn, and Pisces. These are useful to determine the sex of the unborn child, or of a thief.

Signs can be grouped as a cardinal (movable)--Aries, Cancer, Libra, and Capricorn--of which Aries and Libra are equinoxial, and Cancer and Capricorn solstitial. The mutable or common signs are Gemini, Virgo, Sagittarius, and Pisces, of which Gemini, Sagittarius, and Pisces are bicorporeal. I have seen events repeated when the moon was in bicorporeal (double) signs. Another instance illustrating the use of double signs is the chart of the recent Townsend Thorenson ferry disaster, where Saturn, ruler of doors, was angular in the double sign of Sagittarius, for they were double doors that were left open. When judging timing, mutable signs can indicate that something will take less time than if fixed signs were involved.

Fastest are cardinal signs. If the Ascendant or its ruler and predominance of planets are in cardinal signs, the likelihood is that something will be started but not finished due to lack of staying power. In questions about changing residence or jobs, cardinal angles quickly decide it's time to move. If the Ascendant and its ruler are in mutable signs, the resolution is firmer (what can happen is that the individuals involved will be firm and resolute for some time, then later change and be firm and resolute in another way).

If the Ascendant or its ruler is in a fixed sign, it shows continuity of purpose, and a person who is true to his word.

The water signs are considered fruitful, and thus are useful in pregnancy questions. Barren signs are Gemini, Leo, Virgo, and Aquarius.

Gemini, Virgo, Libra, and Aquarius are known further as human signs. In the case of a lost animal, those signs show it is where humans inhabit. Animal signs are Aries, Taurus, Leo, the last part of Sagittarius, the first part of Capricorn. For some reason Leo and Sagittarius are called *ferral*. Mute signs are the water signs, especially if Mercury, the planet ruling the voice, is in them.

Three signs are called *running*. They are Aries, Sagittarius, and Leo (do they walk fastest?). *Standing* signs are Gemini, Virgo, and Aquarius; *sitting* signs are Taurus, Libra, and Capricorn, and *lying down* signs are Cancer, Scorpio, and Pisces.

Signs commanding and obeying are those equally distanced from the solstice points. The ancients invented many more.

The virtue of this information is that it makes you look carefully at the sign in which your chief significator is positioned, and to deduce as much information as possible from it within the context of the question. It is a detective game.

Quadrants or Quarters

The first quadrant, which extends from the east to the Midheaven, that is, from the line of the first house to the line of the tenth house and containing the tenth, eleventh and twelfth houses, is called Oriental, Vernal, masculine, sanguine (blood red), and Infant.

The second quadrant, from the cusp of the Midheaven to the cusp of the seventh, containing the ninth, eighth and seventh houses, is called Meridian, Estival (summer), feminine, choleric, and youthful.

The third quadrant, from the cusp of the seventh to the cusp of the fourth, containing the sixth, fifth, and fourth houses, is called Occidental, autumnal, masculine, melancholic, and the quadrant of Manhood.

The fourth quadrant, from the cusp of the fourth to the first, containing the third, second, and first houses is considered northern, feminine, winter, phlegmatic, and of Old Age. [7]

This gives about five years to each house.

In a horary question, if someone asked what part of life would be best, (and I must admit nobody has asked me that, although someone asked Lilly), you should find the position of the benefics, and judge by their house positions as listed above. Conversely, if you are asked to determine the worst time, judge by the positions of the malefics. In that old example Lilly gives, [8] he found Mars in the eighth house and judged that around twenty-five would be worst age for that particular person.

Manilius, who lived about the time of Christ, put forward this theory of ages in his *Astronomica*. He wrote:

> The curve which stretches from the orient to the topmost point of the circle claims the earliest age and infant years. The slope which sinks down from the summit of the sky till it reaches the occident succeeds to the years of childhood and includes in its province control of tender youth. The portion which appropriates the setting heaven and descends to the bottom of the circle rules the period of adult life, a period tested by incessant change and chequered fortunes. But the part by whose return to the orient heaven's course is

done and which with enfeebled strength slowly ascends the backbent arc, this part embraces the final years, life's fading twilight, and palsied age. [9]

One can see here the continuity of an idea for 1,647 years at least. An idea recently contradicted by the whim of modern writers. The proof, however, is in its use.

Unlike Manilius or Lilly, Ptolemy associates ages, not with quadrants, but as is more familiar to us, with planets. "Up to the fourth year the Moon rules, producing suppleness and lack of fixity in its body, its quick growth and the moist nature"...then, "for ten years Mercury rules, there is the beginning of articulation and the intelligent logical part of the soul" is developed. Venus then takes over for eight years with an impulse toward love, "a kind of frenzy enters the soul." Next the Sun rules for nineteen years with "desire for substance and position," after which Mars rules for fifteen years introducing "severity and misery into life", then Jupiter for twelve years bringing retirement and dignity, and lastly Saturn which "lasts for the rest of life." [10]

The quadrants also show directions. From the Ascendant to the M.C. is southeast, from M.C. to the Descendant is southwest, from Descendant to I.C. is northwest, and from I.C. to the Ascendant is northeast. [11] If the Moon is stronger than the chief significator in any chart or is natural ruler of the object lost and in these positions, it indicates direction. Lilly seems to use the Moon to locate lost cattle especially, maybe because the sign of the Moon is in their horns and the Moon is exalted in Taurus.

This information is used as well as direction by sign. Yet in practice, I usually have found the most reliable indication to be the sign in which the chief significator is placed, or the Moon where it is more appropriate (as with a fugitive, wandering thing, or animal). But that is a subject which demands a chapter of its own. Lilly advises we use the stronger body, the significator or the Moon. [12]

Further Divisions of the Ecliptic

As we have seen in a previous chapter on the evaluation of planets, the signs are further divided into unequal segments called the *terms*, each ruled by a planet, and again into the faces, also ruled by planets.

In antiquity there were yet further divisions of sections of two-and-a-half degrees each, called the dode*catamoria* by which all signs of the zodiac were contained within a sign, starting with the sign being divided. [13] The dodecatamoria were then subdivided into five sections, one for each planet, and each small section contained only half a degree, in order- -Saturn, Jupiter, Mars, Venus, Mercury--to each dodecata- morion. I have not used these refinements and cannot write about them except to say they show that astrology was highly developed in the days of Manilius and early Greeks who tell us of them. [14]

Of course, signs are also divided into degrees, and every degree has its particular quality. The meanings of several degrees are still remembered and de Vore lists them in his *Encyclopedia*, [15] as does Carter at the back of the *Encyclope- dia of Psychological Astrology*. [16]Very ancient is the knowledge of those degrees which affect the sight, but there is a whole list of other degrees: dark, light, dusky, void, and of increasing and decreasing fortune--but you must read Lilly for those. Thus, every degree held a subtle nuance of meaning.

The *Via Combusta* is still another division. Some say it maintains the influence of the fixed stars that were once in that section of the sky. So there are divisions and subdivi- sions, dispositors, and minor dispositors, and intermixing and mingling, from which judgment is derived. It is by no means clear cut. Manilius calls this inter-relatedness, the hospitality of signs. Al Biruni mentions a Hindu division into three and one half degrees.

The Decanates

The decanates are a division of each sign into three sub-sections of 10 degrees, each of which is ruled by a sign. This differs entirely from the faces, which are ruled by the planets in the Chaldean Order. According to Al Biruni the decanates are of Hindu origin. This is apparent really because methods that have been passed on to us through Greece and Rome emphasize the planets.

The decanates divide the signs thus:

Signs	1st dec.	2nd dec.	3rd dec.
Aries	Aries	Leo	Sagittarius
Taurus	Taurus	Virgo	Capricorn
Gemini	Gemini	Libra	Aquarius
Cancer	Cancer	Scorpio	Pisces
Leo	Leo	Sagittarius	Aries
Virgo	Virgo	Capricorn	Taurus
Libra	Libra	Aquarius	Gemini
Scorpio	Scorpio	Pisces	Cancer
Sagittarius	Sagittarius	Aries	Leo
Capricorn	Capricorn	Taurus	Virgo
Aquarius	Aquarius	Gemini	Libra
Pisces	Pisces	Cancer	Scorpio

At the end of the last century and the beginning of this, work was done on the relationship between decanates and physical appearance. In 1938, David Anrias produced an amusingly illustrated book in which he drew a representation of each decanate of each sign as it rises. [17] He connects such characteristics as short necks with Libra and tallness with the third decanate of Gemini. (This is surprising as an aphorism says that tallness is associated with the beginning of signs.) It becomes more difficult to give accurate descriptions of

physical appearance as the races mix, yet certain characteristics persist. For example, large, uneven front teeth are
connected to Jupiter, and Moon-like, pale, circular faces with
a strong Moon.

Chapter 9

Cautions
and Strictures

Before judging a horary chart you must look to see if it describes the situation. This alone requires some experience. You need to identify the querent in the context of the question. Then you must consider if the chart is valid according to the following time-honored rules and cautions:

1. *The chart is valid when the ruler of the hour and the Ascendant or ruler of the Ascendant are the same planet, or of the same triplicity or nature.* In the best charts this is present. I find some of Lilly's maps have the ruler of the Ascendant or the Moon in strong aspect to the ruler of the hour. The original chart (not the turned chart) is the one that counts here. (Opinion is that some charts obviously do describe the situation, yet the hour does not accord. There is a message somewhere here. It may simply indicate a poor outcome, or it may be that it is not an excellent chart.) Some charts give a clearer and more accurate description than others. This is a rule I sometimes disregard, yet I think we should be aware of it.

2. *When 0, 1, or 2 degrees ascend, especially in signs of short ascension, it is no use judging,* unless the querent is very young and his body, complexion, moles, and scars agree with the sign ascending.

3. *If 27, 28, or 29 degrees ascend in any sign it is not safe to judge,* unless the querent's age corresponds to that number of degrees. I find a late degree can indicate despair.

4. *It is not safe to judge when the Moon is in the later degrees of a sign,* especially Gemini, Scorpio, or Capricorn. (Having told us that, Lilly does judge sometimes when the Moon is in later degrees, though not in those named signs. I can only suggest we keep to the rules until we are as proficient as Lilly.)

5. *When the Moon is in the Via Combusta.* This, you may remember, is from 15 degrees Libra to 15 degrees Scorpio. Discard these charts. The Ascendant in the Via Combusta is not a stricture at all, although some past astrologers have distrusted it, Henry Coley, for instance. Such a chart may be judged.

6. *When the Moon is void of course,* "all matters go hardly," says Lilly, "unless the main significators are very strong." And yet it is not so bad if the Moon is in its own signs or those of Jupiter (that is, Taurus, Cancer, Sagittarius or Pisces). Usually I find there is nothing the querent can do, as in the example later of a chart with a void of course Moon about a missing rabbit. In that instance there was a satisfactory result, for the answer can perhaps be judged from the strong significator instead. Notice Lilly never says the chart cannot be judged.

7. *If the seventh cusp is afflicted, or the ruler of that house is retrograde or impedited, if the question is not about a seventh house matter.* Such a position shows that the astrologer's judgment will not please anyone. The rule as we have it referred, of course, to Saturn and Mars afflicting the seventh

cusp. Whether the outer planets also count I am not sure, but I do not think so. Of course, if the question is about some tragic case such as murder, the seventh cusp is likely to be afflicted, because it opposes the first, the house signifying the physical body.

8. *If Saturn is in the Ascendant, especially retrograde*, the matter seldom or never comes to good. Be warned, but you can read the chart. Be careful that you are not upsetting the querent.

9. *If Saturn is in the seventh* it is either a sign of the poor judgment of the astrologer because the seventh house shows the astrologer, unless he is the querent, or shows the matter will go from one misfortune to another. Again, this is not a stricture in a seventh house question. (In my opinion if Saturn is in the seventh house, but in the sign adjacent to the one on the cusp and far from the cusp this stricture does not apply.)

10. *If the ruler of the Ascendant is combust.* Usually this means that the astrologer has not been given enough information to get the correct answer, and may even have been misinformed. Lilly says the configuration shows the querent is in some great fear (is very worried).

11. *If the ruler of the seventh is unfortunately placed*, in its fall, or in the terms of an infortune, judgment will not be good, (unless the chart refers to a seventh house question.)

Regarding numbers 7, 9, and 11 above, these strictures are made assuming the astrologer is signified by the seventh house. But if the astrologer is the querent and signified by the Ascendant and ruler of the Ascendant, (when the astrologer asks his or her own question, it is doubtful if these particular strictures apply. I am of the opinion they do not).

12. *The same question cannot be asked twice.* There are

astrologers who do not want to accept strictures, but I do not advocate this. It is always tempting to bend the chart and find some pleasant reply, but when you find one of the traditional, obvious strictures, I recommend you discard the chart. They are there for the protection of the astrologer, a warning to leave it alone. Once you have determined the chart is valid, consider the significators and decide if they do truly represent the persons or things concerned. A chart should describe the situation, and the querent is represented within the chart*[1] and described to the extent to which he or she is involved in the question personally.

As for the same question asked twice, it is my opinion that there can be only one chart for each question. Consequently, political questions are worthless, because you never know where or by whom they were first asked. I refer to such questions as, "Who will win the General Election?".

Michele Karen writes, "Horary, as the I Ching or the Tarot, is a means through which divine guidance expresses itself. Asking twice the same question supposes that we have not cared to listen to the first reply, or that it did not fit with our expectations more likely to be dictated by our little self than by wisdom. Asking twice therefore stems from a profound misunderstanding of the respect we owe to that which encompasses us in the mystery of creation."

There are some who say we should not ask large questions, but only small personal ones. But it depends where your mind ranges. We ask those questions with which we are deeply concerned, wherever they range. Does God restrict prayer?

Barbara Watters points out that if a planet in the querent's nativity is situated in the early degrees of the sign concerned, exactly on the horary Ascendant, the chart can be judged, and the planet will be particularly significant in the judgment.

Chapter 10
Collection

Natal astrologers have difficulty with the importance of the comparative speeds of the planets. When asked to draw a diagram of "Collection" even experienced natal astrologers often have no idea at all which planet is applying to which. Collection is so simple they probably can't believe it. Collection occurs when two lighter planets that do not aspect each other both make an aspect towards another weightier planet. This weighty planet then collects, or catches the light of the two lighter planets and produces an affirmative answer. It is important to be able to recognize it because if you don't, you will give the wrong answer.

The collecting planet also must be friendly or it might hinder rather than help. One would be wary and, for instance, usually discount the opposition of Mars to Saturn, thinking, "Will Saturn really want to help Mars?" But Jupiter usually helps, it all depends on the context of the question.

Figure 10.1: "Should C. and S. go to Gibraltar to see the Comet?"

Regiomontanus House System

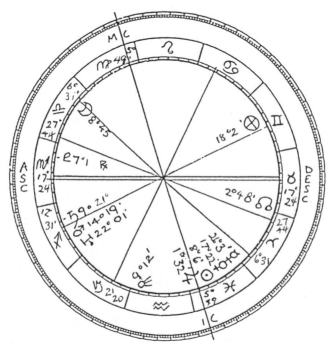

♀ **is the Comet**
27 February 1986
12:05 A.M. G.M.T.
London 51° 33' N 0° 10 W

But can you recognize this in a chart? I reproduce here a horary that contains such a configuration. The question was, "Should C. and S. go to Gibraltar to see the Comet?" Here we see the querent--"C.," our hero--represented by the Ascendant and Mars, ruler of Scorpio, and the Moon. "S.," the certain young woman, is represented by the seventh cusp and its ruler Venus.

That there will be fluctuation of objectives is shown by the Moon in the eleventh (the house of objectives). The Moon applies to Saturn on the querent's second house of cash, and a blocked feeling in this direction ensues. He insists that the journey is a short one to him and a third house matter, so the Moon is also indicating his approach to the journey. His ruler, Mars, is in the second, suggesting extravagance and outgoing of cash, especially since it is opposite Fortuna. The Moon shows this fact. Its next aspect is to sudden and unexpected expense in the shape of Uranus, to say nothing of its trine to Fortuna.

On the whole I think he will go, but will he go alone? Venus, the young woman, is departing from a dexter square of Mars, and as she moves faster than Mars, does not appear at first glance to be involved in this matter. However, have you seen it? Mars goes to a conjunction of Uranus, and Venus to a square of Uranus. Uranus, therefore, collects them up, so they are in this together. Uranus is the natural significator of airplanes and flights.

Certain other configurations show the delights of the excursion. But Mercury, ruler of the tenth house of success (and of Fortuna--and after all, the goal of the chart is to see the comet so Fortuna may symbolize that in a way), is detrimented, void, and peregrine, and in so damp a sign I wondered if they would get a good view of the comet after all.

Ideally, in collection the faster planets receive the heavier in one of their dignities, demonstrating the sympathy between them. However, it can also work without this, as demonstrated here.

The forecast proved correct, for those of you who are curious about the judgment. Weather was damp in Gibraltar and as C. and S. climbed the Rock the sky was cloudy. Then suddenly the clouds parted and they had a clear view of the comet, with lights shining in its tail--worthy of the grand trine between the Moon, the Comet, and Fortuna.

Figure 10.2: Collection

12° 13° 14° 15° 16° 17° 18° 19° 20° 21° 22° 23° 24° 25° 26° 27° 28° 29°

Imagine here two chicks running away from each other and the mother hen collects them and brings them together. There was another one further along which the mother hen cannot collect, because it has run to a higher degree.

Chapter 11
Sorting Out
the Jumble

Beginners have told me that their charts look like a jumble and they don't know where to start.

Once you have written down your question, drawn your chart, and determined that it is fit to be judged, it is a good idea to decide upon your main significators. When this has been done the chart begins to take on form, it begins to make sense. It no longer looks like a jumble.

As I have already said, the sign on the Ascendant and the planet ruling it, and the Moon always represent the querent--so find these. Look at the house the Ascendant ruler is in; each house describes a department of life. The house your symbol is in will describe where you are. If it is in the sixth, it shows you are at work. If it is in the fifth, you are having a good time, in the fourth you are at home. If it is with another planet you are not alone.

The sign containing the planet that symbolizes you is like an adjective.

The chart should describe the situation asked about. The Ascendant, the planets there, and the ruler of the Ascendant should in some way describe the questioner especially if they are involved in the situation. The house ruling the quesited should produce a planet describing the person or matter asked about. It may not be easy at first to be sure if your chart does so describe the situation. If you ask a question, do not judge your own question if a sign that is entirely alien to your nature rises, (or alien to yourself in the context of that question). At times when you are traumatized the Ascendant may differ from when you ask a normal, quiet question like, "Where are my spectacles?" Nevertheless, with practice you learn to recognize the aptness of the description. Gadbury suggests the Ascendant may be similar to your solar return ruler.

The Moon is co-ruler of the querent and usually shows where your true interest lies. This is useful if you are not judging your own question, for it will tell you, the astrologer, the true emphasis of interest of the querent. If a mother asks if her son will live abroad, for example, and the Moon is in her fourth house, you might surmise that her true interest is whether she will consequently be obliged to move house. There is no need to voice this, for what you say should be confined to answering the question. Nor should voice be used to criticize the character of the querent, thus discouraging questioners.

So the Moon is different from the Ascendant ruler. The Ascendant ruler states fact, the Moon indicates interest. If the ruler of the Ascendant is in the sixth you may be "at work" or ill, but if the Moon is there this is what you have in mind.

Having identified those two, turn to look at the quesited. The planet that rules the house of the matter asked about symbolizes the quesited. If the question is about partnership, the planet ruling the seventh cusp or a planet positioned in the seventh house symbolizes the partner.

The literal placement of the symbol often will tell you the literal placement of the person or thing asked about. If they are isolated planets, they are alone. If they are with another, the quesited is with another.

The condition of the quesited can be gleaned from the

condition--fortitudes or debilities--of the planet symbolizing him. A person with a good opinion of himself will be shown as a planet exalted. The chart is strangely like a play with the characters decked out round the stage. The Moon is the most powerful. The Moon shows the action, yet if the Moon is powerless in the chart a conclusion still can be found from the application or separation of the symbols of the main characters.

In a very simple question position alone may provide the answer. In questions such as "Which is the best direction to go for our holiday?" look where the main significators are. "Will I get the job?", (the inferred question is "Will I be in a position of having the job") will be answered "Yes" if the querents main significator is in the tenth house. The main significator approaching the ninth cusp gives an affirmative to "Will I go abroad?" If it is the Moon only that is there, you hope to go.

Usually the question is more involved than that. In asking where something is we also want to know if we will find it. Action is involved, and with action, aspects, receptions, translation of light or collection, and the whole complex structure of the chart. For example, if you ask if someone is at home and his significator is angular, then he is. (If the person does not mean anything in particular to you, take the seventh ruler as his indicator, but if he is an intimate friend take the eleventh house ruler). If the significators are in succedent houses the person is not far from home; if they are in cadent houses the person is far from home. If your significator perfects an aspect toward the symbol of the quesited, then you will meet each other.

Everything on this earth belongs to one of the houses, and the secret is knowing which one. If you use the wrong house you will give the wrong answer. Therefore, carefully study *Christian Astrology*, pages 50 to 56. Do not be misled by astro-wafflers. Many modern matters are not mentioned by Lilly and you have to think hard to understand the underlying implications of the houses. For instance, the fourth house is your base, your beginning, your end, the soil, your source, your ancestry, your father. Once you know the meaning of a house there is no reason to refer to books of house rulership, which can be misleading.

I emphasize that a knowledge of traditional house rulerships is essential for horary. Houses sometimes have similar properties to signs, but not always. For instance, the stomach belongs to the fourth sign, Cancer, but to the fifth house. This may be because the solar plexus would be associated with the fifth house. However, we must remember that they are not identical, although the anatomical symbolism often is.

In considering houses, remember that a planet within 5 degrees of a cusp belongs to the following house.

Confronted with some questions, it certainly can be very difficult to decide which is the relevant house. Let us say, for example, the army is under consideration. A young man about to join the army in peace time might consider that it is a sixth house, employment matter--a service. A politician assessing the resources of his country might say it is an eleventh house matter, for the kingdom is ruled by the tenth and resources are always contained in the following (here, the eleventh) house. In the seventeenth century when every town had its army, the town was signified by the fourth house, and the fifth (its resources) ruled ammunition and the army. [1] To a general who was about to lead his army on exploits, the army would be a first house matter--"ourselves," "we." He might ask, "What shall we (the army) do?" Or he might consider it a resource of "ourselves," that is, a second house matter. The astrologer must understand the implications.

I will give another example. If a king is shown by the tenth house (which he generally would be), then his wife, the queen, is shown by the fourth. Yet in a country such as ours (United Kingdom) where we are ruled by a queen, the tenth house represents her. If she should ask the question she would be signified by the first house, but if her mother asked the question the queen would be shown by the fifth.

A succedent house represents the resources of the preceding angular one.

The list I have given of what is ruled by houses is brief. It is merely the underlying principle of house rulership that must be understood. I sometimes think your own questions work out best because only you fully realize what is implied.

You must decide which house your question concerns. If you are asking about your son or daughter, look at the fifth house. The ruler of the fifth symbolizes your offspring. Let's consider the question, "Will I visit my daughter?". Are the rulers of the first and fifth approaching an aspect or separating? Does another planet translate light from one significator to the other? Does the Moon contact them both? Is there a heavier planet to which they both make aspect? With that most popular question, "Shall I leave my husband?" take the ruler of the seventh for his significator and the ruler of the Ascendant for yours (or the querent's). Remember the Sun is a natural significator of men, and so is Mars, whereas the Moon and Venus are natural significators of women. Do the relevant planets draw together or separate? Consider the aspects. In which house is his significator? Is it alone, or with a planet representing someone else? This can be a difficult question if the man asks the question about his wife, because the moon usually symbolizes the questioner as well, and so one is often not sure if the Moon is the querent or the woman. Each case needs individual attention and study.

If you, the astrologer, ask the question, the Ascendant and its ruler and the Moon signify you, the questioner. But if the question is asked on behalf of someone else, consider the house that represents that person. If the question is asked on behalf of a husband or wife, turn the chart mentally so that the seventh ascends. I do not like referred questions, although technically the chart can be turned more than once.

Suppose you ask a question on behalf of your husband's brother. Turn it to the seventh, then to the third from there, e.g., the ninth. That would do for your husband's brother, or for your partner's car. (One would hope you didn't get a question involving both of those at once!) Suppose you want to find your mother's book. Your mother is of the tenth house and her possession is the second from there. e.g., the eleventh. The book is symbolized by the planet ruling the sign on that cusp, but it also is ruled by Mercury, the natural ruler of books. The sign containing the planet that is the significator of the book will describe, as an adjective does, where the book is. Suppose it is in Virgo. Virgo describes a place south from where you are, somewhere that work is carried out, low down, perhaps on the floor, or in a cupboard. The house position helps too, as for instance, in an angular house the object asked about is at home.

It is very awkward with referred questions when you are asked on behalf of "a friend" because most relationships and also partnerships are seventh, but close friends are eleventh. I prefer not to judge these questions.

Next decide on the other main actors on the scene--who is the thief, if any, the buyer (first), seller (seventh), the overseas holiday (ninth), price (tenth). Look at the planet ruling the sign on the cusp and at any planet in the house. Look at the dispositors, both by sign and term. Now we begin to see that one planet can represent several people or things, and that one person can be represented by several planets. It can be complicated. Of course, if it is too difficult don't judge it! Wait until another question is asked which may be more helpful.

Some planets are not main significators at all. Do not waste time with them, as they may not be relevant to your question. If the Moon casts no approaching aspect to them they may show something in the past which has little bearing on your answer.

A question that seems to worry some people is: "If many people ask the same question, how do you know which chart should be judged?" To this I can only give my opinion which is based on the rule that you can't ask the same question twice, and that only the first time a question is asked is it valid. Of course, most questions are domestic ones, and you know if you have asked them before, but questions such as "Who will win the General Election?" seem useless to me because you do not know who the first questioner was.

Other people want to know if a chart can answer more than one question. Yes, if the questions are at the forefront of your mind at the same time, and you write them down. One chart will, of course, answer more than one questioner. It will describe also every event that is happening in that place at that time, and it will give a variety of answers according to the question and significators used.

Mrs. Watters gives a rule for deciding between two objects: an old car and a new one. The third rules cars. Your third house is your car now, and the third from the third is your next car, she says. [2]

Another way to differentiate seems to be to use the first sign in the third house as the first car, and the second sign in the third house as the second car. I am told by Paddy Balentine that the first sign rules the score in the first half of a game, and the second sign rules that in the second half. I prefer this way.

Horaries will never be judged by computers because although you may think they depend on so many set rules, really they depend on judgment--judgment and visualization. You have to learn the rules at first, as you do when you learn to drive, but it is judgment that makes a good driver. And Jupiter rules judgment.

Recently some misleading misunderstandings have arisen. One might, for instance, ask a question about a child. The fifth house rules children, so you look at the sign on the fifth cusp and you might see Taurus. Therefore, Venus is the planet that is symbol of that child. Or, if you see Leo on that cusp, then the Sun would be symbol of that child and the sign the Sun is in would tell you about the child. But you *cannot* look at the chart and say, Leo is the fifth sign so it rules children. Leo does not rule children. It is, in fact, a barren sign--fiery, hot, dry, angry, commanding, eastern, ruling places like forests and deserts, palaces and castles. Not a hint of children anywhere. If the symbol of the child is Venus and Venus is in Taurus, the child might be lost in farmland; or, the child might be fair and sturdy, depending on the question.

The misconception has led to a further misunderstanding:

the idea that the planet ruling the sign belongs to the sign. For instance, the misconception might be that the ninth house is connected with Sagittarius and therefore Jupiter is ruler of the ninth house. This is wrong. The ninth house is ruled by the Sun. It has always been known as the House of God. The sign is subservient to the planet. If Jupiter is well-placed here it is through the Chaldean order of planets. By this arrangement Saturn is well-placed in the first, Jupiter in the second, Mars in the third, the Sun in the fourth, Venus in the fifth, Mercury in the sixth, the Moon in the seventh, and so on. It is true Jupiter is strong in the ninth, but for other reasons the Sun rules that house.

Chapter 12
Perfecting the Matter

There are various ways in which to reach an affirmative conclusion to a question, or, as they used to say, of bringing the matter to perfection. You usually need more than one indication to produce a certain, or even probable answer, such as the significator of the querent drawing to a conjunction with the significator of the quesited without difficult intervention of a malevolent or unsympathetic planet.

If the conjunction takes place in an angular house, and the significators involved are moving fast, and if they are strong in dignity, essential or accidental, then the matter occurs, or your affirmation occurs sooner. If the planet symbolizing the quesited is also the dispositor of the querent this is even better (assuming the question was a positive one). If the conjunction takes place in a succedent house it will take longer than if it occurs in an angular one, and in a cadent house longer still. Yet in some questions, according to Lilly, the rule is reversed and the angular houses take longer.

If the conjunction occurs in the sign of the joy of the planet, that's a help, for instance: Saturn in Aquarius, Jupiter in Sagittarius, Mars in Scorpio, Venus in Libra, Mercury in Virgo.

The trine and sextile bring affirmatives; so does the square, but with difficulty. With a square especially consider the houses from which planets apply towards an aspect, whether they are fortunate or not, and if the planets involved are dignified, or even accidentally dignified, it may bring the affirmative.

The position and dignity of a planet is more important than the nature of the aspect. A trine indicates ease. The opposition is a separative aspect, and the matter usually comes to nothing. If there is mutual reception by sign between rulers it may bring some result of a temporary nature that you would regret, but even then the Moon would need to confirm, by translating light from the quesited to the ruler of the Ascendant, or similar.

You can get an affirmative answer by translation of light. You can also get it by collection, both of which have been described earlier. Of course, if there is no application between significators or other helpful factor the answer is negative. Sometimes the very presence of a planet in a house can give an affirmative answer.

Suppose you desire a certain job. The tenth is the house of profession. If the ruler of the tenth is in the first (your personal house) the job is yours--it comes to you. If your main significator is in the house of the matter, you go to it. It is yours. [1] This holds true in very simple questions, or in parts of questions, but not where action is involved. This ruling is not relevant to your co-ruler, the Moon.

Planets that are main significators in mutual reception by sign also can sometimes indicate an affirmative answer even if there is no aspect between them, provided there is no contradiction elsewhere, such as the Moon opposing Saturn. Mutual reception by house is another possibility. If your significator were in the tenth and the ruler of the tenth in the first, then you would get the job. The kind of mutual reception every natal astrologer knows is reception by sign. If you want a relationship with someone and that person's significator is in the sign your significator rules, and vice versa, that's fine.

The relationship will happen. A weaker mutual reception also can be by triplicity, as Moon in Aries and Jupiter in Virgo, or by term, as Mars in 28° Aries and Saturn in 2° Scorpio, or by face, as Sun in 18° Gemini and Mars in 25° Capricorn. If there is reception, but a square aspect, the answer is affirmative but with difficulty. The weaker mutual receptions will not of themselves give an affirmative, but acknowledge an acquaintanceship.

Reception can take place between triplicity and sign or any dignities, but by sign is the strongest. Bonatus said that significators in mutual reception "abate all malice." [2] It gives a way of escape, and is beneficial.

In mutual reception the planets exchange degrees. They exchange places entirely, otherwise how could planets exchange place by term?

To enlarge on this a little, there are certain positions, or dignities--such as a planet's own house, sign, term, exaltation, triplicity, or face--which are advantageous to a planet. If the planet does not occupy such a position but another does, the two planets can change places, and are thereby transferred back into their dignity. Lilly says "the use of it is this much, for many times when as the effecting of a matter is denied by the aspects, or when the significators have no aspect to each other, or when it seems very doubtful what is promised by a square or opposition of the significators, yet if mutual reception happen betwixt the principal significators, the thing is brought to pass, and that without any great trouble, and suddenly to the content of both parties." [3] He qualifies this statement by stipulating that the planets should be benevolent and in good houses, and that the dignity should be by house (sign), and that it is particularly good when the planets are in the signs of their joy. [4] He gives an example of the rules about mutual reception, that if the planets apply even by square or opposition, if there is mutual reception there can be a favourable reply, though with much labour. [5] In this latter case we are told there should also be translation of light by the Moon. [6] In fact, plenty of back up is needed. Those who argue (how they argue!) that Lilly did not use reception by term or face can see an example on page 402 of *Christian Astrology*.

We understand then that the planet has a strength in that position to which it is exchanged, yet one cannot start using aspects from that place as if the planet had been there radically. It is a reflection only.

Chapter 13
Antiscia

This technique is used in nativities and horaries, but is particularly useful in synastry. Firmicus attributes its discovery to Hipparchus (who lived in the second century B.C.), and gives an interesting example of it in the *Mathesis.* [1]

The procedure is this: draw a mental line between 0° Cancer and 0° Capricorn--the solstice degrees--and mirror one side of the chart onto the other. So if a planet is at 3° Capricorn, its antiscium (the Americans call this its solstice point) is at 27° Sagittarius. Or, if a planet is at 10° Cancer, its antiscium is at 20° Gemini. It is the same number of degrees on the other side of that imaginary line. The contra-antiscion degree is then 20° Sagittarius. It acts rather like a conjunction. The antiscium of Saturn on a promising planet can spoil your hopes!

Tables of the Antiscia in Signs

Gemini = Cancer
Leo = Taurus
Virgo = Aries
Libra = Pisces
Scorpio = Aquarius
Sagittarius = Capricorn

Any planet in Gemini sends its antiscion into Cancer, or from Leo into Taurus.

Figure 13.1: Antiscia

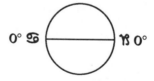

The Antiscion with regrad to degrees	The Antiscion of the planets with regard to minutes	
1 = 29	1 = 59	16 = 44
2 = 28	2 = 58	17 = 43
3 = 27	3 = 57	18 = 42
4 = 26	4 = 56	19 = 41
5 = 25	5 = 55	20 = 40
6 = 24	6 = 54	21 = 39
7 = 23	7 = 53	22 = 38
8 = 22	8 = 52	23 = 37
9 = 21	9 = 51	24 = 36
10 = 20	10 = 50	25 = 35
11 = 19	11 = 49	26 = 34
12 = 18	12 = 48	27 = 33
13 = 17	13 = 47	28 = 32
14 = 16	14 = 46	29 = 31
15 = 15	15 = 45	30 = 30

Below is an example that demonstrates the effectiveness of antiscia. See reference to the charts of Hitler and Nero in the History section of this book, Part Five.

"Will we stay together?"

The Sun and Ascendant represent the querent, and Saturn represents the quesited. The Moon is co-ruler of the querent. The Sun, being the fonder of the two persons in the relationship, has gone right over to the quesited's side of the chart.

There is no applying aspect between the main significators, and to confirm the negative outcome, the antiscium of Saturn falls on the Descendant throwing the contra-antis-

Figure 13.2: "Will we stay together?"
Regiomontanus House System

26 January 1985
4:17 P.M. G.M.T.
51° 32' N 0° 43' E

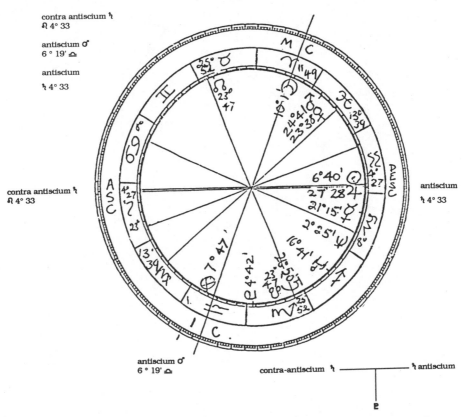

cium to the Ascendant. This forms a T-square with Pluto in the fourth, which showed the querent being ejected from her house.

Despite the approaching conjunction of Venus to Mars natural significators of male and female, Venus is in the degree of the Nodes, a fateful degree.

The final aspect made by the Sun is sextile to Uranus, the planet of divorce or separation and rearrangement.

There is reference in history to the use of the equinoxial points in a similar way to the solstice points. This technique was called *equipollent*, or the commanding and obeying signs. If the planets are also in aspect, their connection is fortified.

Remember, too, to use midpoints!

Chapter 14

Fixed Stars

"The Fixed Stares give great gifts and Elevate even from Poverty to an extreame height of Fortune, the Seven Planets do not so." [1]

The fixed stars have always been the means by which we measure our position in the Universe. They were first categorized by their colour and were associated with the characteristics of the planets thereby.

They were named according to their effects and most of the names we know are Arabic in origin.

A fixed star in conjunction with a planet of the same character greatly emphasizes the qualities of that planet. [2] If the star is of contrary nature it will hinder the planet.

The effects of the fixed stars are long-lasting and slow, thus the stars are inappropriate for judging passing matters, certainly they are not for ephemeral domestic horary questions, and probably not even for nativities. Their use in nativities is, in any case, undesirable because of the stark interpretations that can be attached to these stars, except when they appear on the Ascendant. They were used for the foundation of buildings or towns. Dee used Regulus in the chart for the Coronation of Elizabeth I. Flamsteed used it for establishing Greenwich. Malefic stars were conspicuous at the launch of the Titanic and the Space Shuttle. Therefore they should always be considered in Mundane astrology, events, and at the times of eclipses especially when they conjunct the eclipse or important significators or angles. Similarly, they are considered at Ingresses and Great Conjunctions.

Many people have told me they do not use fixed stars in interpretations because there are so many, but we consider only a few, far fewer than Ptolemy listed. Ptolemy described for us the ancient arrangements of the constellations, where each constellation in itself had significance. For instance, Argo affected shipping, Cygnus and Aquila influenced birds, as did Virgo and Sagittarius, which were both winged signs. Cancer and the Dolphin affected the sea, and Perseus influenced humanity.[3] Unfortunately Algol is in Perseus.

The constellations Ptolemy knew did not encompass all stars. There were some outside any constellation and they were called "scattered." Ptolemy described the stars within the constellations giving their position and characteristics. [4]

Modern astronomers have rectified the shapes of the constellations to make them neater, and tidied up the old arrangements to include all the stars. This has been disastrous for interpretation since stars of differing properties are now contained in one modern constellation. Moreover, these astronomers have changed the names not only of the stars but of the constellations. This means it is extremely difficult to identify some of the stars named in antiquity. George Noonan, who is an expert on Ptolemy, has written a book that will identify the Ptolemaic constellations and stars with the modern names and enumerations of today's astronomers. [5]

When reading old books remember that the precession of the equinoxes has moved the tropical zodiac over the position of the fixed stars, so that they appear to have moved at a rate of about 50 seconds a year, whereas Algol was at 20° Taurus at the time of Lilly it is now at 25° 55'. Apart from their movement against the zodiac, fixed stars do have a slight movement of their own, one toward another, but this is slight and of astronomical interest only. [6] Stars vary in brightness, and since the brightest are those that have a strong effect on Earthly life, perhaps their influence varies from century to century.

One problem astrologers must deal with, and about which they have various opinions, concerns the distance a star is from the ecliptic. Some stars have great celestial latitude. Ebertin suggests it makes no difference [7], other astrologers think it does. I follow Ebertin.

Lilly used only about forty fixed stars and found that number adequate. You can use an orb of one degree if it is a powerful star in a powerful place, but usually half a degree is sufficient.

Among the brightest stars in the sky are Regulus, Arcturus, Sirius, and Aldebaran. All of them are Suns--a concept beyond the imagination.

Chapter 15
The Part of Fortune

No horary chart is complete without the Part of Fortune (Fortuna). We have been taught to calculate it by adding together the number of degrees of the Ascendant and the Moon, and then subtracting the number of degrees of the Sun from that. So, if the Ascendant is at 3° Taurus (that's 33 degrees), and the Moon is at 4° Scorpio (214 degrees) adding those makes 247 degrees. If the degree of the Sun is 20*[degree] Leo (140 degrees) subtract this from 247 degrees, leaving 107 degrees, which is 17° Cancer. The Part of Fortune therefore would be at 17° Cancer.

This is the same as counting the number of degrees from the Sun to the Moon, and extending them from the Ascendant. The Moon is to the Sun what Fortuna is to the Ascendant. [1]

The Part of Fortune signifies substance. Where the Part of Fortune is in a chart, there is your treasure--literally or metaphorically. It is written like a kiss with a circle round it. It has no orb [2] and casts no aspect.

For years I had paid no attention to it in my birth chart because its position seemed irrelevant. Unfortunately, I had read that its house position indicated the department of life where your substance would increase, and this was so inappropriate in my own case that I had begun to wonder if the calculation should be reversed in a woman's chart. As a matter of fact Vettius Valens, Al Biruni, Manilius, Firmicus, and many others do so reverse the calculation in nighttime charts. Ptolemy, however, calculated day and night charts the same way, the way Lilly handed down to us.

Ptolemy also left a clear description of the way to understand the Part of Fortune. Here we are told the Part of Fortune informs us about material acquisition, and it should be judged by the dispositor, the planet, that is, ruling the sign in which the Part of Fortune is placed. Note the dignities of the dispositor, evaluate it, and find out its relation to the preceding syzygy (new or full Moon), to fixed stars, or if it is in an antiscion degree. If that dispositor is well-placed and strong the querent will be rich, especially if the Part of Fortune is aspected by the luminaries.

Ptolemy states that if Saturn is the dispositor (or governing planet) riches come from building, agriculture, or (and this I can hardly believe) shipping. If Jupiter, from inheritance, trusteeship, or priesthood; Mars through military operations and command; Venus through gifts and women; Mercury through eloquence or trade. [3]

The Part of Fortune is used in other ways also. The aspects between the significators of children or of acquaintances to the Part of Fortune will indicate how fond of them you will be, or how charming or fortunate they are. In synastry, when both significators and the Part of Fortune fall in the same sign this brings a secure friendship. If the positions in both charts accord, it is a friendship through need.

In Roman times the Part of Fortune was of great importance, and a statue to Fortuna was in every temple. It was then one of the four hylegical places, preceded by the Sun, Moon, and Ascendant only. By Lilly's day it was considered one of the five hylegical places. Lilly says the Ascendant, M.C., Sun, Moon, and Part of Fortune are called the five hylegical (or principle) places, and that direction to them will show "most

Figure 15.1: Lilly's Table to Help You Determine Fortuna's Strength in a Chart

		Score
Strong and fortunate by signs	in Taurus, Pisces	5
	Libra, Sagittarius, Leo or Cancer	4
	Gemini	3
	Virgo in terms of ♃ or ♀	2
In ☌ with ♃ or ♀		5
In △ with ♃ or ♀		4
In ✶ with ♃ or ♀		4
In ☌ with ☊		3*
Strong by house	In 1st or 10th	5
	7th, 4th, or 11th	4
	2nd or 5th	3
	9th	2
	3rd	1
Fixed stars	Regulus	6
	Spica	5
Not Combust or under the Sun-beams		5

		Minus score
Weak in	Scorpio, Capricorn, or Aquarius	5
	Aries	0
In ☌ with ♄ or ♂		5
In ☌ with ☋		3
In ☍ with ♄ or ♂		4
In ☐ with ♄ or ♂		3
In the terms of ♄ or ♂		2
Weak by house	in 12th	5
	in 8th or 6th	4
With Algol (the fixed star)		4
Combust		5

* Dubious

of the affairs and contingencies belonging to every man and woman in the natural course of life." [4] Lilly, in *The Effects of*

Directions Nativities, directs both the Part of Fortune and its dispositor to show increase or decrease of fortune. (This is for nativities.) [5]

Contrastingly, fragments of remains of interpretations of ancient Greek horoscopes and the literature of the Arabic astrologers, mainly Al Biruni, confirm the importance of the Moon in night charts. According to these sources, at night you count the degrees from Moon to Sun in the direction of the flow of the signs and extend them from the Ascendant to find the Part of Fortune. [6] I am now persuaded to change my calculation for night charts. The trouble is probably that we have had very few night charts as historic examples because most important people are born in the day, and most nativities have been made for important people.

Early Greek Horoscopes contains charts of Vettius Valens and others using a particular technique called the Circle of Athla. [7] Fortuna was regarded as the Ascendant of the Lunar Horoscope, and that is what Al Biruni was still calling it in the eleventh century. One then counted round in the order of the flow of the signs, eleven complete signs, and the resulting place is called the eleventh "loci of Accomplishment" (not to be confused with the original eleventh house "Bonus Daemon"). This was an extra and secret dimension. The original house and house ruler on which it fell were used in interpretation. Other houses, too, were counted from Athla. In the Introduction to Manilius' *Astronomica*, (Loeb edition, translated by Goold) there is an illustration of the Circle of Athla, [8] but the order of the matters ruled by houses is jumbled and does not accord with the interpretations of the old Greek charts in the above mentioned book. I can only assume that this was a purposeful coverup of what would have been a carefully guarded trade secret for the select few. This technique was used in charts for nativities and events.

The Lot of Fortune (which is the same as the Part of Fortune) is only one of many. There are lots of lots. In horary we often use the lot of marriage, of illness, of surgery, of death, of danger and of legalizing. The books of Ivy Goldstein-

Jacobson [9] are a good source of information in this area. Al Biruni gives 97 lots, [10] including those of commodities,[11] which should be useful for stock market astrologers. Some of these lots are calculated differently for day or night, and some are extended from places other than the Ascendant. *The Fortunes of Astrology* by R.H. Granite provides clear instructions about their use for those who cannot obtain Al Biruni's *Elements of the Art of Astrology*. Nicholas de Vore's *Encyclopedia* also gives a very useful list. Studying astrologers of the seventeenth century, such as Lilly, gives us a helpful stepping stone to understanding the more ancient astrology and opens the panorama of the past. I hope that more manuscripts will surface and be translated by future astrologers. The trouble has been that translators often are not also astrologers.

So far I have come upon no historical evidence of the Nodes being used in the way Fortuna is used in the Circle of Athla.

If the Moon aspects Fortuna it is not void of course. See the illustrated Coronation of Elizabeth I where Dee used this. He would not have elected so important an event with the Moon void.

Apart from the Lot of Fortune and its use in the Circle of Athla, the use of other lots seems to have been developed by the Arabs and Jews. Al Biruni, writing in the eleventh century, gives the work of the famous Abu Ma'shar as one of his sources.

I certainly advocate the use of the lots as an adjunct to our Western methods in horary. My own experience with them leads me to use the unturned, radical chart to find their positions. Following are some lots from Al Biruni. *Fortuna:* Count from Sun to Moon and extend from Ascendant. Change in nighttime chart.

Daemon: The Lot of the Sun. (The unseen, and religion.) Count from Moon to Sun and extend from Ascendant. Change in a night chart.

Marriage: (from Hermes) Count from Venus to seventh cusp and extend from the Ascendant. Do not change for night chart.

Death: There are two ways: 1) Count from the Moon to the eighth cusp and extend from Saturn; do not change at night. 2) The way explained by I.G. Jacobson, which is Ascendant plus eighth house cusp minus the Moon. Both seem strong. Do not confuse the Part of Death with the Lord of Death, ruler of the eighth house.

Urgent Wish: Count from the lord of hour to lord of Ascendant, extended from the Ascendant and changed at night.

Injury in Business: Lord of Ascendant to Fortuna, extend from Ascendant; do not change at night.

Illness: From Saturn to Mars and extend from the Ascendant; do not change at night.

Chapter 16

Regiomontanus, and House Systems

The best results are obtained in horary astrology by using Regiomontanus house division. This is a division of the equator into equal arcs of 30° which are projected onto the ecliptic. Some authorities maintain the method was in use for centuries before the life of Regiomontanus and that he popularized the mathematical concepts of Abraham Ibn Ezra or some earlier astrologer by making tables available. [1] Others ascribe the method to Regiomontanus himself. These tables for all latitudes were called *Tabulae Directionum* and were used for navigation and exploration. It is known as the Rational Method. [2]

Joannes Regio Montanus is a name for Johann Muller, who was born on 6 June, 1436, in Konigsburg, Germany at 4:40 P.M. (Julian Calendar). His nativity can be seen in John Gadbury's *Collectio Geniturarum.* [3] and it was preserved for us by Origanus. His chart, illustrated, shows a preponderance of Geminian planets.

He was a famous mathematician and astrologer who wrote books other than the *Tables*, and who found a way to extract the nativity of the son from that of the father. (I would like to read that!) He was invited to Rome by the Pope to be Court Astrologer, to help reform the calendar. There he suffered a violent death at the age of forty-two. I don't know how he died, but with four planets including both luminaries in the eighth, and Mars conjunct Sun there, I wonder if he was burnt or stabbed?

Figure 16.1: A Nativity from Regio Montanus, from John Gadbury's *Collectio Geniturarum*

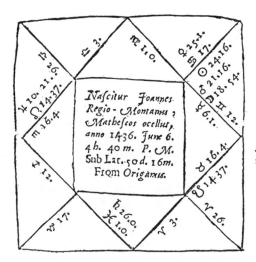

THis is the Nativity of that excellent Mathematician and Aftrologer, *Regio - Montanus,* (as *Origanus* hath it, fol. 724. *de Effectibus*) who framed thofe excellent Tables of Directions, for all manner of Latitudes : before which time, Aftrologers were at fuch a lofs , that they could not direct one Nativity then , in that fpace as now they may do ten.

His method was generally used. But there was another system, ascribed by some to Magini, and popularized with Tables by a Perugian monk and mathematician, Placido Titi (born in 1590). It was a merely unfortunate accident that the nineteenth century *Raphael's Ephemerides* published these Placidean Tables making them easily available to all. [4]

In practice, the cusps are most important in horary, for instance, in timing a planet can be symbolically directed to a cusp. The Regiomontanus method gives best results and therefore was used by most successful astrologers.

For example, I have used symbolic direction of a planet to the sixth Regiomontanus cusp to find the time of an animal's death, in accordance with the words of Nicholas Culpeper, "The Lord of the eighth very strong in the ascendant, gives you fair warning death is a coming."[5] In the chart I did, the lord of death (ruler of the eighth) was 1 1/2 degrees from the animal's Ascendant (sixth cusp), and death occurred one and a half days later. This would not have been shown by other house systems.

Lilly shows us a similar example of a soldier about to go abroad. His significator was two degrees from the ninth cusp (Regiomontanus) and the soldier went away in two months.[6]

This does not imply that timing is always to a house cusp. Every chart is judged on its own merit. You have to look at where the indications are. In the chart I did for the animal above, I was looking at the possibilities of death and it was there: the eighth house ruler was at the Ascendant (the body), standing clear and undeniably like a spectre. In Lilly's chart for the soldier, he was thinking of the journey so he looked at the ninth cusp. (But timing is more frequently made by the Moon to the next planet it aspects, or from one main significator to another, either by symbolic direction or from the Ephemeris.)

Sometimes timing can be made according to when a planet changes sign, or when a planet moves to the planet symbolizing the quesited. Lilly, for example, judged the brother would reach home when his symbol (Venus) reached its own terms, that is, a place where he was at home. [7] In my horary, "Shall I go to Australia" (Figure 20.4) I judged by the change of Jupiter into Sagittarius, of travel, which rules the ninth cusp. These are judgments a computer cannot make.

To revert to the subject of houses, if the Regiomontanus system gives the required results why change to another, no matter how clever the higher mathematics involved in its calculation? For people who would like to find precise, simple information on houses there is Marie Lorenz book, *Tools of*

Astrology, showing contrasting systems. [8] Systems in use before Regiomontanus were those of Porphry, an extremely ancient method, Alcibitius, and Campanus. During this time calculation depended on the astrolabe, for there were no tables. To understand something of house division in the past you needed to be a great mathematician.

One such man, a mathematician and doctor, was Alabitius or Albucasis, who lived in the tenth century and wrote a famous book on surgery called *The Method*. Another was Campanus. The house sizes in Campanus' system are more varied than in that of Regiomontanus, and although we do not use his system, we are indebted to him for the part he played in the renaissance of astrology in the thirteenth century.

There has always been talk of Ptolemy's own system, and some people think he used Equal House. He lived near the equator and, of course, all houses are equal there. But that does not mean he would have used it if he had lived further north, because for Ptolemy the M.C., the tenth house was the most important. It ruled Glory and those persons in command. You would not find that in an Equal House chart, where the M.C. and tenth cusps do not coincide.

In his recent and brilliant book *Classical Scientific Astrology* George Noonan tells us of a fragment from Rhetorius (sixth century) that gives Ptolemy's own method. [9] Perhaps natal astrologers will use it one day.

I can only tell you the system I find yields good results for horary, appears to be that of Abraham Ibn Ezra, a system named after Regio Montanus.

The reason I prefer the chart format found in this book is that every degree is given its space, every sign its 30 degrees, and the houses are assigned their true areas. One can see midpoints more easily, and how close or far the fixed stars are to any planet. In the sky surrounding us we do not have some degrees bunched up and others elongated. Every house, every degree, has its space. Why distort them?

Part Two: Specific Questions

Chapter 17

Regarding Specific Questions

Some readers may consider the subject matter in the following questions rather trivial, for although these are the type of questions that occupy our minds with such intensity and are vitally important to us, they are not necessarily of consequence to the world at large. This is the wonder of astrology and the answers we seek from it, that the smallest and seemingly insignificant object is comprised of the same pattern that permeates all existing things. The slightest ripple, the brush of a butterfly's wing, reacts to the same vibration that is in the enormity of the Universe. I understand that scientists are now rejecting the idea of the separateness of objects and concluding that there is an underlying relatedness in all things. [1] Such an idea is inherent in astrology.

Horary charts are, as I have said elsewhere, much like photographs, and one likes to show the best. The definition should be crisp and clear, the content easily identified; and yet it is not the solution to the question asked that is of major importance (the discovery, for instance, of the place where the front door key is), but the affirmation of the universal laws of astrology, the deciphering of the code, the one indisputable clue which is so valuable--that is the object of our work. Finding that if the symbol of the lost object is in an earth sign the object really is south, or if it is in a water sign it is in the north, or if it is in the twelfth house it is imprisoned, *that* is our treasure trove.

Small personal questions can absorb our minds to the exclusion of all else. Since they are personal, nobody else has asked them. The trouble with large and important questions is that every astrologer, capable or incapable, is asking them. "Who will win the next election?" they ask. As discussed before, a question can only be asked once, it cannot be asked hundreds of times by hundreds of astrologers in different locations. Therefore, such questions are a waste of time-- unless, perhaps you are yourself the Prime Minister, in which case it may truly dominate your thoughts. But for the average questioner there may be other questions that press more urgently on the mind, questions such as, "Will I be late for my appointment?"

Great matters may be better decided from event charts. The rules regarding these charts differ slightly from horary; for example, the first house rules the initiator of the action rather than the querent.

Yet if your question is a great one and nobody else has asked it, it is possible it will yield great results. William Lilly solved some very great questions such as, "How long will the Presbytery last?" He also solved some that were trivial, such as his most famous of all about his lost fish. By his brilliance in astrology he traced the thief and retrieved some of the fish. An early surviving example is from Palchus, famous in the fifth century A.D., is of a chart to find the lost linen of a slave girl.

A question is best framed in simple words, as in prayer. Prayer is our supplication to God, the pattern of heaven His answer back to us. And so I ask you as you read my examples to work them through if you can, search out the rules behind them and do not be distracted by the subject matter. Consider this: It does not matter if a car is a magnificent Rolls Royce or a small Austin Mini, it is no good without an engine. It must work and it must be possible to demonstrate that it works. Much astrology today is unprovable waffle. The advantage of horary questions is that they work and can be seen to work.

Chapter 18
Partnership Questions

"It [the seventh house] giveth judgment of Marriage and describes the person inquired after, whether it be Man or Woman, all manner of Love questions, our publique enemies, the Defendant in a Law Suit, in Warre the opposing party...whether Man or Woman, wives, sweethearts, their shape and description and condition." [1] Notice the word "describe," because the participants in a horary question are described by the chart, and if they are not the chart is not valid. There is, however, no need for a horary astrologer to enter into a detailed psychological discussion of the querent or quesited. The first house, after all, refers to the body, and it is more apt to give a physical description than a psychological one to identify your significators.

In judging this matter, as with nearly all questions, the Ascendant and its ruler and the Moon represent the querent, man or woman, and the sign of the Descendant represents the quesited.

In addition, the Sun and Mars are natural significators of men, the Moon and Venus are natural rulers of women. Saturn is the natural significator of older people, usually the father figure. This additional rulership is not required in all questions, but occasionally these planets help when the resolution of the horary is not apparent from the accidental rulers. This natural rulership has been recognised for thousands of years. It is not a matter of opinion.

In his *Introduction to Astrology*, which is meant to be an edited version of Lilly's work, Zadkiel gives the opposite information, contradicting astrological tradition.[2] I warn those who are trying to understand horary from Zadkiel to beware; he confuses the significators, using the Sun for women.

In practice I find that the headline answer in partnership questions, the "Yes" or "No," can usually be found from the main significators alone, and from the major aspects. This is usually what your clients want to know.

The applying aspects of planets are much like a meeting, and the perfection of the aspect is when the meeting takes place. As soon as the planets start to separate even by six minutes it is like two people parting.

Now is the time to use the knowledge of the techniques that we have studied in the first part of the book, before attempting judgment. What we require is to see the perfection of aspects between the significators of querent and quesited. This gives an affirmative reply. (See Chapter 12.) This aspect can be between the main significator of the querent or the Moon, and the significator of the quesited. It needs to be a good aspect out of good houses. Translation of light or collection can achieve the same outcome. But if there is no perfecting aspect, or if the aspect is by opposition, the answer is negative. [3]

If there is a square with reception, we can say that a marriage will take place, but with difficulty. With a square or opposition without reception, the matter comes to nothing.

In these charts then, there is often no necessity to evaluate the planets. However, if a more detailed account is required, there is no doubt that a careful assessment of planets in the light of what we have so far learned will clarify much detail. The longer you work with a chart, the greater the degree of detail you will be able to elicit.

Figure 18.1: "Shall we stay together or split up?"

Regiomontanus House System

10 November 1984
12:45 P.M. G.M.T.
51° 13' N 1° 25' E

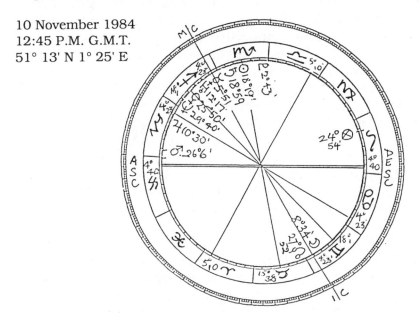

"Shall we stay together or split up?"

This is perhaps the simplest chart with which to begin.

The querent is shown by the Ascendant and its ruler, Saturn, the quesited by the Sun, they are near cazimi, showing a close relationship. It could hardly be closer. Also, look at Fortuna in the seventh; their fortune is in their partnership.

But the Moon contradicts the two main significators. They stay together for the present, but Moon moving to the opposition of Uranus will bring disruption in about four months.

She is the fonder, represented by the faster planet. (Yes, they did move house, incidentally, as you may wonder since the Moon is in the fourth, but, of course, that was not the question. The Moon often shows what the querent is thinking.)

Fig. 18.2:"Will my wife come back to me and what shall I do?"

The querent, as ever, is represented by the Ascendant and the planet ruling the sign on the Ascendant, and the Moon. Saturn, therefore, symbolizes the husband. His wife is symbolized by the planet ruling the sign on the seventh cusp. The Sun, therefore, symbolizes his wife.

Saturn is at 7° Scorpio and the Sun is at 13° 30' Scorpio. As the Sun moves faster than Saturn, we can see that the wife is leaving, for the Sun cannot retrograde. This is the short answer to the first part of the query. The answer is "No."

The separation is confirmed by the movement of Venus, natural significator of women, from Mars, natural significator of young men, in the seventh house. Venus is square Neptune, showing deception. She deceives him. She has hopes of going to University, and the Sun pursues Mercury, planet of book learning. But Mercury moves faster than Venus, and thus eludes her, disappearing into the next sign before she can catch him. She never succeeded in getting into University.

The husband asked what he should do about his future and, fortunately, here we can soften the blow of his wife's departure. The Moon shows by its applying aspects what will happen. Its first aspect is to the conjunction of Uranus, the planet that symbolizes divorce and upheaval. It then goes to the conjunction of Jupiter, the greater benefic. It is the ruler of the tenth house of career, Jupiter, in its own sign, angular and strong, showing success in his career as a probation officer, which he was studying. The Moon is in the ninth house of further education, and his study did bring him excellent results. The Moon's position and its aspect to Jupiter speak clearly of the aspirations of this man.

The Part of Fortune in the first house also confirms this, for it is judged by its dispositor, the well-placed Jupiter in the tenth. I suggested that he give all concentration to his own affairs and successful examinations.

The sign Cancer on his sixth cusp aptly describes his

Figure 18.2: "Will my wife come back to me and what shall I do?"

Regiomontanus House System

6 November 1983
1:50 P.M. G.M.T.
51° 13' N 1° 25' E

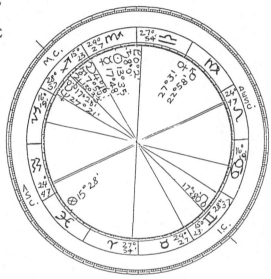

	0 1 2 3 4 5 6 7 8 9	10 11	12 13 14	15 16	17 18 19 20 21	22 23 24 25	26 27 28 29
	♇ ☽ ♄		☉	⊗	☿	♂	♀
	0° 4° 7°		13°	15°	17°	22°	27°
	2' 16' 50'		35'	28'	48'	58'	3'
	♏ ♐ ♏		♏	♓	♏	♍	♍
	♒		♃		♉		
	7°		13°		☊		
	50'		33'				

chosen work of welfare and looking after others. Even the South Node in the tenth house did not spoil his career, but shows only that he decided on such a career quite late in life. Fortunately, there is no planet in the same degree as the Nodes. He has been highly successful.

The aspects of the Moon to Saturn and to the Sun are ignored because they are only semi-sextile and do not give a main answer to the question.

Fig. 18.3: A Husband Asks About His Marriage

There is usually a stricture against the judgment of charts where only a few degrees ascend, but Barbara Watters points out an exception to this rule. [4] If the querent has a natal planet in the degree in question, then that planet is considered important in the interpretation of the horary and is taken as the horary ruler; the chart can be judged. I, therefore, asked this querent when his birthday was, and on hearing that the Sun was in 3° Cancer in his nativity I judged the chart. He was a very Cancerian man, who cared deeply for his wife. He was usually unemployed, though he did collect antique articles to sell. He had a round face and a brown beard.

The querent was represented by the Moon, ruler of the Ascendant, in the second house, peregrine. His wife is symbolized by Saturn, ruler of the seventh house. Notice that Saturn is conjunct another planet--Mars, representing a young man, a policeman. His wife, too, was a police officer in the docks. Her natal Sun was in Scorpio, and she had a firm square jaw.

By its position in the ninth and tenth houses the Sun shows how the querent went to a job overseas. The Sun is ambiguous in its symbolism. As ruler of the tenth from the seventh it also represents the man's Leonine mother-in-law, an overbearing lady who half-owned his house. (Note Leo on his fourth cusp of "house.") She also lived overseas, and she was to send him some letters full of harsh words (Moon to opposition Mercury), in addition to which he had the difficult situation of his wife with her lover, (Moon square Saturn and square Mars). Finally, there was his financial trouble with his mother-in-law (Moon opposition Sun from the second house of finance), about the house.

He left the country about five months later, leaving all, very much the loser, for the Moon is peregrine. The house had not sold and the policeman was living in it with the man's wife (Venus, natural ruler of money and love, is in mutual reception by term with Mars).

Perhaps the period of time until the querent's departure

Figure 18.3: A Husband Asks About His Marriage

Regiomontanus House System

Wednesday 15 February 1984
12:19 P.M. G.M.T.
51° 13' N 1° 25' E

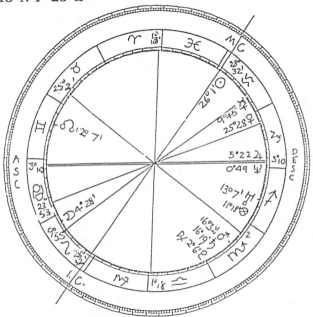

0 1 2 3 4 5 6 7 8 9	10 11 12 13 14 15 16 17	18 19 20 21 22 23 24	25 26 27 28 29
Ψ ♇ ☽ ♃	☿ ⊗ ☊ ♅	♄	♀ ☉
0° 2° 4° 5°	9° 11°12°13°	16°	25°26°
49' 6' 28'22'	45' 18' 7' 7'	19'	28' 1'
♑ ♏ ♌ ♑	♒ ♐ ♐	♏	♑ ♒
		♂	
		16°	
		32'	
☽ ⚻ ☿ △ ♅ □ ♄ □ ♂ ⚹ ☉		♏	

can be judged from the degrees between the Sun's present position and its entry into a new sign. This indicates a new career (on the M.C.) in about five months.

The trine of the Moon to Uranus was, I think, when he heard of his new job abroad.

Fig. 18.4: "Will I ever go off with my lover?"

The Ascendant and its ruler, the Moon, symbolize the querent, and indeed, her natal Ascendant was Cancer. She has gone over to "The Other" completely, in the seventh, and would do whatever he suggested!

This is much to her disadvantage, for the Moon is detrimented in Capricorn. The Moon moves to a conjunction of Mars, a contact in which it is always the Moon that is hurt. The Moon in the seventh house shows change of partner, because the Moon is very changeable, as was this woman. The quesited, (the lover), ruler of the seventh house is Saturn, in mutual reception with the Moon. He is in her exaltation and face, she is in his sign, indicating some sympathy between them and reciprocity of feeling. Yet as the Moon is the faster planet, she is by far the keener in the relationship. She applies hopefully towards a trine to Saturn.

This adds up to an affirmative answer and I thought she would unfortunately go with him. She did; she left her husband and children and went away with her lover. But, ten days later he went back to his wife. Notice he is in mutual reception by sign with Venus (his wife), which is even stronger than the reception with the Moon. He was two-timing them.

Venus had recently squared him--perhaps suggesting a quarrel--but now the mutual reception gave him a way out.

The Moon had aspected towards Saturn but after one and one-half weeks (1 1/2°) she had met Mars. Perhaps that was a quarrel. Anyway, Mars provided the prohibition that prevented her reaching the perfection of a trine aspect with Saturn.

Our querent, the Moon, was then left greatly hurt and disadvantaged. Although the main actors in this episode are the Moon and Saturn, the Moon's husband may be indicated by the Sun, natural ruler of men, in the angry sign Aries. It was a year before he would be reconciled to her. The Sun is 1 degree from Taurus, the exaltation of the Moon, where she would feel at home. She went back home to him in one year.

Figure 18.4: "Will I ever go off with my lover?"

Regiomontanus House System

The hour of Venus, which is cold and moist.
The sign of Cancer, which is cold and moist.

20 March 1971
10:25 A.M. G.M.T.
51° 13' N 1° 25' E

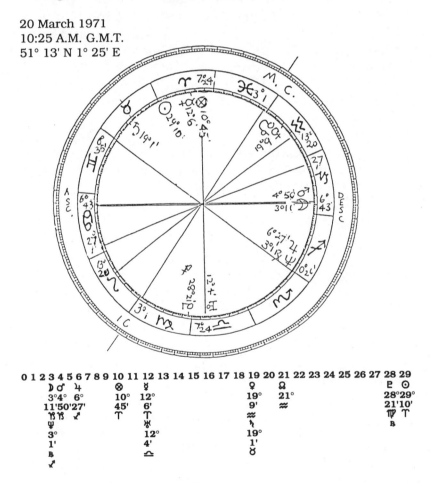

	0 1 2 3 4 5 6 7 8 9	10 11	12 13 14 15 16 17 18	19 20	21 22 23 24 25 26 27	28 29
	☽ ♂ ♃	⊗	☿		♀ ♌		♇ ☉
	3° 4° 6°	10°	12°		19° 21°		28° 29°
	11'50'27'	45'	6'		9'		21'10'
	♑♑ ♐	♈	♈		♒ ♒		♍ ♈
	♆		♅		♄		ᴮ
	3°		12°		19°		
	1'		4'		1'		
	ᴮ		♎		♉		
	♐						

The fifth house of her children contains Uranus, which always shows upheaval and rearrangement. Here it is exactly in opposition to Mercury, natural ruler of young people.

Fig. 18.5: "Will anything come of this love affair?"

The chart shows that it is the seventh house and not the fifth that rules love affairs, and illustrates prohibition.

The querent is represented by the Ascendant and its ruler, the Sun, and also by the Moon. (The Moon is always co-ruler).

The Sun is void of course, moreover it separates from any aspect towards the ruler of the seventh, the quesited. The Sun is in its detriment. The Moon, co-significator of the querent, does, however, make a dexter sextile toward the ruler of the fifth, Mars, and if the fifth house rules loves, this would have provided an affirmative answer. It is prevented in its dexter sextile towards Saturn because it first meets Mars. If Saturn, ruler of the seventh, is significator of the lover, the answer is negative. The answer was negative.

Fig. 18.6: "Is this the right time to separate from my husband, and what would be the probable outcome?"

The Ascendant and its ruler, the Sun, represent the querent; so does the Moon. The querent's appearance is reminiscent of the Aries decanate of Leo, for she is small and lively with blonde hair that sprang upward and big blue eyes. Saturn, the ruler of the seventh, represents her husband. The Sun is in the fourth, at home, newly entered into Sagittarius, an independent sign. It is disposited by sign and term by Jupiter, ruler of the fifth house of pleasure, and part ruler of the later part of the seventh, her next partner. Jupiter itself is disposited by Venus, the planet of love, which is strong and

Figure 18.5: "Will anything come of this love affair?"

Regiomontanus House System

17 February 1982
2:59 P.M. G.M.T.
51° 13' N 1° 25' E

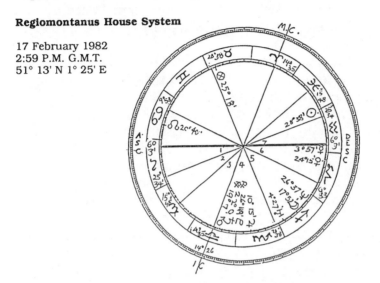

Figure 18.6: "Is this the right time to separate from my husband, and what would be the probable outcome?"

Regiomontanus House System

24 November 1980
9:40 P.M. G.M.T.
51° 13' N 1° 25' E

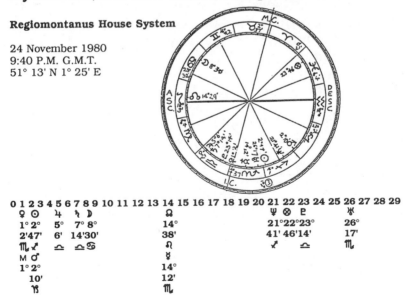

0 1 2 3 4 5 6 7 8 9	10 11 12 13 14 15	16 17 18 19 20 21 22 23 24 25	26 27 28 29
♀ ☉ ♃ ♄ ☽	♌	♆ ⊗ ♇	♅
1° 2° 5° 7° 8°	14°	21°22°23°	26°
2'47' 6' 14'30'	38'	41' 46'14'	17'
♏ ⚹ ♎ ♎ ♋	♌	⚹ ♎	♏
M ♂	♉		
1° 2°	14°		
10'	12'		
♑	♏		

angular in this chart. There is a midpoint, Mercury equals Venus/Uranus, showing thoughts of love. The querent was apparently in love.

The Moon usually shows what a querent is thinking and here it is strong in the eleventh house of the Good Daemon, indicating strong hopes and wishes. Since it is in its own sign it shows, I think, her hopes were well founded, especially as it will eventually trine Fortuna. It last passed over Mars of quarrels, and will next pass over Jupiter, a benefic. (This is a technique suggested by Jacobson in *Simplified Astrology*.)

The angles of the chart are fixed, showing she would not move immediately. Her husband, Saturn, is not alone; he is with another planet. She told me he was having an affair. There he is, in the third house, a short distance away. She had not liked that news. (The Moon moves from the square of Jupiter and Saturn.)

She must stay at home and organize her finances, which are the trouble, as seen from Mercury, her cash at present in the degree of the Nodes. Her money and her earnings are in the home. Mercury, ruler of her money, is in the fourth house, and Venus, ruler of the tenth, is on the fourth house cusp.

I said I thought she should wait at home shrewdly, but that she *would* be able to go, with some difficulties, (Moon square Pluto of ejection) and eventually, the Moon's trine to Uranus in the fourth house shows re-organization of her home affairs. Uranus is the natural ruler of divorce. I thought that she would re-marry because the Sun was nearly conjunct the Part of Marriage, and both in a dual sign. I thought she would do this when the Sun reached 16° of Sagittarius by 1 degree symbolic direction, and entered a new chapter (house). That could have been fourteen or fifteen months because Sagittarius is a mutable sign and the Sun angular.

The querent is a local acquaintance of mine, so I telephoned her in 1984 to ask when she did leave home and when she remarried. She left home "about three months after the question, and she re-married on February 19, 1982"; that was fifteen months after the question. The virtue of this example is that we know the outcome.

The Moon enters the twelfth house in 15 degrees from its present position and also squares Pluto in 15 degrees. It perfects its trine to Fortuna in 14 degrees. Notice the Moon rules the twelfth house of self undoing and sorrow, (for which, perhaps, she had unknowingly wished?). The aspects of the Moon in Cancer, succedent, can be counted as months.

I asked if she was happy, and she is, but with reservations. She is worried about his health and other difficulties. (The contra-antiscion of the Moon is conjunct Neptune). She also told me I had been right about the great money difficulties of her former husband. The ruler of the eighth, his money, is conjunct Saturn, and Fortuna is conjunct the antiscium of Saturn. Because of this he had stayed on at home. Eventually he left and she felt justified, both to herself and for the law, in going off. He returned, however, and when the day came for her to finally leave the house there was great unpleasantness. This difficulty is expressed by the Moon's square to Pluto of ejection. Then she had re-organized her life (Moon trine Uranus) and, as I say, remarried.

Presumably the three months to her departure is accounted for by Sun's aspect to sextile dexter Jupiter, the ruler of her freedom, in 3 degrees. In so complicated a chart, one planet can play many roles, and the antiscium of Saturn with Fortuna affected the husband and wife differently--he in his cash, she in her hopes of a successful second marriage.

Fig. 18.7: "Will my husband ever go? Will there be a divorce?"

The querent is symbolized by the Ascendant, Virgo, and its ruler Mercury, and, of course, by the Moon. She was a secretary, tall, with long legs, who dressed carefully in fawns and pinks and in a practical way. She was good-looking and rather elegant, reminiscent of Garbo. (See Figure 18.7 on the following page.)

Her husband is shown by the sign on the seventh cusp and its ruler, Jupiter, and in a secondary way by the Sun.

Their disruption is clear from the Moon inconjunct the Sun exactly. The husband's significator (Jupiter) is not alone; it is with Saturn--someone else--and living at the querent's expense, for Jupiter is in the second house of her possessions. He is in her house openly having an affair, and he is in no hurry to move. Jupiter is just turning retrograde, the most dilatory position. His new partner is already receding, but he will be after her.

The querent, too, is interested in someone else as can be seen by her significator approaching conjunction with Mars. She had a friend at her place of work, which is a large chemical factory.

I associate Pluto with ejection, and as Jupiter reaches Pluto in November 1981, I thought her husband would leave then. So he did, but he returned. She had to sell the house to be rid of him. Angular Uranus was an undeniable testimony of divorce, and on the fourth cusp it shows re-organization of her home. The Moon reaches sextile Uranus in 27 degrees. At the time of the question we could not believe that meant months. I thought twenty-seven weeks more probable. However, the divorce took place in twenty-seven months, in April of 1983.

Another detail confirmed by the chart shows the Moon, the querent, trine Venus in the fifth, which describes her closeness to her daughter. The angular Moon on the Ascendant shows that change was at hand, and that the querent is

Figure 18.7: "Will my husband ever go?" "Will there be a divorce?"

Regiomontanus cusps

Jupiter stationary

22 January 1981
7:20 P.M. G.M.T.
51° 13' N 1° 25' E

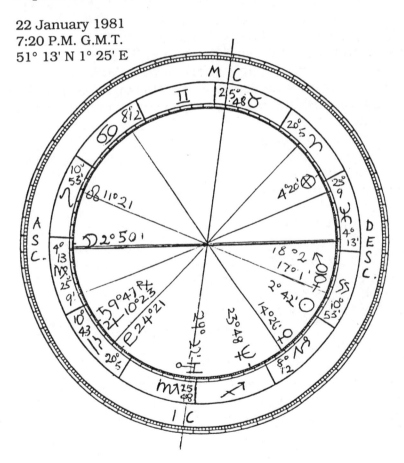

wondering what is going to happen to the child. In the modern sense of the word, the Moon is beseiged between Mars and Saturn. (Traditionally this is too wide to have been accounted beseigement.) Yet it may express the feeling the querent had of not knowing which way to turn.

* * * * * * * * * * * * * *

Lilly considered that you can tell which partner in the relationship is the fonder by looking at the faster planet, and I recall two of his example charts which illustrate this. The ancients believed that you could tell this by house position: if the ruler of the first is in the seventh the querent is fonder, and vice versa..

Chapter 19

Questions Concerning
Things Lost or Mislaid

To Find Something Lost or Stolen

The rules for finding objects mislaid are different from those
for finding objects lost. The lost article is symbolized by the
planet ruling the house of possessions, the second, and the
Moon as co-ruler. Of course, you must decide who owns the
object before you can decide which house rules it. If it is your
daughter's, take the second from the fifth, that is, the sixth;
if it is your father's, take the second from the fourth, that is,
the fifth.

It is always simpler if the querent asks his own questions,
then at least you know who the first house rules.

If the planet is angular, the lost article is indoors. If it is in
the first, or if the planetary hour ruler is in the first, the item
is in the part of the house most used by the querent, and with
the things he likes best. If it is in the tenth it's in his shop or
workroom, or in the living room or the first room after entering
the house. If it's in the fourth, the object is in the room

frequented by the father of the household or the most elderly person, or in the oldest part of the building. Since the elderly like warm rooms this could be in the centre of the house. And of course, the seventh house shows the place of one's partner.

The nature and quality of the place is known by the signs the symbols are in, including the Part of Fortune. The greater number of relevant symbols in airy signs show the article is high up, or upstairs; or, if it's outdoors, it's on a hill or hillock, or on a plant or tree.

If the signs are fiery, the item is near a fire or chimney or where there is iron; or near the walls of the house, if the walls are brick (because bricks have been fired).

If the signs are earthy it is on the ground, floor, or earth under the pavement or floor. If it's out of doors, it can be near a bridge or stile.

If it's in watery signs the lost object is near water.

If the symbol is between two signs or near a cusp of a house, the object could be near a door or threshold, between two rooms, or has fallen down behind something. It is higher or lower according to the sign.

I have found the place is known by the sign where the chief significator is. This piece of advice I have found extremely useful. However, Lilly also tells us that if the Moon is stronger than the main significator, judge by the Moon. [1] In judging by the Moon, consider sky position, that is, above the horizon as south; below as north; on the Ascendant side, east; and on the Descendant side west.

He also suggests the following analysis regarding direction; consider the sign ascending, the sign of the Ascendant ruler, the sign of the fourth, and the sign of its ruler, the sign the Moon is in, the sign of the house of possessions, and the sign containing Fortuna. One then finds the direction most of them indicate. It was in this occupation that Mr. Lilly found great merriment, though I must say I find it rather tedious.

The Moon's role is extremely ambiguous. Not only can it be the querent, but it also can be the goods or the indicator of timing. It is particularly important in the charts of fugitives, who vary their flight according to the Moon. Therefore, in the case of a lost creature, note the Moon, yet if the creature is locked in somewhere it has not lost its way, and is not so subject to the Moon. It is also strange that cattle have a particular affinity to the Moon, because the Moon is exalted in Taurus; the Moon's curve is shown in the shape of their horns.

If the Moon aspects its dispositor or vice versa, it shows the return of the animal or goods. If the dispositor of the Moon is with the ruler of the hour, that shows return. The dispositor by term of the Moon is also important, and if these are angular and aspecting the ruler of the first the querent will have his goods back.

If the symbols are in succedent houses the goods are not far away. If they are in cadent houses they are far away.

Remember, too, that if the symbol of the goods is retrograde is shows a returning.

To Find a Mislaid Object

If you have mislaid an article in the house, that is, put it down in the wrong place and then forgotten where, the rules for chart judgment are different from those used to find a lost article or animal. It is not always easy to decide if something is in the lost or mislaid category.

In either case, the second house rules the possession, and

if the querent owns the article, the planet ruling the sign on the second house symbolizes it.

If this planet is angular, or the planetary hour ruler is angular, or the Moon, it shows the article is within doors and that there is likelihood that the article is mislaid. Neptune is usually prominent in these charts because of the forgetfulness it portrays. Or, the fourth house of your residence is stressed. If you see these indications it is well to apply the following rules for finding mislaid things.

Look at the planet ruling the sign on the fourth house. This will describe where to look. If it is Saturn, look in a dark place, or an unpleasant place. If it is Jupiter, the object is near wood; if it is Mars, it's in the kitchen or near a fire; if the Sun, it's in the main room, hall, or where the owner of the house is; if it's Venus, it's in or near a woman's clothing or where fabric or cloth is; if Mercury, it's near books, pictures, or carvings; if it's the Moon, it's near water or a pit.

Consider *the sign that the ruler of the fourth is in.* If it is in Aries it indicates the roof or ceiling, or near plastering; Taurus, cellars and rooms low down; Gemini suggests walls or hall, or rooms where games are played, or in chests; Cancer shows cellars and washrooms; Leo tells us it's near a chimney; Virgo, in a study, or cupboards; Libra indicates upstairs, attics, one room within another, or on shelves; Scorpio shows sinks and kitchens and where there is water or dampness; Sagittarius, upstairs or near a fire; Capricorn, low, dark places near an entrance; Aquarius upstairs or in high places; Pisces, in damp, watery places. The planet will show you the place, not the sign on the fourth cusp.

It can be seen that the ruler of the second house sign does not help in these instances with finding the object. Its application by aspect to the ruler of the first, or the application of the first to the ruler of the second may show the time of recovery, but it does not show location.

The article's natural ruler may also help. For instance, if the question was about keys, the position of Mercury near a cusp might show the keys were near a door, wall, or boundary.

The second house ruler representing the object should describe it in the following way. If the ruler is Saturn, then the article contains lead or iron, is a black garment or article, or is made of hide or animal skin. If it's Jupiter, the object is white, or has tin or silver in it (Jupiter is exalted in Cancer), or has yellow and white in it. If it is Mars, it belongs to fire or might be knives or something that cuts. If it's Venus it belongs to women--rings, silks, soft things, and such. If it's the Moon it may be animals or country things or something to do with liquids. If it's Mercury it's money, books, or something of mixed color. This list sounds very similar to the list of what each planet naturally rules, but it is a strange fact that often the ruler of the second house and natural ruler are the same.

This list is apt for interpretations of charts about lost articles as well.

For those who would like to draw up a chart for an object mislaid, here are particulars of an example. "Where are my mislaid car keys?" 10 September 1971. 51° 13' North 1° 25 East. 3.35 P.M. G.M.T.

Saturn rules the querent and the keys which contained saturnine metal. Taurus rules the fourth house cusp so Venus indicates that their location is connected with women's clothes or fabric, and Venus' position in Virgo points to cupboards and storage space. They were in the querent's overall pocket in the cupboard where paint things were kept. Mercury is by a cusp and the overalls hung on the back of the door (near a cusp shows near a boundary, and Mercury is the natural ruler of keys). The Moon applies to the conjunction of Saturn, the keys, in 3°. The keys were found in three days. There is no astrological indication that the keys were indoors except that Jupiter, part ruler of the second, is angular. Reason, however, told me they must be, otherwise how did I drive home? To quote Lilly, "combine art with discretion."

It is also helpful to discover what the querent was doing before the fit of absent mindedness, and this can be found by the planet from which the main significator last separated. Lilly considered Saturn shows forgetfulness, but nowadays we associate it with Neptune. He suggests that if it separates from Saturn it is because of some cold or sickness; if from Mars, through a quarrel, fear, or sudden temper, enmity, or fire; if from the Sun, through someone important; if from Venus, through enjoyment, drinking, singing, or "dallying"; if from Mercury, because of writing or sending letters; if from the Moon, because of frequent use, or because of some ordinary, unimportant person.

Fig. 19.1: "Where is Max the cat?"

Max had been missing for ten days. (See Figure 19.1 on following page.) He is a glossy black cat who lives in a third floor flat in Clapham South. His territory includes roof tops and ledges, chimney pots and drain pipes. Once he had managed to reach ground level, but he hurt his legs in the achievement; it must have been a difficult journey.

His distraught owner, Jeremy, wondered now if Max had done this again and perhaps become victim to the traffic of the South Circular, or discovered a new home. Jeremy and his brother William had climbed about on precarious ledges, but had been unable to find Max on the rooftops. Despair set in.

When I heard of Max's long disappearance I was extremely upset. He is such a charming cat.

Suddenly I knew it was the moment for a horary.

Nobody had asked me the question so I simply took the

Figure 19.1: "Where is Max the cat?"

Regiomontanus House System

8 September 1983
8:35 P.M. G.M.T.
51° 13' N 1° 25

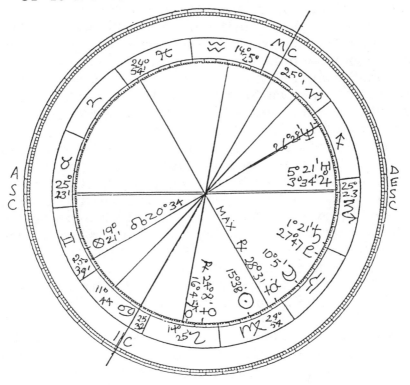

0 1 2 3 4 5 6 7 8 9	10 11 12 13 14	15 16 17	18 19 20 21 22 23	24 25	26 27 28 29
♄ ♃ ♅	☽	☉ ♂	⊗ ☊	♀	♆ ♇ ♀
1° 3° 5°	10°	15°16°	19° 20°	24°	26°27° 28°
21'34' 21'	5'	38' 45'	21' 34'	8'	28' 47' 3'
♏ ♐ ♐	♎	♍ ♌	♊ ♊	♌	♐ ♎ ♍

sixth house as the house that represents small animals and used that cusp as Max's Ascendant. Virgo ascended, therefore, and Mercury, its ruler, was there in the first house. I knew then that Max was on his home ground, that he had not fallen. The Sun, ruler of the twelfth, was in the twelfth. He was a prisoner. Mercury, his symbol, was in Virgo, a southern sign. It was angular and important, therefore I decided he was south and near the edge of his territory (28 degrees). The Moon, always important in the charts of fugitives was in Libra, signifying Max was high up, in such a place as a garret or flat place. Libra is a human sign, so it suggested a place where humans inhabit and not down a chimney. Libra, too, indicated a place near windows. [2] It was clear he was imprisoned because the Sun, ruler of the twelfth of imprisonment was positioned in the twelfth. [3]

It was late at night but I telephoned Jeremy in London. "He has not fallen," I said. "He is not far from where you are now, but in a southerly direction, dry, in a location used by humans, near windows, a room, perhaps a garret, an attic, because the ground is level like a floor. [4] He is imprisoned. If you don't go and look for him he will die (Moon moving eventually to the ruler of the eighth). But you have a good chance of finding him (Mercury retrograde)

"Good Lord," said Jeremy. "I can't go climbing over the roof past people's windows at this time of night, but thank you very much." Jeremy climbed out over the ledges in the morning. He climbed southward towards Balham, and at the very end of the block was a room with three fastened windows. Two windows he couldn't budge, but the third he forced open. It was a disused attic, a garret, and in the corner lay Max, very thin. There was a joyous reunion. Of course, Max was very thirsty, for he had drunk nothing for ten days. Algol on the Ascendant before I turned the chart had made me suspect he was injured in the neck, and I expect his throat hurt. He drank a whole bowl of milk. I now realize that Algol is in Perseus and will hurt a human, but may not affect an animal.

For those readers who are beginners I will enlarge on the judgment of this chart. Because the sixth house rules small animals the chart is turned so that 24° Virgo becomes the Ascendant for the cat. You need not literally re-draw the chart that way, just visualize it. Mercury rules Virgo, therefore Mercury symbolizes the cat. We see Mercury in the cats first house, and planets angular mean "at home." This is how I knew Max had not fallen off the roof. If the cat's symbol had been in a succedent house, he would have been quite far from home. If it had been in a cadent house Max would have been very far from home. Another way to judge this is the distance of the animal's symbol from its owner's symbol, here Venus, ruling the Ascendant, which is only in the next sign.

So Mercury is the main significator in this chart and if we want further adjectival detail we must look at the signs. When we consider the qualities of Virgo we find it is south, dry, at floor level, and where things are stored and dried. Virgo is called a human sign, so it describes a place frequented by humans.

Do not ignore the Moon! Its position in the air sign Libra suggests airy, high up, windy, upstairs rooms, attics, windows. Libra rules flat ground, so combined with Virgos information, it sounded like an attic floor. If there had been new building, he would have been there, but there wasn't any. (The Moon in a cardinal sign might show new buildings.)

The Moon also shows action. Its past action reveals what has happened, how Max got shut in there. The Moon has passed the sinister sextile of Uranus and Jupiter in Sagittarius. We had had some wild (Sagittarius) storms (Uranus retrograde) about the time of his disappearance, and I think the owner of the property might have gone up and closed fast a banging window; because Jupiter is in its own sign, Sagittarius, it is his own house. The Moon next passes over Pluto, a planet which brings things to light.

Fig. 19.2: The Happy Story of Blackberry the Rabbit

He was a fine, regal rabbit, tawny-colored and with a ruff. His symbol in the chart being the Sun, ruler of Leo which is on the sixth house cusp, the house of small animals. (See Figure 19.2 on the previous page.)

The Moon is weak and void of course, so it is of secondary importance in this chart. In fact, the chart is only good because the main significator is so well-placed on the M.C. with Jupiter, otherwise the void Moon could be a caution.

Blackberry was not only lucky (Sun with Jupiter) he was inventive (Sun semi-sextile Uranus). Uranus is not a main significator and, therefore, can help describe the Sun. He was also lonely (Sun in Capricorn) and bent on procreation (Sun on the fifth house cusp of the turned chart).

Blackberry ran due south (Sun in Capricorn reinforced by its position in the southern angle) and was, in fact, seen in the town car park (parking lot) about one mile directly south of his home.

In the car park, the man from the fish bait shop caught him and protected him, seeing that he was a tame rabbit. (The fish bait man is symbolized by Jupiter.) Later he sent Blackberry to his sister, here shown by Saturn, who kept rabbits. There Blackberry stayed until his owner's (the querent's) advertisement was seen and answered, and the querent went to bring him back home.

You observe that Jupiter goes to dexter sextile of Saturn, his sister. Mars, the querent, also goes to a dexter trine of Saturn. I will not tell you how long it was before the rabbit returned home, but leave you to ponder. If you write to me I will tell you. The time is clearly stated by symbolic direction.

In the view of the rabbit it was no doubt a void adventure, because when he arrived back at the point from which he had departed, he was neutered. But, as consolation was given a companion.

For those who suggest this chart should not be judged with

Figure 19.2: "Where is Blackberry the rabbit?"

Regiomontanus House System

5 January 1985
11:40 A.M. G.M.T.
51° 13' N 1° 25' E

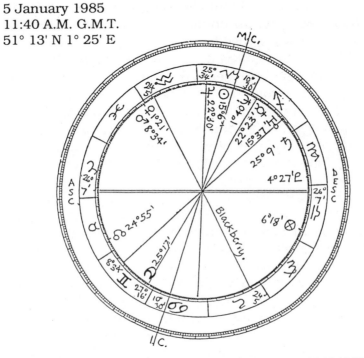

	0 1 2 3 4 5 6 7 8 9	10 11 12 13 14	15 16 17 18 19 20 21	22 23	24 25 26 27 28 29
	♀ ♇ ⊗ ♂		☉	☿	♌ ☽
	1° 4° 6° 8°		15°	22°	24° 25°
	21' 27 18' 34'		6'	23'	17'
	♓ ♏ ♎ ♓		♑	♐	♊
	♆		♅	♃	♄
	1°		15°	22°	25°
	40'		37'	30'	9'
	♑		♐	♑	♏

☽ void
☉ to ♂♃

Saturn in the seventh, I reply that it is far from the angle, and not in the sign on the Descendant. And, the chart did exactly describe the situation, for we must mix reason with judgment.

Fig. 19.3: "Where is Teddy?"

When I answered the telephone on 2 January 1985, a friend, Eve Jackson, had a question for me. "Where is the cat?" she wanted to know. "What is his name?" I asked, seeking to identify him in some way. "Teddy," she said. "Where is Teddy?" My heart went out to him for it was Arctic weather. "I'll do a horary straight away," I said. The time was 5:50 P.M. G.M.T.

The first house represents the querent, together with the Moon. Eve, therefore, is symbolized by the Sun in this particular question, because the Sun rules the Ascendant. It is placed in the sixth house of small animals, a matter on which her attention was pivoted. Capricorn is on the cusp of the sixth and so Saturn, ruler of Capricorn, symbolizes the cat. I find cats are represented by the sixth house without turning the chart. Apparently living creatures do not always count as possessions, but exist in their own right.

Saturn is in Scorpio. From this sign we can derive the description, condition, and whereabouts of the cat. I assumed he was black--Saturn and Scorpio have affinities with that color--and that he had white on his face or head because Jupiter is in the first house and rules white.*[5] Saturn in Scorpio mixed with the Moon in Taurus led me to the conclusion he would be stocky and square. Eve confirmed this later, and it is important because you want to be sure you are considering the correct house, especially as it transpired it was a neighbor's cat. Yet the question had not been framed in that way, so I simply looked at the sixth. Eve had been left in charge of him when the gentleman who owned him had gone to the hospital, and Teddy had panicked and run away.

Signs show the sort of place Teddy is in. Scorpio gives us the following range of choices: damp, wet, northerly, cold, places where there are beetles, gardens, orchards, vineyards, kitchens, larders, and wash houses. This made me think he wasn't on the road.

Since Saturn is near a cusp, I knew he was by a door, wall or boundary, because a planet within 5° of a cusp is consid

Figure 19.3: "Where is Teddy?"

Regiomontanus House System

2 January 1985
5:50 P.M. G.M.T.
51° 13' N 1° 25' E

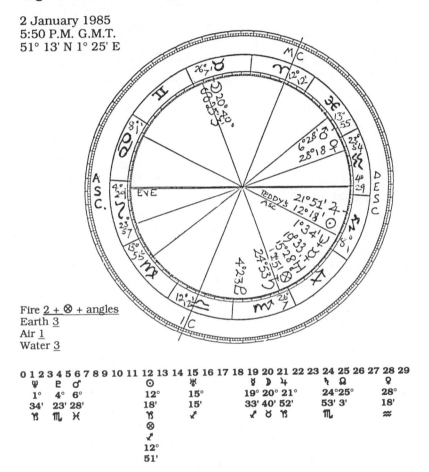

Fire <u>2</u> + ⊗ + angles
Earth <u>3</u>
Air <u>1</u>
Water <u>3</u>

0 1 2 3 4 5 6 7 8 9 10 11	12 13 14	15 16 17	18 19 20 21 22 23	24 25 26 27	28 29
Ψ ♇ ♂	☉	♅	☿ ☽ ♃	♄ ☊	♀
1° 4° 6°	12°	15°	19° 20° 21°	24° 25°	28°
34' 23' 28'	18'	15'	33' 40' 52'	53' 3'	18'
♑ ♏ ♓	♑	♐	♐ ♉ ♑	♏	♒
	⊗				
	♐				
	12°				
	51'				

ered as being in the following house.[6] Saturn is in the twelfth house of imprisonment. As you will see, he was inside. I realized that it was likely he was locked in, perhaps in an outhouse (outside loo), (Saturn's position in Scorpio!) Since Saturn has no dignity here and is not in mutual reception, I judged that his condition was sad, unhappy, and out of place.

Earthy signs showed him low down, and indeed Scorpio is often so. Certainly he was not upstairs or westerly because of the lack of air planets. The Moon applies to a trine of Jupiter in one degree. In addition to being the greater benefic Jupiter is the lord of the terms of the Moon. I interpreted that to mean Eve would have him within twenty-four hours. Another hopeful indication was that the Sun was in Teddy's first house, and that shows recovery unless the Sun is in Aquarius or Libra where it is weak.

I telephoned Eve to tell her she could hope to see Teddy within twenty-four hours, and that he might be in an outhouse (loo) to the north of the house, locked in or near the door. I also told her that she must continue her search, he would not come to her. (This is because the Sun moves faster than Saturn, so she must go to him.) The Moon, also Eve, encounters Jupiter (by aspect) before Saturn, signifying that there would be an intermediary who would take her to the cat. Had the planet first encountered by the Moon been obstructive it would have prevented her reaching Teddy. However, Jupiter is benefic, disposited by Saturn, the cat, and in Teddy's first house. Therefore, Jupiter helps her. Eve said she had already searched the outhouses in her vicinity. I was sure she would find him soon; he wasn't far away because the Sun and Saturn are in the same quadrant. Another point was that the Moon next passed over Pluto which indicates something coming to light.

I wondered if what would lead Eve to the cat was a tin of liver (Jupiter).

What happened is this. After hours of exhausting and freezing searching Eve asked the caretaker of the block of flats next door if she could look in the locked up basement. The flats were not due north, as I had indicated, but east north east. The caretaker accompanied Eve, and unlocked the door to the basement, a very Scorpionic dark place Eve said. There was Teddy, very frightened. The helpful caretaker had played the part of Jupiter, the intermediary. Teddy still ran from Eve, for the Moon opposition Saturn is separative, but the caretaker produced a tin of cat food and Teddy was captured. (I wondered if it contained liver!)

For days I was vexed that Teddy was not due north, since the water signs rule north. Lilly says that, "if the lord of the sixth be in watery signes, North," in a low place. I realize now I had judged the chart as I had judged that of Max, by the chief significator. But in this chart the significator was weak and the Moon was strong. The Moon was in the south east quadrant, and with the Moon you must consider the quadrants. Therefore, I should have tempered the judgment north by adding southeast of north.

The Moon's trine to Jupiter had kept its promise and Teddy had been found within twenty-four hours.

Finally, Teddy was taken to the lady he often stays with, no doubt the final aspect to Venus reached by the Moon in this story, when she will translate the light from Saturn to Venus at 28° Aquarius.

Figure 19.4: Street Plan Showing Eve's House and Teddy's Flats, and Where He Was

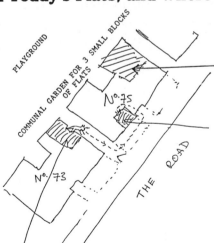

N

W ──┼── E

S

Woman in basement flat let me in and brought tin of cat food (liver?).

Teddy found in basement lumber room here. He must have gotten through front door of block (N 75°) which usually is kept shut. Either lumber room door was closed or he was too frightened to come out where people come and go. He couldn't have gotten back out of block once front door was closed.

E.J.

Teddy's flat on ground floor: exit through kitchen into passage between two blocks.

Our flat roughly above Teddy's, on first floor.

196 Horary Astrology Rediscovered

Fig. 19.5: "Where is Chloe?"

Although my success with Teddy had only been partial,
Eve must have found it of assistance, for she telephoned on 16
February to ask "Where is Chloe?" a male cat who was lost. Eve
had tried this one herself, so I could not ask the same
question. Instead I asked her for particulars of the chart she
had judged, and worked on that.

Eve is shown again by a Leo Ascendant and the Sun is,
therefore, her symbol. It is in the seventh house, with the
symbol, Mercury, of her neighbour, to whom the cat belongs.
You can see by this picture that Eve had just left her
neighbour. On Chloe, the white hairs were slightly lower on
the body, as Jupiter is further from the Ascendant.

The beauty of this chart is the clarity with which time is
shown. The cat was missing five nights, and there are 5
degrees between Mercury, symbol of the neighbour, and Saturn, symbol of the cat. Also, if you look in the ephemeris, you
see that Mercury, Moon, and Sun have reached the degree of
Saturn on the early morning of Sunday/Monday. He turned
up at 2:30 A.M. He was on the window sill.

I asked if Chloe had fled in panic, and was told there had
been some workmen in the home, so perhaps he had been
northwest by north. He also may have been by a fire, with the
Moon in Sagittarius.

Figure 19.5: "Where is Chloe?"

Regiomontanus House System

14 February 1985
4:09 P.M. G.M.T.
51° 52' N 0° 20' W

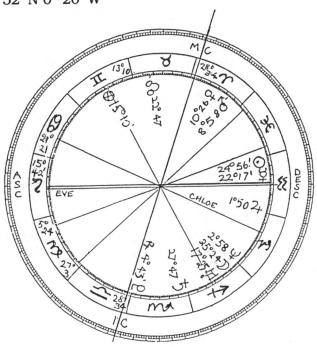

0 1 2 3 4 5 6 7 8 9	10 11 12	13 14 15 16 17	18 19 20 21	22 23	24 25 26 27 28 29
♃ ♆ ♇	♀	⊗ ♅		♉ →	☉ ☽ → ♄
1°2° 4°	10°	15° 17°		22°	24° 25° 27°
5' 47'	26'	10' 25'		17'	56' 24' 47'
♒ ♑ ♏	♈	♐		♒	♒ ♐ ♏

Fig. 19.6: "Where are my spectacles?"

The spectacles are lost, not mislaid at home. The querent here is symbolized by the Ascendant and its ruler, Venus. The spectacles being movable possessions are shown by the ruler of the second house, Mercury. The whole chart must describe the situation. Mercury identifies the item as "implements," that is, equipment. (Or, Mercury could have indicated pictures or books or paper.) In this chart it is particularly apt that the querent was a doctor, and Lilly mentions that Venus and Mars in the sixth house makes a good doctor. [7] The sign Scorpio, too, accords with such a description. As for the spectacles in Capricorn, they were the doctor's working spectacles, nothing fancy. The house position of Mercury is interesting, showing he had not left them at home (in that case Mercury would have been in an angular house). Mercury instead is in the ninth house of travel, and the doctor had just arrived on a long distance bus from the south, (Capricorn rules the south).

The condition of the planet should be considered, and here we see Mercury is retrograde. This is by no means all bad as some modern writers think, but is extremely fortunate if it concerns a lost article or person, since it shows change of direction, and that the article will be found. There are three meanings to retrograde:

1. Someone or something will be found or return [8]
2. Something happens suddenly [9]
3. It delays [10]

Having considered the possible location of the spectacles, we want to know what happens. Action is known mainly from the Moon. Note the planets to which the Moon makes major aspects before it leaves the sign it is in. Its past aspects show what has happened and its approaching aspects show what will happen. Other planets, too, make aspects and show events, but the Moon moves so much faster that it is the main

Figure 19.6: "Where are my spectacles?"

Regiomontanus House System

Sunday 25 December 1983
1:35 P.M. G.M.T.
51° 13' N 1° 25' E

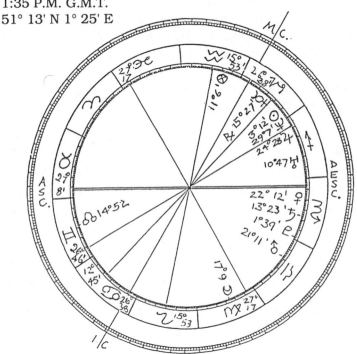

Moon translates light from trine Venus to sextile Venus.
Mercury is retrograde.

Figure 19.7: Moon Translating Light from Mercury to Venus

13   14   15   16   17   18   19   20   21   22   23   24   25   26   27   28

indicator of action. It is simple to set out the planets under your chart as I have shown in Figure 19.7 .

Notice that only the main significators, the Moon, Mercury, and Venus have been used to give the main answer in this chart. In this example chart the Moon recently trined Mercury and next sextiles Venus. This is translation of light by the Moon, and shows the conveyance of the spectacles to the owner. The doctor telephoned the long distance bus company, who had found his spectacles and handed them to him as he boarded the bus for his return journey. The Moon is 5 degrees distant from Venus, however it was fast moving and produced the spectacles within four days.

"Where is the front door key?"

It was late at night when a friend telephoned to say she had lost her front door key. She was already indoors but worried about leaving the house in the morning. (See Figure 19.8 on the following page.)

The Ascendant matched her nativity, with Libra ascending. This signifies the querent, together with Venus and the Moon. The Key, being her possession and thus a second house matter, is also ruled by Venus.

Venus is not angular so one might easily think that the key is not indoors, but Mercury, natural ruler of keys and ruler of the hour *is* angular. The ruler of the hour angular indicates the goods are "in the owner's hands. [11]

The Moon moves to trine Venus, showing satisfaction to the owner. An article is where the chief significator is by sign. I thought, "Sagittarius is east, it is also inward toward the center of the galaxy." Sagittarius also made me think of hips. Venus rules women's clothing or bedding. Jupiter conjunct Neptune shows absentmindedness. I could not think of the solution, except that she would find the key. It was there somewhere. Lilly says, "If it be Venus it signifyeth the place of the seat of a woman or Bed or Clothes." [12]

He also writes, "Behold the Lord of the terme of the Moon,

Figure 19.8: "Where is My Front Door Key?"

Regiomontanus House System

19 January 1984
10:41 P.M. G.M.T.
51° 32' N 0° 5' W

Hora ☿

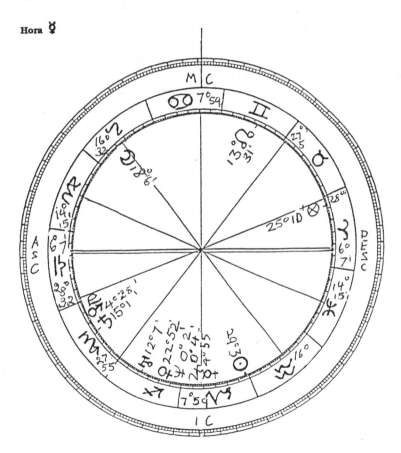

the which is signifier of the substance stolne to be recovered.
If the Lord of the terme of the Moon and the Lord of the House

of the Moon be increasing both in motion and number, and free from unfortunes; it shows it shall be recovered whole and sound, and nothing diminished thereof.[13] It was past midnight. I gave up and telephoned back to her. She had gone to sleep, and yes, she had found the lost key. "I had on a new skirt with two pockets and I had turned it 'round so the pocket with the key was at the back, and I had forgotten," she said. "So the pocket was on your hip?" I asked, thinking of Sagittarius. "Yes." "What color was your skirt?" I asked. "Deep blue with a bit of Neptune green," she told me. Jupiter conjunct Neptune! The fact that it was on her actual person was well described by Venus ruling the first and the second.

Chapter 20
Miscellaneous Questions

A frequently asked question is about change of residence. Be sure you understand the situation and whether the querent has a particular house in mind or is asking in a general way.

At the outset it may be advisable to frame the question as "Shall I stay or shall I move?" and follow Lilly's detailed instruction on how to assess the relative value of the first, representing the querent as he is, or the fourth, his house, or the seventh, the house to which he will remove, noting too if the angles are movable or fixed.

It is not until the querent has a specific house in mind, and one which he is definitely and seriously thinking of buying, that you can set up and judge a chart in the way the following two are judged. That is, to consider the first as the querent (whether buyer or seller), the fourth as the house. The sign on the fourth will describe the house and its site, whether dry or damp, high or low, or if wooded. The seventh is the seller, or the other person, and the tenth shows the price. Nowadays a lack of direct aspect between the ruler of the first and ruler of the seventh is not unusual, but there is usually an intermediary, showing the agent.

Fig. 20.1: "Will we get the house?"

The querent is represented by the Ascendant, Cancer, and its ruler, the Moon. The house to be purchased is represented by the chart's fourth house, the sign on its cusp, Virgo, and its

Figure 20.1: "Will we get the house?"

Regiomontanus House System

13 March 1984
10:58 A.M. G.M.T.
51° 13' N 1° 25' E

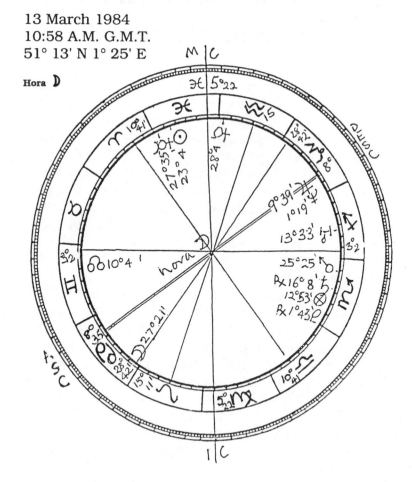

ruler, Mercury. The querent had dark curling hair, a round face, and slightly uptilted nose. She was a nurse and a mother of small children, complying with the lunar description.

The angles are not fixed, showing change. The Moon, which reveals what happens, makes a dexter trine to Mercury. This in itself is the affirmative reply.

Counting a degree as a day (since the Moon is in a cardinal sign, angular) I realized that the very day she asked the question would be best for the purchase. Time is usually ascertained from the Moon or the chief significator, and in this case the Moon is also the chief significator. I telephoned to say that today the house would be bought. I was told it was so arranged.

The seventh house and its ruler, Saturn, represent the seller, the other. Jupiter here shows the seller will deal honestly and keep his word.

The price is shown by the tenth house. The Sun here suggests that it was high. The combustion of Mercury indicates some confusion. The confusion was about the querent's husband's money being available to purchase the house. The Sun is the natural ruler of husbands. In this chart, it is part ruler of the second house, linking up these matters. Cancer is actually on the second cusp and the money spent was to be partly hers and partly his.

At one time, such negotiations took place directly between purchaser and seller, but nowadays an agent is involved. Here the agent is represented by Mars. Mars also rules the eleventh, the querent's wishes. The Moon, symbol of the querent, translates the light from Mars to Mercury, the Sun trines Mars--that is, the husband's money goes to the agent--and then the Moon translates from Mars to Mercury, the house.

The fact that the Moon last passed over Mercury shows that the querent had just been looking at the house. Previously, when the Moon had made a sinister trine to Saturn, symbol of the seller, it was a friendly contact. Both hoped for the sale. The Moon's aspect to Mercury was dexter, indicating that the querent felt a compulsion to buy the house.

Virgo on the fourth cusp describes the soil, which was dry and good for agriculture. But Mercury in Pisces and a preponderance of water signs made me wonder if there was a well.

Figure 20.2: "Shall I buy the house?"

**Regiomontanus House System
Answer "Yes"**

15 May 1985
12:36 P.M. G.M.T.
51° 13' N 1° 25' E

Wednesday
Hora ☿

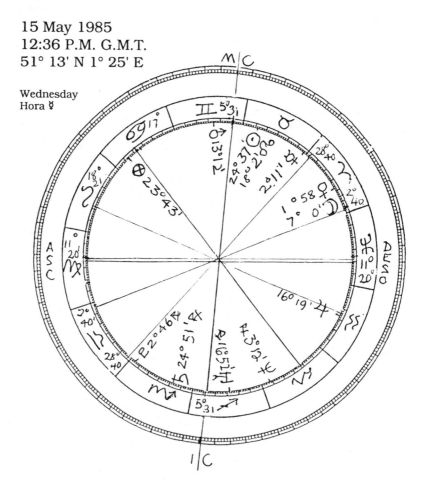

The house was bought that day, and has so far been an unlucky house for the purchasers. The ancients considered a grand trine very unfortunate.

The validity of the chart is confirmed by the planetary hour, the fifth hour on a Tuesday, the hour of the Moon, which harmonizes with Cancer, the sign on the Ascendant.

Fig. 20.2:"Shall I buy the house?"

The Ascendant and its ruler and the Moon symbolize the querent. She is a practical and sensible person, quiet and well spoken.

The fourth cusp and its ruler describe the house she wanted to buy. The tenth and its ruler relate to the price.

In attempting to describe the house I noticed Jupiter, (ruler of Sagittarius) symbol of the house, in Aquarius. So I looked up the properties of Aquarius and decided which of those adjectives were relevant. The character of the town precludes the first word "hills," but certainly the ground was uneven and the soil was full of flint stones. From the words "near some little conduit or spring," together with Neptune in the fourth I deduced there was likely to be water, or a well on the property. Yet none of us was prepared for the surprise Uranus near the fourth cusp gave us: over two thousand gallons of water were discovered under the concrete out in the yard. Here we see support for the ancient's association of wetness with Aquarius.

From the sign Sagittarius on the fourth I gathered the house might be situated high in comparison with its sur-roundings, and there are about six steps up to the front door. I also thought large dogs might have been kept there and that the fireplaces would be an outstanding feature. So they were.

Mercury, the main significator, does not aspect towards Jupiter, representing the house, but the Moon, the co-signi-ficator, does. In that aspect is the affirmative outcome, the perfection.

Before the Moon reached the dexter sextile of Jupiter it

conjuncts Venus the natural significator of money, in the eighth, indicating a loan. It then proceeds to sinister sextile Mars, the price. Again Mars connects the eighth of loans with the price of the house, yet since the sign on the tenth identifies with our querent she did not mind it; it was a fair price.

Jupiter on the sixth cusp indicates the great amount of work that had to be done on the house, and that it would be done satisfactorily.

The Moon is between the benefics and the querent loves the house, which contains gracious rooms with early seventeenth century panelling, for Jupiter is associated with wood.

Fig. 20.3: "Will I make money at this (professional) job?"

The querent is represented by the Ascendant and its ruler, Jupiter, and also by the Moon. She has a pale face like ivory because Pisces ascends in her natal chart as here. With her natal Sun in Taurus, she works very hard for money.

Her career is represented by Jupiter, ruler of the tenth in this horary chart, for she identifies with it. (She is an accountant.) The Sun, Fortuna, and Venus natural ruler of money, are in the sixth house of hard work. The placement of Jupiter in the eleventh is traditionally the most favorable possible for the Greater Benefic, for that is the house it naturally rules. [1]

Venus, accidental ruler of the second and natural ruler of money, trines Jupiter. This is emphasized by the translation of light by the Moon from Venus to Jupiter. The two benefics ensure a fortunate outcome. The retrogradation of Jupiter makes this happen even more suddenly. (Some might say this is not strictly translation of light since Venus is already in trine to Jupiter, however, Lilly says that translation occurs whether or not the significators are in aspect.)

If you look at the diagram of degrees and planets below the chart (Figure 20.3) you can see plainly that the Moon is between Venus and Jupiter. Drawing the degrees and planets this way is a great help. [2]

Figure 20:3: "Will I make money at this (professional) job?"

Regiomontanus House System

7 August 1984
8:15 P.M. G.M.T.
51° 13' N 1° 25' E

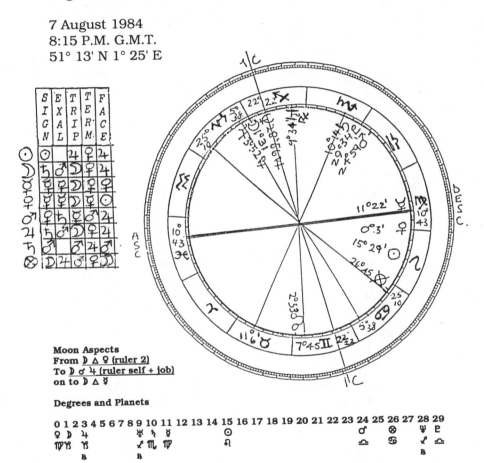

Moon Aspects
From ☽ △ ♀ (ruler 2)
To ☽ ♂ ♃ (ruler self + job)
on to ☽ △ ☿

Degrees and Planets

0 1 2 3 4 5 6 7 8 9	10 11 12 13 14	15 16 17 18 19 20 21 22 23	24 25	26 27	28 29
♀ ☽ ♃	⚨ ♄ ☿	☉	♂	⊗	♆ ♇
♍ ♑ ♑	♐ ♏ ♍	♌	♎	♋	♐ ♎
B	B				B

The diagram of dignities at the top left of the chart is also helpful. There you can see the lesser mutual exchange of dignities between Venus and the Moon, Venus being in the triplicity of the Moon and the Moon being in the terms of Venus, bringing a natural sympathy.

Fig. 20.4: "Shall I go to Australia?"

The Ascendant and its ruler, the Moon, represent the querent. The validity of the chart is emphasized by the Moon's nearness to the degree of the querent's natal Sun. The Moon rules both the planetary hour and the sign on the Ascendant.

The ninth house with Pisces on its cusp and the ruler of Pisces, Jupiter, symbolize the distant country, Australia, to which the querent may go. The querent is in a dilemma. She has the offer of a good job at the B.B.C. in London, or she can accept this offer to go to Australia to sail yachts.

The cardinal sign rising indicates the restlessness of the querent, for the Moon loves change and is always fluctuating. A cardinal sign on the fourth cusp also shows change of residence, (she now lives in London).

The Moon is appropriately placed on the fifth cusp of enjoyment (which is what she is thinking of). So are Mars and Saturn there, signifying hard work, yet pleasure at the same time. These planets are appropriately in Scorpio and Sagittarius, signs which both love the deep sea. The only major aspect made by the Moon is a square to Jupiter (which rules the ninth of overseas and the sixth of work). In fact, the Moon moves between Venus, ruler of the eleventh in the chart (hopes), to Jupiter, ruler of the ninth. Again, we have this fortunate contact between the Benefics.

The rule about square aspects is that a square can bring an affirmative answer if the planets are placed in good houses and have dignity where they are. Jupiter certainly has dignity because it is in mutual reception by sign with Saturn, (which deserves a score of 5). But the Moon, except that the fifth house is considered lucky, has no essential dignity. Nevertheless, from the general indications of the chart I judged she would go. As we might expect, the square brought difficulties: she had almost left her decision too late. (Notice the late ascending degree.) But with telephone calls and some effort all was arranged, and in a month she went. This is shown by the fact that there are approximately 4 degrees before Jupiter

Figure 20:4: "Shall I go to Australia?"

Regiomontanus House System

2 February 1986
3:05 P.M. G.M.T.
51° 13' N 1° 25' E

Querent's Planet ☽
Quesited's Planet ♃
Planetary Day ☉
Planetary Hour ☽

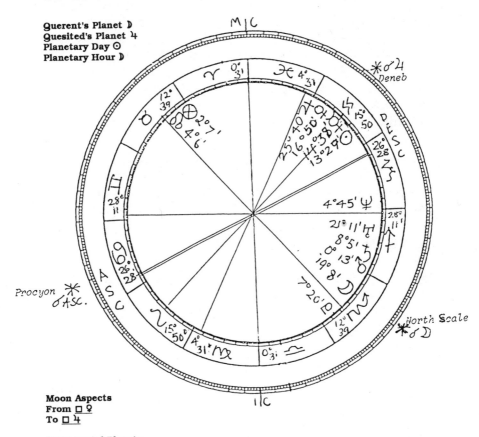

Moon Aspects
From □ ♀
To □ ♃

Degrees and Planets

	0 1 2 3 4 5 6 7 8 9 10 11 12	13 14 15	16 17	18 19 20	21 22 23	24 25 26 27 28 29
	♂ ⊗ ♆ ♇ ♄	☉ ☿	♀	☽	♅	♃
	0° 2° 4° 7° 8°	13° 14°	16°	19°	21°	25°
	13 7 45 20'5'	29 39	50	8'	11'	40
	♐ ♉ ♑ ♏ ♐	♒ ♒	♒	♏	♐	♒
	♌					

reaches its own sign. The contract was to be for a year, or, as she was going so late, it would be just under a year. The Moon is 11 degrees from the end of a sign.

The Moon with the North Scale shows scope for distinction and personality. The Ascendant with Procyon puts thoughts into action, gives drive and a sharp mind, though some imprudence. [3]

The Moon midpoint Mars and Pluto shows audacity, daring, energy, and resolution, signifying a determined woman.[4]

Aries on the Midheaven suggests a pioneering career. Fortuna in the tenth is extremely fortunate, especially since it is disposited by Venus.

She went to Australia, and the following December wrote that it had been great fun but hard work. She sounded exhilarated.

Fig. 20.5:"Where is Ann Lock?"

A young woman was missing and there was much newspaper and television coverage about it. She had been married only a month before, and she was employed by the British Broadcasting Corporation.

For those who may not have followed this case, British television showed a film about the events of Ann Lock's last day. She received a telephone call asking her to put in some extra work at the B.B.C. and she went up to London especially (I think it was at the weekend). It was a day on which she didn't have the car, so she had to cycle to the station. There she left her bicycle in the bicycle shed. She put in her day's work, said good-bye to her colleagues in a normal way, and was never seen again. When she had not returned home by a late train, her husband went to the station to find her. Her bicycle was no longer in the shed. She did not arrive on any train. He informed the police, and an extensive search took place.

I do not like to dwell on such matters, but a journalist asked me to do a chart in case it could be helpful.

To be valid a chart must describe the situation, and

Figure 20.5: "Where is Ann Lock?"

Regiomontanus House System

Friday, 30 May 1986
9:45 A.M. G.M.T.
51° 13' N 1° 25' E

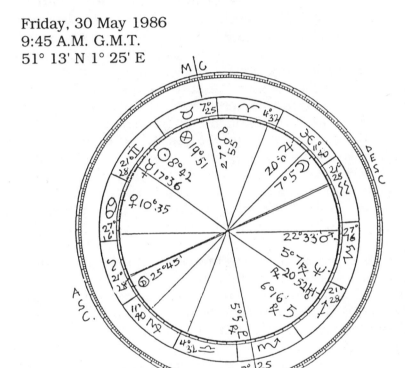

0	1	2	3	4	5	6	7	8	9	10	11	12	13	14	15	16	17	18	19	20	21	22	23	24	25	26	27	28	29
					Ψ	♄	☽	☉		♀							☿		♃	⊗		♂			⊕		♌		
					5°	6°	7°	8°		10°							17°		20°	19°		22°					27		
					7'	16	5	42		35							36		0	♒		33'					55		
					℞	℞	♓	♊	♋								♊		♓	20°		♑					♈		
					♑														52										
					℮														℞										
					5°														♐										
					5'																								
					℞																								
					♏																								

Translation by Moon from Saturn retrograde to Sun.

usually say something of the querent. Here the Ascendant is my own, and the Sun is in Gemini with Mercury, symbolizing my journalistic friend. The square of the Moon to the Sun shows my dislike and reluctance to be involved in a newspaper or publicity matter. This clear description in the chart shows that the Ascendant should be used to signify the querent(s), despite Lilly's instruction that when a question is asked about whether an absent one is dead or alive in a general way, and when that person has no relation to the querent, the Ascendant, its lord, and the Moon represent the absent person. [5] If, in this case, the Ascendant, the querent had not so clearly described us, but had shown the absent one more obviously, I would have used it for the quesited. If you can see the picture in a chart you will know which way to judge it.

Because of the nature of the question I accepted Saturn, ruler of the seventh, retrograde and void, not as an indication that the astrologer's judgment would be poor, because the judgment concerns the seventh house, the other: Ann Lock. As we were asking about the probable victim of a murder we could not expect her significator to be other than poorly placed. The seventh cusp in the turned chart is the Ascendant of Ann Lock and Saturn is her symbol. As ruler of Aquarius, Saturn represents a polite and pleasant person, for Aquarius is the joy of Saturn.

The retrograde position of Saturn shows she will be found. Saturn poorly placed and retrograde suggests damage to her. Saturn at 6° Sagittarius is 2 degrees from the opposition of the Sun at 8° Gemini, now the ruler of her seventh house and symbol of her husband. The Moon at 7° Pisces translates the light from Saturn to the Sun in 2 degrees; her body was shown to him in two months.

Saturn in Sagittarius tells us she will be found on higher ground than the surroundings, and the Part of Fortune in Taurus indicates farmland, with bushes and trees not far off.

The Part of Death ascends, and undoubtedly the evidence of the chart inclines to show death.

The villain, Mars, lurks in ambush on her twelfth cusp.

Mars in Capricorn describes him as thin, dark, with a small head and dark hair. Mars is in 22° Capricorn and, as Dennis Elwell will tell you, that is a degree area prevalent in the charts of murderers. (Dennis has quite a collection of murderers' nativities showing this, and I remember in the sixties John Addey pointed it out in connection with the Tow Path murders.) It is the antiscium degree of Antares, connected with violent death. Apparently even good people whose charts have this area stressed find difficulty in realizing their fellow human beings are people and tend to regard them as things.

When Lilly was asked if a brother was dead, he considered both the eighth of the turned chart and the eighth of the radical chart. [6] It is, therefore, a more complicated matter to judge a turned chart than an unturned one.

In the radical chart Jupiter, Lord of Death, is in the eighth, and the Moon is on its cusp (any planet within 5 degrees of a cusp is read as being in the following house). In the turned chart Mercury is Lord of Death, on Ann Lock's fifth cusp of generation opposite Uranus which is on the unturned fifth cusp, both square to Jupiter, Lord of Death in the unturned chart. This I think describes her rape and death.

Mars departs with haste from this dreadful configuration. Being in a higher degree than all the other planets he no doubt thinks he has escaped. However, the Moon catches up with Mars and I think the criminal will be caught.

In the ephemeris, the Moon perfects its conjunction with the man two days after the date the chart was drawn, and I wondered if anything would be discovered then. However, it was not. It is more usual to decide timing from symbolic direction, but it is sometimes done from an ephemeris.

Mars departs from contact with Jupiter, which is the second house ruler of the turned chart. He had been at her possessions. The bicycle and her bag were later discovered abandoned. (Did he go back to the station where he had seen her leave her bicycle in the morning and take it along the footpath later, to mislead?)

From the foregoing I realized it was not the husband who

could be guilty as some people had suggested.

Ann probably fainted from shock, I deduced, because her symbol, Saturn, is mid Neptune/Pluto, which shows dark foreboding and decline of powers. Jupiter's involvement in this configuration is merciful. For such information alone I half hoped the newspaper would publish what I said, as I thought it might comfort her husband. (It was not published.)

Mars, the villain, in Capricorn in the sixth house suggests a manual worker. Its connection with the ninth of long journeys made me think of long distances covered by railways. In the context of the crime I put forward my theory that the murderer was probably a railway worker.

With the Moon at 15 degrees from Mars I wondered if the criminal will be caught fifteen months after the query.

The police did indeed catch a criminal railway worker later on and he was convicted of two similar rapes and murders in early 1987. His hair was dark, but reddish (Mars!). They were unable to prove he murdered Ann Lock, although the police thought he had done so. He was extremely short, as Capricorns often are. Mars was in its own terms.

Fig. 20.6: "I have fallen in love with a 1937 Bentley. Will I be able to buy it?"

The querent is symbolized by the Ascendant, its ruler, the Sun, and by the Moon.

The car is represented by the third house, Libra, and its ruler, Venus.

The querent is concerned about being able to pay for the car and his co-ruler, the Moon, is showing concern in the second house of cash. It is peregrine. Indeed, he has not enough money. Fortuna, his treasure, is in the possession of others, in the eighth house.

The main significator of the querent has gone right over to the other side of the chart--he has gone over to the salesman, the other, and is anxious to please him at all costs. The salesman is symbolized by the seventh house and its ruler

Figure 20.6: "I have fallen in love with a 1937 Bentley. Will I be able to buy it?"

Regiomontanus House System

15 February 1987
4:42 P.M. G.M.T.
51° 13' N 1° 25' E

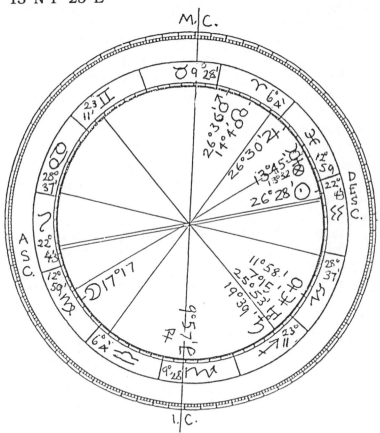

Saturn. He is a dark-haired, long-faced, pale gentleman, tall because his symbol is in the terms of Mercury.

Venus, symbol of the car, is in the querent's fifth house. She is his Joy; beautiful, her names are many: Cytherea, Aphrodite, Phospherus, Ericina, the evening Star Hesperus, or the Morning Star Lucifeli. She is shining and clean (polished?), feminine, full of mirth and jollity. Her sounds are quiet and subdued, for Venus has a soft voice, but may be overly fond of drinking (expensive in fuel); she is musical, charming, with large headlamps.

In tradition, Venus is in her joy in the fifth house, and the colours associated with the fifth are black and white or honey colour. Although at first I thought the car might be dark because it is disposited by Saturn, I eventually judged it was honey-coloured, as Venus is so strongly placed. I told the querent this and he confirmed it was true.

Libra ruling the third cusp suggested the car was airy, and, I thought, a two-seater, conducive to partnership. (Although she was mainly a two-seater there was some small space for two back seats.)

The ruler of the querent's money, Mercury (ruler of the second), is in its fall in the eighth, the house of other people's money. That is where the money has gone, to pay for the car. Jupiter, the planet of plenty, is also in the eighth, suggesting money ready to be borrowed, perhaps from some large corporation?

It won't be easy for the querent with two squares and an opposition. The square from the Moon in his second house to Uranus indicates a monetary shock. My judgment is, considering the chart as a whole, that he will deplete his wealth (Mercury in fall in the eighth and Moon peregrine in second), borrow heavily from some large corporation, (Jupiter in the borrowing eighth--and indeed, the car may technically remain theirs). Yet this large loan gives him possession of the car because Jupiter is mid-point Sun/Mars, which is described by Ebertin as the act of taking possession.

Venus rules not only the third house, but the house of

success and achievement, the tenth, the crowning Glory of our querent.

The Sun sextiles Mars ruler of the final fourth. I hope this will be enough to secure success. If the loan from Jupiter is eventually achieved (and with the opposition of the Moon, the querent must expect some refusals) then, because of the nature of oppositions, I think he will regret his financial commitment.

According to tradition and William Lilly, the first house rules white or grey, the second green, the third red or yellow or saffron, the fourth red, the fifth black and white or honey colour, and the sixth black. The seventh rules "dark black," and the eighth green and black. (I surmise that the eastern side of the chart rules the light colours and the western side the dark colours, and that since there is a distinction between black and "dark black" the sixth is not so dark as what we understand by black.) When we are told that the eighth is black and green, I also wonder if this includes a colour made by the mixture of green and black, which I call "bottle green." The ninth house rules green and white, so does this mean also jade green (which is a combination of green and white)? The tenth house is connected with red and white (pink?), the eleventh with saffron yellow, and the twelfth with green.

The planets also rule colour we are told. Saturn rules a dull, leaden colour, or ashy colour, or black; Jupiter rules blue, purple, ashy, yellow, or green. Mars rules fiery red and yellow; the Sun rules gold, scarlet, and some say purple. Venus rules white or milky sky-colour mixed with brown or a little green, (this sounds to me like pale turquoise blue). Mercury rules mixed colours like the neck of a stock dove, and many colours mixed in one, and of course, the colour of quicksilver, or "dusky silver," Lilly wrote. The Moon rules silver-white, and pale yellowish white (a colour I would call cream), and the colour of mother of pearl.

Traditionally, there is also a connection between colours and signs as follows. Aries, white and red (pink); Taurus, white and lemon (cream); Gemini, white and red (pink); Cancer, green or russet; Leo, red or green, (this red is Chinese red, I think); Virgo, black and blue; Libra, black or dark red; Scorpio, brown; Sagittarius, yellow or green sanguine (this is a sort of goldy-green, I think); Capricorn, black or russet; Aquarius, sky blue; Pisces, glistening white.

As a matter of fact, the querent who asked about the Bentley told me there was another car there at the time which was black and white and had light blue upholstery. It was too expensive and he was persuaded to try instead for the honey-coloured one. My first thought was that the car was black and white and blue, but as I say, from the general pleasure shown I eventually ruled out black and decided on honey.

What transpired is this. The querent sold all he could to raise the money for the Bentley, and when he went back to buy it, it had gone. He bought a less expensive black and white one. He sounded happy about it, but it was the honey one he had really loved first, and about which the question was asked.

Fig. 20.7: The Tragedy of the *Herald of Free Enterprise*
"Where did the water get in? Was it human error that caused the accident?"

This chart came from Sue Ward, and the interpretation is hers and mine. Saturn on the seventh cusp could be an apt warning if a querent asked a personal question in such dreadful circumstances. It would be wiser to remain silent. But in this context angular Saturn clearly portends disaster to the ship.

The Ascendant and the Moon represent the ship, and Mercury symbolizes those that sail in her. [7] The Ascendant reflects the name of the ship: Mercury, the Herald. Mercury is retrograde, in detriment, which in a question of this sort shows it will travel for only a short while, and is in danger. Malefic planets angular suggest danger. Saturn indicates drowning or running aground. Mars in an earth sign also shows running aground.

Figure 20.7: The Tragedy of the *Herald of Free Enterprise*

"Where did the water get in? Was it human error that caused the accident?

The parts of the ship

Aries, the prow of the ship
Taurus, under the prow (toward the water)
Gemini, the stern
Cancer, the bottom of the ship
Leo, the top of the ship above water
Virgo, the belly of the ship
Libra, the part that sometimes is above
    and sometimes is below water, the trim
Scorpio, the crew's quarters
Sagittarius, the crew
Capricorn, the ends of the ship
Aquarius, the master of the ship
Pisces, the oars (or means of propulsion)[11]

The three culprits are the malefics ♄ ♂ and ☋. Put them together with the signs they are in and you see where the fault lay.

Regiomontanus House System

7 March 1987
10:09 A.M. G.M.T.
51° 32' N 0° 45' E

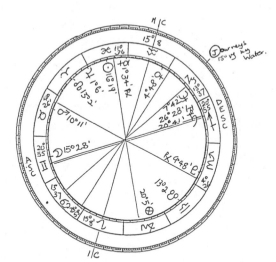

Moon Aspects
From
To ☽ □ ☉ ☍ ♄ ☍ ♅

Degrees and Planets

0 1 2 3 4 5 6 7 8 9 10 11 12 13 14 15 16 17 18 19 20 21 22 23 24 25 26 27 28 29

Different signs relate to different parts of the ship, and the signs in which the malefics are placed show where the danger and damage is. In this chart Saturn is in Sagittarius, sign of the mariners, the crew. Mars is in Taurus, showing the prow of the ship near the water line. The South Node, Cauda, is in Libra, the balance, (and ballast?). (Saturn, Mars, and the South Node are the malefics in traditional astrology.) This answers the question. The fault lay with the crew, and the part of the ship below the prow and the ballast.

Since the Ascendant is the body of the ship, any opposition to this place is dangerous, [8] and here we see Saturn, symbol of drowning. Saturn is also natural ruler of doors, and to look for the adjective to describe a planet, one looks at the sign containing it. Here the adjective is supplied by Sagittarius. They are double-bodied doors. Saturn, the seamen, and Saturn, the doors, show clearly the cause of the trouble. The Moon, ruler of the second house, the cargo, is also afflicted by Saturn. When the Moon reaches the Ascendant, it will square Fortuna and oppose Saturn exactly; Fortuna will be midpoint Moon/Saturn. This is reminiscent of the Titanic, for it shows "much prejudice by sea and sailors, and loss of credit." [9] The square to Saturn indicates loss of movable and immovable goods and waste of fortune. Incidentally, all this points specifically to a Saturnine person, or persons.

Venus sextile Saturn does alleviate the tragedy to an extent. Venus is the natural significator of money and much money has been collected for the relief.

It is very relevant that most planets are above the horizon, keeping the boat only half-submerged. In fact, I do find the chart a graphic picture of the situation. Saturn, like a fulcrum, shows the doors half-submerged below the water line, across the horizon. Mars, a malefic, is above, and Cauda below--the ballast weighing it down.

The ship started out late and was probably in a hurry. Bellatrix on the Ascendant shows recklessness, and so does Rigel with the Moon. Ettanin with Uranus brings dishonor. [10]

The signs and the parts of the ship to which they correspond are written on the chart.

Fig. 20.8: "Is AIDS a manmade disease?"

Before proceeding with the main interpretation, one identifies the querent in the chart. (See Figure 20.8.) This question was asked by Jean Elliot, symbolized by the Capricorn Ascendant and Saturn, its ruler, in Sagittarius. The querent, along with all of humanity, is placed on the eleventh cusp of hope and trust.

Figure 20.8: "Is AIDS a manmade disease?"

**A question from Jean Elliott, interpretation
by Olivia Barclay**

Regiomontanus House System

24 October 1986
1:17 P.M. G.M.T.
51° 31' N 0° 5' E

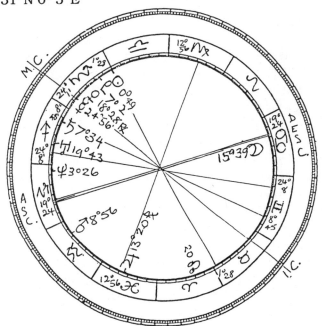

To turn to the question, we see the Ascendant and Saturn as mankind, and in particular as the bodies of mankind, with the Moon as co-significator. The disease is identified with the sixth house, and with its ruler, Mercury, which in the chart also rules the fifth of pleasure and the eighth of death. Mercury is in a position of strength and authority on the M.C.

The Moon, co-ruler of mankind, is half in the sixth of disease and half on the seventh cusp of partnership. (Any planet within 5 degrees of a cusp is read as being in the following house.) The Moon points to a trine aspect of Venus and Mercury, described by Ptolemy as a "preference for young boys." [12] Mercury, the significator of the disease, is in Scorpio, the sign that is associated anatomically with the sex organs, the fixed sign showing long duration of illness. Culpeper states "if the disease comes of love there is not a more pestilent planet in the Heavens than Venus." [13] Venus is with Mercury and the Moon points thereto. It is interesting to note the Greek names for Mercury and Venus--Hermes and Aphrodite, whose child was the Hermaphrodite. Mercury is the planet of communication, and in Scorpio of sex. There is a prevalence in the chart of water and fixed planets, which again points to Scorpio. In ancient times a grand trine was considered unfortunate. All this describes the disease as water-borne.

Jupiter, the planet of plenty, is in the second of wealth. Here it is retrograde, and at the time the question was asked, funds were being withheld in Britain, but Jupiter soon turned direct and further funds were forthcoming. The plentitude of Jupiter opposes the eighth cusp, and will bring many deaths. It was the ancient symbol of nature for it proliferates (read the *Hermetica*), and in this chart we see the separation of the Moon--ourselves--from nature.

Mars is important as the dispositor of the Scorpio planets, and it ascends in this chart. We also must remember its association with blood and anguish.

Mercury, symbol of the disease, is in the fixed sign Scorpio, 5 degrees and 4 minutes from Sagittarius, representing slightly more than 5 years until it will be disposited by Jupiter.

At that time I hope our wealth will be able to cure the disease.

Neptune is the vague, unknown enemy here on the twelfth cusp, part symbol of this wasting illness. Venus is not helpful, either. Apart from Culpeper's canny remark, it is part ruler of the eighth and ruler of the fourth, both unfortunate houses. The Sun is at 0° Scorpio which de Vore calls a degree of sensuous passion.

And so to sum up, I do not say that the chart shows AIDS is now primarily spread by homosexuals--not at all--but that its origin was there, maybe in one act. I see no astrological evidence that human beings scientifically manufactured it. Capricorn ascending can signify the animal facet of humanity.

I would like to add further that Jean's significator, because she was the querent, is semi-sextile Pluto in the ninth. This shows the depth of thought to which she plumbed and brought forth this deep question.

Part Three: Mundane

Chapter 21
An Introduction to Mundane Astrology

Many people associate Mundane astrology with political events and political knowledge. Yet really it means any events of wide interest, such as volcanos and earthquakes, as well as politics. Charles Harvey leads the way in this field.

It is certainly useful to have access to the charts of countries, and Nicholas Campion has just produced a comprehensive book of national horoscopes and of many towns and cities which, with the exception of his charts for the United States, I recommend. (I use a Gemini Ascendant for the States.) Event charts can be judged as horary charts except that whoever initiates an action is represented by the first house. Also, of course, there are no restrictions to invalidate a chart, because an event happens when it happens.

Of course, there are many great events which happen at an unknown time. When did the radiation first leak from Chernobyl? The advantage of horary is that you know the time.

But horary charts concerning world events are rare because one must know what to ask. You cannot ask every day if a plane will crash or if a ship will sink. Even if you did it would not be a true horary question, where the mind is tuned in to the moment, and then the planetary hour would be wrong, or other inappropriate positions occur.

When an event has occurred you need to ask your horary question about it soon, or hundreds of other astrologers will have asked first. The trouble with large and important questions is that every astrologer, capable or incapable, is asking it. But an event chart of Mundane interest can be drawn up at any time.

Mundane events are usually, though not always, depressing. They are easier than horary because you know the outcome. For this reason you find more people give talks about them than about horaries. Besides, they sound more important!

The Disaster at Bhopal

In searching for an astrological explanation of the Bhopal tragedy, it seemed appropriate to find that it occurred as Neptune, ruler of gas, entered Capricorn, the sign ruling India. Saturn, which rules Capricorn, was at 21 Scorpio conjunct the fixed star Unuk, the Neck of the Serpent.

Despite many indications of misfortune in the chart drawn up for the time of the tragedy, it does not by itself describe anything so horrific as occurred. To find out that we should heed the words of Ptolemy, "The first and most potent cause of such events lies in the conjunctions of the Sun and Moon at eclipse and the movements of the stars at the time." [1]

The chart of the eclipse preceding the event as seen in Bhopal at 6:27 A.M. on November 23, 1984, therefore should be studied and compared with the chart for the time of the disaster.

In the eclipse chart (Figure 21.1) 0° Scorpio ascends with Pluto and Saturn (ruling India) in the first house. The eclipsing luminaries stand at 0° 47' Sagittarius, at mid-point between the Ascendant and Neptune, and oppose the eighth cusp of death, (since death is the subject of our enquiry) which is at the degree of a fixed star cluster known as the Pleiades, noted

Figure 21.1: Eclipse Preceding the Bhopal Disaster

Regiomontanus House System

Time in India: 4:27 A.M.
23 November 1984 (22 November in India)
10:57 P.M.
22° 30' N 77° 30' E

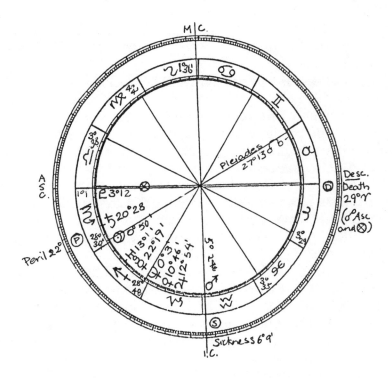

since time immemorial for affliction to the eyes. [2] De Vore in his *Encyclopedia* says the Pleiades can cause blindness, [3] and Elspeth Ebertin collected a great many examples of diseases of the eyes and blindness in connection with the Pleiades. Lilly mentions wounds to the eyes and arms. Ivy Goldstein-Jacobson calls the Pleiades "The Weeping Sisters" for if they are prominent there is always something to weep about. [4]

In this chart the Part of Death is at 29° Aries, opposing the Ascendant (House of Life) and the Part of Fortune. Mars, ruler of the chart, is in mutual reception with Saturn, which it squares, and is conjunct the Part of Sickness. It is the only planet in an air sign. Saturn, ruler of India is only 2 degrees from the Part of Peril. Jupiter is lord of the eclipse, but cadent and peregrine, disposited by Saturn.

The Moon, from which the sequence of events is learnt, moves from the midpoint of Asc/Neptune (*Combination of Stellar Influences* describes this position as "disharmonious states of soul expression, illusion and deception of the senses, and its biological correspondence to the act of running about like ants,") to midpoint Neptune/Pluto ("strange states of soul expression, high degree of sensitiveness, response to every influence, treacherous or deceptively painless states of disease, and its biological correspondence to disturbances and trouble of slow or lingering development. Confusion and grievous loss."). [5] It goes on to aspect Mars, (ruler of the Ascendant and sixth of illness), which is conjunct the Part of Illness. Although the aspect is sextile, this contact can do the Moon no good.

Despite these configurations the event did not occur until 3 December 1984 (Figure 21.2). At Bhopal at that time Virgo ascended and its ruler, Mercury, had come to the conjunction of Neptune in the fourth house of home territory. This is a symbolic picture of the people (Mercury) being gassed (Neptune) on their home territory or town (fourth) in India (Capricorn). But the full horror of the event and the attack on their eyes can only be read when comparing both charts. It may be significant that two days after the eclipse, Mercury was eclipsed by the Moon.

In this chart of December 3 the Moon is at 7° Aries (described by de Vore as a degree of life and death). It aspects the Sun, ruler of the twelfth and conjuncts Rastoban, a fixed star indicating property loss. [6] The Sun approaches Uranus at its South Node.

The Fixed Star Unuk that conjoins Saturn in this chart is described by Ebertin as often dangerous and destructive, associated with chronic diseases which are not easily detected, resulting in a weakened state of health, and accidents. He mentions disease and poisoning. [7] De Vore mentions the bronchial tubes.

Figure 21.2: The Tragedy at Bhopal

Regiomontanus House System

Time in India:
3 December 1984
7:30 P.M. G.M.T.
22° 30' N 77° 30' E

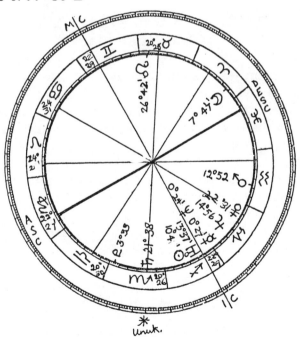

In comparing the two charts it is interesting to see that the Sun on the third of December reached the degree of Venus in the eclipse where she was ruler of the eighth cusp of death, and Venus (in Figure 21.1) reached Saturn by sextile aspect (in Figure 21.2). There are other observations you may also wish to note, such as the stress on 0 degrees.

Although the Virgo Ascendant and consequent significance of Mercury with Neptune located the disaster geographically, there must have been many surrounding places that shared the Virgo Ascendant. What may have singled out Bhopal, with 22° Virgo ascending, could be that Saturn, dispositor of the Mercury/Neptune conjunction, was exactly midpoint Asc/Venus (the eclipse death indicator), standing only a degree from the position of Saturn on the eclipse chart. Of course, there also must be factors in Bhopal's founding chart to contribute further reasons for the tragedy to have occurred in that particular location.

Fig. 21.3: "Where will the Libyan reprisals take place?"

This question was asked the day after the United States had bombed Libya, using air bases in England.

The planetary hour here is of the Moon, (the twelfth on a Tuesday) and its nature is cold and moist, as is the nature of Venus, ruler of the Ascendant.

My first reaction when I looked at this chart was the reprisals would come via Ireland, for Taurus was on the eighth cusp. However, on the next *Television News* it was announced that there had been an Irish (Taurus) woman (Venus) at Heathrow, with a bomb in her luggage! I, therefore, returned to the chart to consider it carefully. Here Venus is in Taurus on the eighth.

Every chart must describe the situation, and the querent is also included. I am represented together with most of the British public on the cusp of the eighth--Venus, ruler of the Ascendant, thinking of death for which word "reprisals" is a

Figure 21.3: "Where will the Libyan reprisals take place?"

Regiomontanus House System

Tuesday, 15 April 1986
6:35 P.M. G.M.T.
51° 13' N 1° 25' E

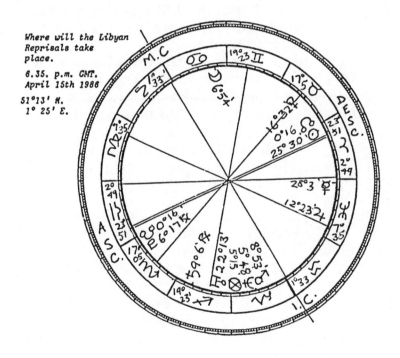

0 1 2 3 4 5 6 7 8 9 10 11	12 13 14 15	16 17 18 19 20 21	22 23 24	25 26 27	28 29
♌				⊙	
♆♇ ♂♄	♃	♀	♅		♉
0°	12°	16°	22°	25°	28°
16'					
48'17' 53'6'	23	3	13'	30'	3
♑ ʙ ♑ ♐	♓	♉	♐	♈	♓
⊗ ♏ ʙ					
5°☽					
15'6°					
♑ 54					
♋					

euphemism. The eighth cusp is the Ascendant at Libya at the time of the previous eclipse, also. In a complex question like this, one planet can represent many things. We, ourselves, are shown by the first house. The Moon, too, represents the general public.

The tenth house signifies people in authority, our government, Leo, and the Sun. It has, as it were, gone over to the enemy, in that it placed us at a disadvantage. (I personally had felt betrayed by our government's action, allowing the Americans to launch an attack from here). The government no doubt felt justified, for the Sun is exalted in Aries, and holds itself in high esteem, confident.

The obvious open enemy at that time was Libya and Kadafi, represented by Mars, strongly exalted in Capricorn, confident it is right. The Moon opposes Mars. In such an aspect it is usually the Moon that is hurt. The Moon trines Jupiter, strong by sign, term and face. Can this signify the United Nations? The Moon is extremely strong, however.

The Moon and Mars both contact Jupiter, (who could be the reconciler). As for the Americans, Mercury rules our eleventh house of allies and friends. Mercury is very poorly placed and void of course, and the Moon never completes aspect to it--the general public in England never really approved the American action. There is a connection between our second house of finances and our seventh of enemies, showing how financially dependent we are. Saturn in our second suggests the situation does not help our economy.

The Sun, our government, is also void of course and leaves the cardinal angular sign in which it is placed in less than 5 degrees. Let us hope this was a one-off action.

But that wasn't the question. The question was about where the reprisals would take place, and again, I return to the verdict of Ireland, and in particular the incident at Heathrow. Taurus can also signify harbours or ports, and our eighth could be read "air" (Gemini) "port" (Taurus), but I was not clever enough for that! Why the situation was saved is open to speculation. Many political ideas are suggested in the chart, as which planets indicate other Arab countries.

The incident at Heathrow was unconnected with the Libyan bombings, say the politicians. It took place the next day, and let astrology speak to astrologers.

Fig. 21.4: The Launch of the Space Shuttle

In comparing the chart for the launch of the Space Shuttle (see Figure 21.4 on the following page) with that of the radical chart of the United States (Gemini ascending version), it is immediately obvious that Uranus on the former is exactly, to the minute, opposite Mars on the latter. Saturn, ruler of falling and drowning when on the eighth, as it is here, is exactly opposite the Ascendant of the States' radical chart.

Mankind ignores astrology at its own peril. Had the astronauts understood the implications of the planetary positions they would never have taken off when they did. The Moon was approaching a square of Uranus, later a quincunx of Jupiter, and then a sextile of Mars. Every sort of Moon-Mars contact would be dangerous. Need we be reminded that Mars rules fire, and is strong here in Scorpio? In fact, the Moon translates the light from Saturn on the eighth cusp to Uranus, and on to Mars.

The shuttle can be identified by the Ascendant and its ruler, Venus. Venus is unfortunately combust. Had this been a horary question I would assume there was something hidden and untold, (or that the questioner was in some great fear), warning the astrologer to leave the question unjudged. In the context of this event the chart shows, too, that there was something hidden that should have been known (a hidden defect), which had not been brought to light.

Mercury is ruler of the second house (all the objects belonging to the shuttle), and it is also combust.

The Ascendant itself is near a fixed star, El Nath, or Hamal, which is of the nature of Mars and Saturn. Ebertin says it is as if these two malefics are fighting for domination, and that life is endangered if the native undertakes climbing, up or

Figure 21.4: Launch of the Space Shuttle Near Titusville, Florida

Regiomontanus House System

28 January 1986
4:38 P.M. G.M.T.
80° 50' W 28° 37' N

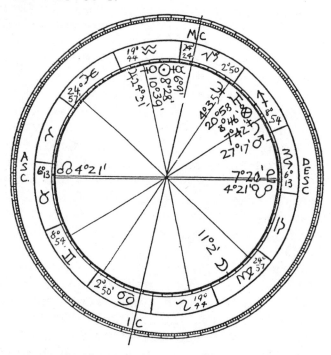

	0 1 2 3 4 5 6 7 8 9 10 11	12 13 14 15 16 17 18 19	20 21 22 23	24 25 26	27 28 29
	♌ ♃♄☉⊗♀☽		♅	♃	♂
	4° 6°7°8°9°10°11°		20°	24°	27°
	21' 9'42'28'46'39'2		58'	31	17'
	♆ ≈ ✠ ≈ ✠ ≈ ♍		✠	≈	♏
	4° ♇				
	35' 7°				
	♈ 20'				
	♏		☽ □ ♅ (⊼ ♃) ⚹ ♂		

down, by leap or dive, into an abyss. Elspeth Elbertin adds an anecdote of a hospital patient who leapt from the window, and others who dived from heights. [8]

Pluto, the natural ruler of ejection, opposes the Ascendant, which is the house of life. Saturn, natural ruler of drowning and falling, is on the eighth cusp, in mutual reception with Jupiter, ruler of the eighth. The position of Saturn alone, without any further investigation, would deter any astrologer from choosing such a moment for a launch like this. Neptune, which perhaps could be called a natural ruler of space (?) is in the degree of the Nodes, described by Watters as a degree of fatality.

(The position of Saturn on the eighth cusp of falling reminds me of the chart of the time of a tragic fall Mr. Lund took from the Post Office Tower in London. He was attempting a "stunt" for the *T.V. Late, Late Breakfast Show*. It went wrong and he fell to his death.)

Fortuna is conjunct Saturn. William Lilly says of such a conjunction, "the consumption of movable and immovable goods, waste of his fortune, and yet he knows not how."*[9] The only place to find the meanings of Fortuna in aspect to planets is at the back of *Christian Astrology* under "The Effects of Directions".

Having also studied the chart of the Bradford fire in England (in the following section), and noticed the same characteristics of sudden flame in both events, the same startling blaze and shock which Mars-Uranus connections express, I am interested to see the two planets emphasized in both instances. At Bradford it was the Mars-Uranus opposition of the previous eclipse reflected in the angles of the founding of the town. Again the same opposition of the planets is present when comparing the Launch chart with the chart of the U.S.A. The Moon makes two major aspects: to Uranus and to Mars.

The midpoints tell the same story. Uranus is mid Saturn-Neptune, showing weakness manifesting suddenly. Pluto is mid Saturn-Neptune, indicating emotional shock and upheaval. Uranus is approximately mid Jupiter-Pluto, suggesting loss of all one's property. This is emphasized by the solstice points of Jupiter and Pluto. Fortuna is mid Mars-Uranus of violent intervention, higher power. There are several squares of planets to midpoints.

Of course the *most* important study when such a catastrophe occurs is comparison with the position at the previous eclipses. Mars, the planet to which the Moon (indicator of events) eventually makes its aspect, is in the degree occupied by Saturn at the time of the lunar eclipse of October 28, 1985. The Moon then was near the Ascendant here, and the Ascendant then was almost conjunct the M.C. here. There are many more comparisons that astrologers with computers could find, but even without a computer the obvious comparisons of angles and the Moon are clear. But consider this: the Eclipse of 28 October falls across the horizon at the location of the Launch at the time of the Launch!

(Here, then, we find the position of the Sun and Moon at the eclipse reflected in the event chart, whereas at the Bradford fire it was the opposition of Mars and Uranus at the time of the eclipse that was reflected.)

Figs. 21.5 and 6: The Bradford Fire

The main indication of 1985 fires and explosions, and probably of football violence, seems to be Uranus at 17° Sagittarius, being opposed by Mars. This configuration, with Uranus at 16° 43' Sagittarius retrograde and Mars at 16° 10' Gemini, was angular across the horizon at Bradford at the time of the solar eclipse on 19 May 1985.

In de Vore's *Encyclopedia of Astrology* he calls 17° Sagittarius a degree of transition, heat flame, and homicide. [10] He appears to be correct, especially when this is emphasized by the opposition of Mars, once known as the god of fire, Pyrois, from which is derived the word pyromaniac, presumably.

The reason I refer to the eclipse is that Ptolemy said that the most potent cause of events lies in the position of the

Figure 21.5: Solar Eclipse Preceding the Bradford Fire

Regiomontanus House System

19 May 1985
9:41 P.M. G.M.T.
53° 47' N 1° 45' W

Terms

☉	♂	♄
☽	♂	♄
☿	☿	☿
♀	☿	☉
♂	♀	♂
♃	♀	☿
♄	☿	♀

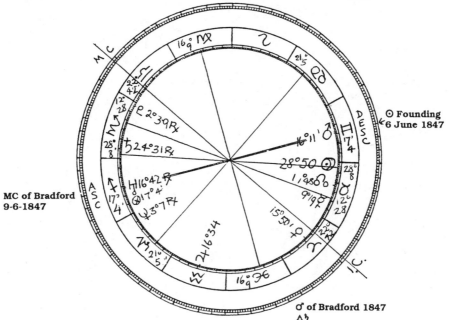

☉ Founding
6 June 1847

MC of Bradford
9-6-1847

♂ of Bradford 1847
△ ♄

	0	1	2	3	4	5	6	7	8	9	10	11	12	13	14	15	16	17	18	19	20	21	22	23	24	25	26	27	28	29
	♇ ♆									☿						♀ ♅ A			♌			M	♄					O	
	2° 3°									9°						15°16°17°			19°			22°	24°					28°	
	40 7									19						50' 42' 4'						23	31					50'	
	℞ ℞									♉						♈ ℞ ⊗							℞					♉	
	♏ ♑															♐ 17°							♏						

♃
16°
34'

♒ ♌
♂ 17
16°48
11'
♊

Figure 21.6: The Bradford Fire

Regiomontanus House System

Source diploma holder with son in the stand

11 June 1985
2:40 P.M. G.M.T.
53° 47' N 1° 45' W

Fire 3
Earth 2
Air 3
Water 2

Terms		
☉	☿	☉
☽	♀	☿
☿	♂	♀
♀	♀	♂
♂	♃	♃
♃	♀	☿
♄	☿	♀

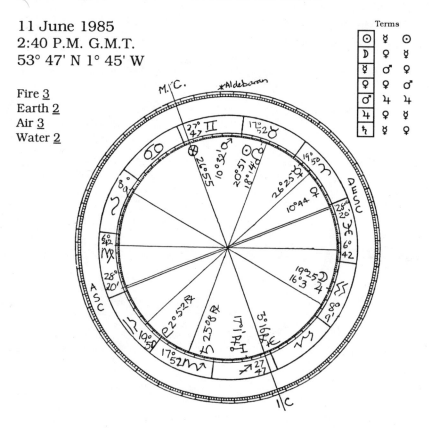

0	1	2	3	4	5	6	7	8	9	10	11	12	13	14	15	16	17	18	19	20	21	22	23	24	25	26	27	28	29
		♇ ♆									♂					♃	♅	♌	☽	☉					♄	☿		A	
		2° 3°								10°						16°17°18°19°20°								25°26°		28°		
		5216								32'						3' 1' 14 25'51'								8' 25		20		
		℞ ℞								♊						♒ ℞		♒ ♉						℞ ♈		♍		
		♏ ♑								♀						♐								♍ ⊗				
										10°																			
										44'									☽ to ☐ ☉ ☐ ♄ ℞ ✳ ☿									
										♈																			

luminaries at eclipses and the movement of stars at that time.

This is the first time I, personally, have found the eclipse to work conversely, but I have often found progressions to do so.

In this chart Uranus is at 17° 1' retrograde Sagittarius.

The ruler of the Ascendant, Mercury, represents the people of Bradford, and Mercury is in the eighth house of, in the context of this question, death. The eighth house is ruled by Mars, who is, therefore, Lord of Death in this chart. Mercury and Mars are in mutual reception by sign, by which I mean (for those not used to event charts) that Mars is in the sign of Mercury and Mercury in the sign of Mars, and therefore they can exchange places. The people (Mercury) can exchange places with death, whom we know was in his guise of Pyrois.

Mercury, ruler of the Ascendant, also rules the twelfth house of self-undoing, and the people were their own hidden enemy in this case.

The Moon, co-significator of the people, was in the fifth house of pleasure, in large numbers, shown by Jupiter, and also having a good time watching a football match. The Moon is natural significator of the populace.

The Founding of Bradford chart (Figure 21.7) shows why the energy of the eclipse hit Bradford. The M.C.-I.C. axis echoes the same opposition that was prominent across the horizon of the solar eclipse. Sagittarius 16° 10' on the M.C. is the position of Uranus at the fire, and the eclipse. The Sun, exactly opposite, is the position of Mars at the eclipse.

Uranus is at 17° 26' Aries, trine the M.C. and sextile the Sun. In my experience the type of aspect hardly matters; it is the contact between planets that counts.

Jupiter on the fifth cusp of pleasure may show the chief enjoyment of the people of Bradford. But in 1847 that degree was conjunct Betelgeuze, an orange-red fixed star of the nature of Mars with a touch of Mercury. Usually with Jupiter it shows honors, and I hear Bradford was winning at the time. Perhaps Bradford has earned honours at sport, but if Betelgeuze is in conjunction with Mars it shows death by lightning,

Figure 21.7: The Founding of Bradford

Source Wigglesworth

9 June 1847   **Placidus**
Midnight
53° 47' N 1° 45' W

	Terms	
☉	♀	♂
☽	♂	♀
☿	♄	♂
♀	♀	☿
♂	♂	♂
♃	♂	☉
♄	♃	♃

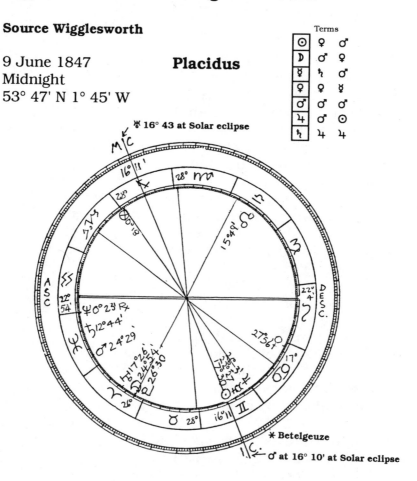

♅ 16° 43 at Solar eclipse

✳ Betelgeuze

♂ at 16° 10' at Solar eclipse

Mutual reception ♂ ♃ sign and terms

Betelgeuze ♂ ♃ on 5th cusp

0 1 2 3 4 5 6 7 8 9 10 11	12 13 14	15 16 17 18 19 20 21	22 23	24 25	26 27 28 29
⊗	♄	☊ M ♅	☿	♂	♃ ♀
0°	12°	15°16°17°	22°	24°	26°27°
18'	44'	4' 11 26'	27	29'	3' 56'
♐	♓	♎ ♐ ♈	♊	♓	♊ ♋
♆		☉		☽	♇
0°		17		24°	26°
23		29		54'	30
♓		♊		♈	♈

fire, and explosion. In this chart Jupiter and Mars are in mutual reception by sign and term. That is, Mars, is in the sign of Jupiter (those unaccustomed to traditional astrology may not realize that Jupiter rules Pisces) and Jupiter is in the terms of Mars. (The terms can be found out by looking at Ptolemy's Table of Dignities, Figure 6.1). Therefore, the planets in mutual reception exchange places and Mars is partly transposed to the degree where Jupiter is.

There is a modern suggestion that when planets exchange places they retain their original degree. I can see no justification for this invention and think the present example illustrates that it is more likely planets exchange places, as Ptolemy says.

The previous solar eclipse, on April 15, 1847, was at Aries 24°.

It is more usual to look at the syzygys preceding the event rather than those after it. The chart of the Preceding New Moon (Figure 21.8) is certainly worthy of inspection. Uranus is at 17° 39' Sagittarius--the degree of transition, heat, flame, and homicide--on the eighth cusp of death, denoting suddenness.

Mars ascends with Algol, the most malefic fixed star, going to the opposition of the malefic, Saturn, retrograde.

Venus is lady of the new Moon, since the new Moon is in Taurus. Venus is badly placed in the twelfth house of self-undoing, and is in mutual reception with Mars.

In the Lunar Eclipse preceding (Figure 21.9) Mars rules the syzygy, the luminary above the horizon being in Scorpio. Mars is 5 degrees from the eighth cusp and, in traditional astrology, is counted as being in the following house. It is, therefore, on the eighth cusp and going to the sextile of Venus, badly placed, though on the fifth cusp, to the square of Jupiter and the opposition of Uranus.

Saturn ascends, retrograde.

There must be many correspondences between these charts that can be found and many midpoints of relevance. I have tried to mention just the headlines. Each one of the charts is worthy of study, but Figure 21.5, the solar eclipse on

Figure 21.8: New Moon Preceding the Fire

Regiomontanus House System

20 April 1985
5:21 A.M. G.M.T.
53° 47' N 1° 45' W

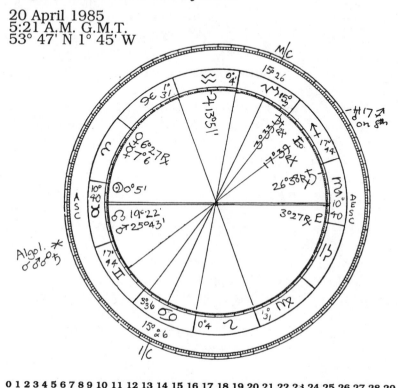

	0 1 2 3 4 5 6 7 8 9	10 11	12 13 14	15 16	17 18	19 20 21 22 23	24 25 26 27 28 29
	☉ Ψ ♀ ☿	A	♃ M	♅ Ω			♂ ♄
	0° 3° 6°7°	10°	13° 15°	17° 19°			25°26°
	5' 33' 27 6'	40'	51' 86	39 22'			43'38
	♉ ℞ ℞ ♈ ♉		♒ ♑	℞			♉ ℞
	♑			♐			♏
	℞						
	3°						
	27'						
	℞						
	♏						

Terms

☉	♀	☿	
☽			
☿	♀	♂	
♀	♃	♂	
♂	♃	☉	
♃	♀	☿	
♄	♄	♀	

Mr. ♀ ♃ -- ♂ ♀ by sign

Figure 21.9: Lunar Eclipse Preceding the Bradford Fire

Regiomontanus House System

4 May 1985
7:53 P.M. G.M.T.
53° 47' N 1° 45' W

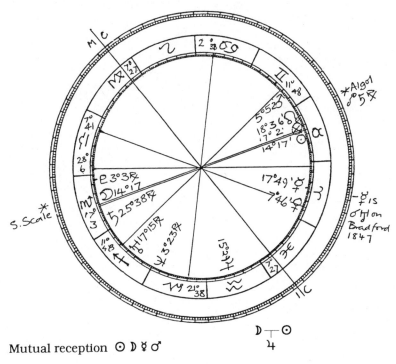

Mutual reception ☉ ☽ ☿ ♂

D ⊥ ☉
4

May 19 seems particularly dramatic. With Sagittarius on the Ascendant I immediately thought of Spain, and waited for an explosive event there. It occurred the Sunday after the eclipse. An oil tanker exploded off the coast of Spain near Algiceras, and approximately three hundred were killed. The lightning speed of the two tragedies showed a resemblance.

Another interesting fact is that on April 15, 1847 there was an eclipse prior to the founding of Bradford. The Moon was semi-sextile Mars exactly at 24° 39' Aries.

Figure 21.10: A Good Way of Setting Out Your Work
on squared paper
The Bradford Fire

```
0 1 2 3 4 5 6 7 8 9 10 11 12 13 14 15 16 17 18 19 20 21 22 23 24 25 26 27 28 29
    ♇ ♆              ♅              ♀  A        ☊          M    ♄              ⊙
    2° 3°            9°             15°16°      19         22°  24°            28°
    40 7'            18'            50'59'                 23'  31'            50'
    ♉ ♉              ♉              ♈ ♈                    ♎    ♏              ♉
    ♏ ♑                             ♂
                                   16°
                                   10'
                                   ♊
                                   ♃
                                   16°
                                   32'
                                   ♅
                                   16°
                                   43'
```

	Figure 21.5
	Solar Eclipse
	19 May 1985

```
                                                          ♈
                                                          ⊙
                                                          24
```
Solar Eclipse
15 April 1847

```
0 1 2 3 4 5 6 7 8 9 10 11 12 13 14 15 16 17 18 19 20 21 22 23 24 25 26 27 28 29
    ♇ ♆              ♂              ♃  ♅     ☽  ⊙              ♄  ♀  ⊗
    2° 3°            10°            16°17°  19°20°             25°26°27°
    25'17'           30'            2'  1'  24'49'             9' 24' 55'
    ♏ ♑              ♊              ♒  ♒  ♒  ♉                 ♏  ♈  ♊
    ♏ ♑              ♀              ♐
                     10°
                     44'
                     ♈
```

21.6
☽ □ ⊙
Bradford Fire
11 May 1985

```
0 1 2 3 4 5 6 7 8 9 10 11 12 13 14 15 16 17 18 19 20 21 22 23 24 25 26 27 28 29
⊗              ♄        ☊  M  ♅              ♀   ♂        ♃  ♀
0°             12°      15° 16°17°           22°  24°     26°27°
33'            44'      46  10' 26'          27'  28'     2' 54'
♐  ♆           ♓        ♎  ♐  ♈              ♊   ♓        ♊ ♋
♆  0°                          ⊙                ☽   ♇
0°  16'                        17°              24° 26°
♓                              29'              53  25
                               ♊               ♈  ♈
```

21.7
Bradford
Founded

```
0 1 2 3 4 5 6 7 8 9 10 11 12 13 14 15 16 17 18 19 20 21 22 23 24 25 26 27 28 29
⊙  ♇    ♀♉    A     ♃     M  ♅  ☊              ♂  ♄
0°  3°  6°7'  10°   13°   15° 17° 18°           25°26°
5'  27' 28'7' 37'   50    24  39' 10'           42'38'
♉  ♆  ♈              ♒    ♑  ♐  ♉              ♉  ♏
    3°
    33
    ♑
```

21.8
New Moon
Preceding
20 April 1985

```
0 1 2 3 4 5 6 7 8 9 10 11 12 13 14 15 16 17 18 19 20 21 22 23 24 25 26 27 28 29
    ♇  ♂  ♀              ⊙  ♃     ♅  ☊              ♄
    3° 5° 7°             14°15°  17° 18°           25°
    3' 51' 46'           17'28'  15' ♉             38'
    ♏  ♊  ♈              ♏  ♒    ♐                 ♏
    ♆  ♈  M                      ♐
    3°     ♍                     ♉
    23                           17°
    ♑                            48'
                                 ♈
                                 A 17°
                                 ⊗ 10'
```

21.9
Lunar Eclipse
Preceding
4 May 1985

Chapter 22

Eclipses and Syzygys

Much predictive astrology in Ptolemy's day was based on the study of eclipses and the new and full Moons (syzygys). It may not be apparent at first that nearly all of the *Tetrabiblos*, Book II is talking about eclipses, and their rulers, and the effects they might have on different countries.

Ptolemy wrote that "the first and most potent cause of events lies in the conjunctions of the sun and moon at eclipse and the movements of the stars at that time." [1] ("stars" is sometimes the translation of "planets").

Like the fixed stars, eclipses and syzygys seem more relevant to events of importance and public interest than to domestic queries, and therefore are considered the realm of mundane astrology. Yet horary questions are sometimes beyond the range of domestic matters too, and horary astrologers should therefore investigate syzygys.

Lilly makes brief mention of eclipses in his volume on horary in *Christian Astrology*. In connection with the first house, he tells us that in a chart drawn up for the time of an eclipse, the first house represents the general public. Later in the book he refers to eclipses in connection with the duration of life, [2] a subject we are reluctant to judge nowadays. Yet I will relate some of Ptolemy's information on this matter for the light it throws on the subject of syzygys.

Certain planets were called *hyleg*, rulers of the length of life. Certain places, too, were of similar importance--the Ascendant and the place of the preceding syzygy. In a day chart the Sun was given preference as hyleg, but it had to be in an acceptable, or prorogative place. If it wasn't, the Moon was considered. If the Moon wasn't well-placed either, the honor was given to the planet that had most "relations of domination" to the Sun, the preceding conjunction (syzygy), and the Ascendant. The phrase "relations of domination" meant the planet that was dispositor by house (old way of saying sign), term, or triplicity. The planet, which would be now "Lord of the Eclipse," would be expected to dominate in at least three ways. If these could not be found, preference was given to the Ascendant. Ptolemy also mentions that the planet's relationship to the angle preceding the eclipse was relevant to its domination.

In a nighttime chart preference was given to the Moon, then to the planet having the greater number of "relations of domination" to the Moon, to the preceding full Moon, and to the Part of Fortune; otherwise, if the preceding syzygy was a new Moon, to the Ascendant, and if it had been a full Moon, to the Part of Fortune. (He had more to say but it did not involve syzygys).

In a new Moon both luminaries are in the same degree, but at full Moon you should consider the one above the horizon.

Ptolemy uses this information about the strength of the planet dominating the syzygy prior to birth to rectify birth charts. But Lilly dismisses such a method and says a birth chart can only be successfully rectified by events, a view with which many astrologers now agree.

If the eclipse is dominated by a fixed star (which then shares in causing the event), the forms of the constellations were taken into consideration in which the eclipse and dominating stars happened to be. Constellations of human form meant the event would affect humans; others would affect animals, birds, fish, rivers, etc.

What puzzles me is that a fixed star cannot be a dispositor by sign, term, or exaltation so must rule by strong position, and therefore, why can't a planet do that, e.g., by conjunction? Jansky suggests in his book *Interpreting the Eclipses* that they do, [3] and I have personal reason to agree with him.

Ptolemy also mentions that a fixed star angular at the time of the conjunction is part ruler.

In Ptolemy's time the luminaries were credited with the entire responsibility for the strength or weakness of ruling planets. They could exert such power because they submitted to eclipse and thereby determined the place of the eclipse and the ruler of these places, so a commentator suggested. This illustrates the traditional reverence for eclipses. It shows that the evaluation of the planets' dignities was bound up with the importance of syzygys.

Having observed the syzygy Ptolemy then occupies himself with the rulership of countries and cities in order to deduce what affinity exists between the eclipse which governs the prediction, and the countries and cities for which it is significant.

The number of people affected and the general extent of the event depended on the length of obscuration of the eclipse, and the relative position of the dominating star to the place of the eclipse, whether occidental or oriental. The people most affected were those in whose birth charts the luminaries and angles were in the same places as those in the eclipse chart, or opposite.

As to the good or bad effect, that depended on the character of the dominating planet or star, as described above. Ptolemy devotes several pages to the characteristics of planets as Lord of the eclipse.

Ptolemy's comments about the syzygy preceding birth are very interesting. He states that where the luminaries are far from, and unrelated to, the Ascendant and do not aspect it, and where the angles are separated by malefics (can he mean by midpoint?) "as frequently occurs in humble nativities" one should look for the last preceding new or full Moon and the lord (dispositor) of it, and of the luminaries of the birth (in the birth chart). For if the places (that is, the important places (the Sun, Moon, Ascendant, and Part of Fortune) all, or the majority of them, are unrelated to the place of the preceding syzygy, *the child will be nondescript.* [4]

I would like to extend that idea by suggesting that if the main places and planets in an event or horary chart are unrelated to the place of the preceding syzygy, the event is not of great importance, and vice versa.

Ptolemy suggests that the duration of the effects of an eclipse equate with the time of obscuration. Jansky does not agree with this, saying he has found it does not work. Mrs. Watters says the next hard aspect from Mars terminates the effect; Jansky thinks the next eclipse does.

Part Four: History

Chapter 23
Egypt

"If you start at the end you will eventually arrive at the Beginning."

"Nothing is as old as the Truth, and nothing is as new as the Truth."

Hazrat Inayat Khan, *The Guyan*

The astrology of antiquity was observational. The Egyptians were interested in the heliacal (meaning near the Sun) disappearances and reappearances of the stars and planets. In other words, when the stars or slower planets are close to the Sun at sunset and are on the ecliptic, they disappear into combustion for several days while the Sun passes in front of them, and then they reappear again just after sunrise. With the Moon, Mercury, and Venus, being faster than the Sun, the reverse happens. After being near the Sun at dawn, they disappear, and days later turn up again in the evening sky, having emerged from combustion. Thus, the New Moon is seen in the evening sky. Nor is it really the new Moon that appears; it was new when obscured by conjunction with the Sun. The Egyptians considered this to be the end of the month not the beginning, and it is still judged by horary astrologers as unfortunate. Understanding the physical phenomena assists us in understanding the meaning of *Combustion* in interpretation, that is, it shows things hidden. If the querent's significator is combust, he or she is overwhelmed and powerless.

It was by such stars as Sirius or Spica that the Egyptians marked their calendar, and from the study of such stars that they learnt of our geometrical position in the Universe. Sirius marked the summer solstice and the rising of the Nile. Sirius, the Dog Star, is associated with hot July days when the dog daisies bloom in English fields.

Cyril Fagan in *Zodiacs Old and New* tells us that in 2791 B.C. Spica, which had a declination of 14 degrees north, and Benetnasch with a declination of 74 degrees north formed a conjunction in right ascension. The Egyptian Pharaoh then held a ceremony in which he or his priest looked through a visor in his headdress to align these two stars with the then Pole Star, Alpha Draconis. The resulting alignment was extended to produce a Celestial Great Circle, and it was upon the axis of such a circle that a temple would be built, so that the line of the stars' light passed centrally between the pillars. [1]

By such computations the buildings of temples at Karnak and Luxor were sited. The temple at Denderah aligns to Sirius, or Isis. The dates of their building can be ascertained from astronomical knowledge. Sir Norman Lockyer explored these sites and discovered that when the Earth, over the centuries, moved on its axis, the Egyptians built another temple adjoining, slightly corrected in direction to adjust to the astronomical positions of the era. And there were temples, too, for the stars of the north that never set: Phact, Ettanin, Capella, Set, and Ptah. [2]

Not only were Egyptian temples aligned to stars, but so were temples in Greece. John Michell writes of the alignment of the Parthenon to the Pleiades. [3]

This discussion of alignments will remind you of Stonehenge and other standing stones of Northern Europe. (As a matter of fact, some standing stones have a hole to be looked through to find alignments, just like the visor on the head-dress of the Pharaoh.[4]) It reminds us of the orientation of churches to sunrise for the day of their patron saints. You may also note a connection with the ley lines and how Stonehenge is at the western end of a ley line and Canterbury Cathedral at the other. [5]

This evolution of tradition between Egypt and Greece, and th similarity between temple alignments, as well as between some Egyptian glyphs and astrological glyphs point to the possibility of the origin of a simple astrology being Egyptian. However, it would have been an astrology that did not include such mathematics as are necessary for the calculation of past or future planetary positions. The Egyptian eye of Osiris reminds us of the symbol of the Sun, the pupil of an eye, and how the luminaries rule sight. The Sun symbol has survived for thousands of years.

My own instinct is that humanity and its cultures (excepting China) stem from Africa. Diodorus Siculus, A.D. 59, said the Chaldoioi of Babylonia were Colonists from Egypt, and enjoyed fame because they had learned from the priests of Egypt. [6]

A famous astrologer priest of Egypt was Manetho. Of his own chart Manetho says, "But I will proceed by a new turn in verse and recall the stars of my own nativity when and in what sign it was the oft-sought Eilithyia delivered me from the womb so that for all time they may teach and prove what Fate granted me to teach, the wisdom and beautiful poetry of the stars. The Sun was in Gemini and there too was beautiful Kypris (Venus) and also beloved Phaeton (Jupiter) and golden Hermes (Mercury) and in Aquarius at the time [were] the Moon and Phainon (Saturn) and Mars was in many-footed Cancer and Centaur was turning about Midheaven, trailing his weapon. Thus the Fates determined my nativity." The date was May 28, A.D. 80. There was another Manetho in the third century A.D.

It was not only the astrology of Egypt that passed on to

Greece. We can see that the early Greek sculptures are like Egyptian work, and that only slowly did they acquire Grecian refinements. The sphinx in Egypt suggests the transition of the age of Virgo to Leo.

Indeed, there are many evidences of very early astrology. Some say the zodiacs were a later invention than the use of the stars and planets, but what is clear is that the early astrology stressed the luminaries. Emphasis was on eclipses, heliacal risings and settings, and phases of the Moon, and the planets. Planets were considered in relation to the luminaries. This concern accounts for the importance later given to the orientality or occidentality of planets to the Sun, a technique that persisted until the time of Lilly, as you can see in his tables for assessing the strengths of planets. Yet I do not see him use this technique in *Christian Astrology*. I, for one, have ignored it because I do not know how to interpret it in horaries.

In ancient Egypt and Babylonia the fortitudes of the planets were known. Ptolemy only recorded them, he did not invent them. Cyril Fagan reckoned he had calculated the year when the planets were in their exaltation degrees: 786 B.C. These positions were apparently crystallized to remain the exaltation degrees. His theory is that it was apparently an extraordinary year in that there was a great lunar Eclipse; the other outstanding event of the year was the removal of Nabu, Mercury, the god of astrology, [7] from one temple to another. But whatever the truth of the matter, they certainly still work.

We cannot doubt the extreme antiquity of the Faces and have mentioned in an earlier chapter their relationship with the hours and days.

These early beginnings are fascinating and may serve to demonstrate to newcomers that astrology was not recently invented, and that it exists apart from psychology. It is our heritage, a tradition that has persisted throughout the centuries. It is our attempt to understand our place in the Universe, tangibly and intangibly.

Chapter 24
Early Astrologers

There is a great advantage in reading books written by astrological authorities of the past.

Legend tells us Mercury founded astrology, for Mercury was the messenger of the gods, and it was Mercury who disclosed their secrets to mankind. It still is.

Much previous knowledge is unknown to us due to the persecution of our art, caused by the materialistic attitude of the West assuming that nothing is credible if unproven scientifically. Yet many of the greatest minds in history have devoted a lifetime to its study.

Manilius and *The Astronomica*

One great man I would like to mention is Manilius, whose beautiful song about the heavens is so graphic that it reminded me of the T.V. series by Carl Sagan. Manilius lived about the time of Christ. Little is known about him except his thoughts.

Instead of picking out the differences of detail between his attitude and ours it is wonderful to consider the continuity of ideas that have survived the centuries and which constitute the tradition of astrology. In his days astrology and astronomy were one, and Manilius was equally interested in the physical reality of the Universe as with its astrological meanings. He was well aware that the Earth is a globe suspended in space, "not spread into flat plains but fashioned into a sphere." He says the sphere is the shape of nature, the shape that continues forever, "round is the orb of the Sun and round is the orb of the Moon..." [1] Such information was learned from eclipses.

He comments that as people live all over the Earth some are beneath our feet but believe they are on top because the gradual curvature of the surface deceives us. [2] (Did you spend your childhood thinking about this and trying to dig down to Australia?)

As might be expected, Manilius wrote that the fabric of the Universe is air, fire, earth, and sea, ruled by a Divine Force. The constellations, in his view, were of fire--"The Ram leads the way, and looks back with wonder of the backward rising Bull" [3]--and so on. He described the constellations and the fixed stars and the legends associated with them. His work is a good lesson in spherical astronomy, with descriptions of the unsetting stars of the northern sky and the Earth on its axis with the sky spinning past.

His conclusion was that since the stars and constellations follow a set pattern their movement is not the result of chance. "For my part I find no argument so compelling as this to show that the universe moves in obedience to a divine power and is indeed the manifestation of God. The Sun never deviates, if the earth were created by chance, the movement of the stars would depend on chance."[4] These words are important, reflecting the philosophy of those early days when belief in free will was not necessarily a virtue, for they imply that since this life is connected to the movement of the stars, our fate, too, follows a set pattern. In Christianity the statement is repeated: "Thy will be done on earth as it is in Heaven."

Both the poem of Manilius and the words of Jesus Christ

were written without the impact of Aristotelian thought to which Ptolemy was soon to subject astrology.

Figure 24.1: The Temples of Manilius

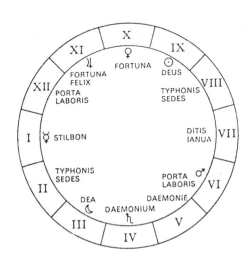

Temple 1: The Abode of Mercury, called "Stilbon," ruling tongue and brain.
Temple 2: "Typhonis Sedes." Typhon was a giant. This also is called the "Portal of Pluto."
Temple 3: The Abode of the Moon, Dea, ruling fluctuations and also brothers.
Temple 4: Daemonium, the Abode of Saturn, ruling parents and heritage.
Temple 5: The Abode of Venus and pleasure.
Temple 6: Laboris, ruling hard work. The Abode of Mars.
Temple 7: Connected with marriage and death. A planet here afflicts the Ascendant.
Temple 8: War. Typhon.
Temple 9: Deus. God. The Abode of the Sun.
Temple 10: Fortuna. Glory. The Abode of Venus.
Temple 11: Fortuna Felix, the most fortunate of all, the Abode of the Greater Benefic, Jupiter.
Temple 12: Labor and misfortune and enemies.

(Reproduced with permission from Manilius, *The Astronomica.* Harvard University Press and Heinemann, Ltd., Loeb edition.)

The beauty of Manilius' poem lies in its imagery. "For I shall sing of God, silent-minded monarch of nature who, permeating sky and land and sea, controls with uniform compact the mighty structure, how the entire universe is alive,...since a single spirit dwells in all its parts and, speeding through all things, nourishes the world and shapes it like a living creature." [5] (Is this antiquity speaking, or is it New Age?)

The poem of Manilius is not long, and is easily accessible. I cannot, therefore, think why so many people who are capable of reading suggest he uses only eight houses when he obviously and unambiguously describes twelve, [6] which I list in Figure 24.1.

Much of what Manilius wrote is comparable to life today. "Vast is the crowd that worship wealth, power, and trappings of office, luxury, diversions of music...yet this will to learn fates law is also a gift of fate." [7]

Some of the sign rulerships he uses are different, for example, the Moon, Diana the huntress, is associated with Sagittarius. Personally, I have always felt an association in the glyph of Jupiter with the Moon's glyph, and think too of the way the Moon void in Sagittarius will sometimes perform.

The houses, of course, were considered more potent than the signs, which is an indication of the kind of astrology then used, for the houses indicate the nature of events. The houses were called Temples as they were the abodes of the gods. The angular houses were called cardinals [8] (like the cardinal points) and, like Ptolemy, he believed the tenth house was the most important.

Manilius also described the characteristics of the signs, sometimes, as in the case of Aries, with sarcastic wit. His descriptions are not identical with those of Liz Greene, who does not enlighten us about which sign makes the best lion tamers. I was interested how much he stresses the triplicities in his synastry.

His first two books are easy reading, but the third describes a system of lots that we have lost. The fourth book is a description of the constellations showing the extent of astronomical knowledge of his times.

Vettius Valens

Vettius Valens lived in the second century A.D. and left a large collection of horoscopes. I am very glad that I may reproduce a chart from his collection here, with the kind permission of the American Philosophical Society in Philadelphia. It is from *Greek Horoscopes* by Neugebauer and van Hoesen. This is the geniture of an eminent man, who lived in the century before Valens. It is dated A.D. 50, October 25, about 4:00 A.M.

Figure 24.2: An Eminent Man, from the Collection of Vettius Valens

About 4 A.M.
25 October A.D. 50
cusps unknown

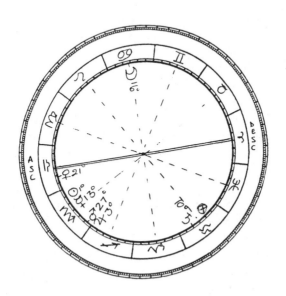

First the astrologer noted that it was a nighttime chart and that, therefore, the Moon was all important. It is strong in its own sign Cancer in trine to Mars. Mars is succedent (called *epanaphora*) and is in its own sign Scorpio, in its own triplicity (Mars rules the water triplicity by night and day), and sect, (remember Mars was given to the night sect). It is, therefore, very strong and shares the rulership of the chart with Venus, ruler of the Ascendant, which is in its own sign, Libra.

The Moon too is very strong. Therefore this is a chart of a noble person with such dignified planets.

In night nativities the calculation of Fortuna is from Moon to Sun (in the order of the signs). Here it is in Aquarius (we are not told the exact degree of the Ascendant). Fortuna is, therefore, in the Locus of Good Fortune, the fifth house. Saturn is here, where he is placed in his own sign and triplicity (for Saturn rules the air triplicity by night).

The astrologer then uses the Circle of Athla, that is, the Lot of fortune becomes the beginning of the circle, and we count eleven equal houses round from here in the direction of the flow of the signs, and reach Sagittarius, in which Jupiter is placed. This is the eleventh loci of Accomplishment (not to be confused with Agathos Daimon).

He then found the exaltation of the nativity which is known by counting the degrees between the Moon and Taurus, here eleven signs. The same number is then counted from the Ascendant, reaching Leo, of which the Sun is ruler, in that most fortunate house Agathos Daimon. The Sun is found in the tenth loci, the Midheaven in respect of the Circle of Athla, which makes the nativity even more illustrious. (Whose can it be!) [9]

The chart brings out the importance of the Moon in night charts and the different way night charts are treated, and the use of triplicity and sect as well as the method of calculating the Circle of Athla. The order of the houses from Athla is the usual order we always use, the Midheaven for career, etc., but in the Introduction to *The Astronomica* by Manilius, (Loeb edition), a different order is mentioned.

In a day chart Fortuna would be calculated in the way shown us by Ptolemy, that is, from Sun to Moon.

Ptolemy

The impact of Ptolemy on astrology and the history of astrology is perhaps greater than that of any other astrologer. He took the idealistic and pantheistic astrology of antiquity, and by applying his cool and mathematical mind, categorized it into what was then considered a scientific and rational system.

Ptolemy was born around A.D. 100 and is said to have lived for about seventy eight years. He resided in Egypt and must have had access to the great library at Alexandria. He was a famous mathematician, astronomer, astrologer, and geographer, and also wrote about optics, mechanics, and music. He discovered the diameter of the Earth and the distance of the Moon.

The *Amalgest* was his great and famous book on astronomy. It is a book to be enjoyed by those with a degree in higher mathematics.

The *Tetrabiblos*, or *Quadripartitium*, (for it is really four books), is Ptolemy's treatise on astrology which has been the authoritative reference for astrologers for nearly two thousand years, although it was not translated into English until 1701 by John Whalley. [10] Unfortunately, there is no longer an original manuscript extant. It might easily have been completely lost if the Arabs had not rescued it when astrology was so persecuted in Europe in the fifth century. It was translated into Arabic, and remained so for centuries, lost to Europe. In the fourteenth century it was re-translated into Greek and into Latin. There have been many translations and versions and commentaries and interpretations, and there are the literary fragments from the original, but it was not until the eighteenth century that it was completely translated into English, and then in an unpraised edition. Of course, some of the content of his teaching had been preserved in the teachings of previous astrologers; also Lilly had included some of

Ptolemy's teachings in *Christian Astrology*, which was published in 1647. The volumes from which Lilly translated had been in Latin (as were all books then), and he tells us he had three versions.

It is not surprising, therefore, that passages in our present editions are dubious or ambiguous, suggesting that some translators may not have been astrologers.

All the astrology of that time was observational, merging with astronomy, using planets that could be seen, and using them in major aspects only. The stress lay with the planets but most of all with the luminaries, and the observed positions of planets in relation to them, such as orientality and occidentality, combustion, and on the velocity and acceleration of planets which determine whether their aspects are dexter or sinister. In the light of observational astronomy our ideas of associating outer planets with signs would have lead Ptolemy to conclude our current thought is confused.

Ptolemy's work is extremely informative regarding eclipses and rulers of eclipses. (I have written about that in the Mundane section). Ptolemy lists all the main fixed stars, their characteristics and positions, and the constellations and their meanings. He tells us of the countries of the world and which planet rules each of them, and why their inhabitants behaved as they did. Beneath his cool objectivity, we glimpse a strange and alien culture where values differ widely from our own.

Ptolemy was interested in the weather and he seeks to relate it to the planets. But for us, these very "scientific" reasons he gives are the weakest part of his argument. We are unconvinced that planetary character causes changes in local weather when we know by our communication systems that it may be sunny in one place and stormy twenty miles away. Again, his rational explanation of a relationship between signs and seasons discounts the entire southern hemisphere. Does the impetus of Aries apply to an Australian Autumn?

All the same, his information on eclipses and their rulers is unsurpassed. There is some sound astrology recorded in the *Tetrabibios* even for horary astrologers--perhaps particularly for horary astrologers--for what natal astrologer is interested that Saturn rules the right ear? Beneath Ptolemy's constant attempt to adapt mundane and horary astrology into a natal framework, the matters concerning the former two shine through.

The book is rich in information on our present techniques. He describes the symmetrical and perfect organization of the planetary rulerships, their dignities and fortitudes, their orbs and qualities. These methods work. It was Ptolemy who defined the start of the tropical zodiac at 0° Aries, and he who tells us also that a planet within 5 degrees of a cusp is regarded as being in the following house. He is most informative about physical appearance and about medical matters. One realizes the importance accorded to Fortuna in that era and how it was one of the four hylegical places. Yet he does not use the Circle of Athla as Manilius and the Greeks did. But it would be foolish to discuss the whole book here; it is better for you to read it yourself, for he was a great man. [11]

Figure 20.8 is a horary chart which I judged using the *Tetrabiblos* as guide.

Names for the Houses or Places at the Time of Ptolemy [12]

1. Horoscopus
2. Gate of Hades
3. Goddess (Moon) Dea
4. Lower Midheaven
5. Good Fortune
6. Bad Fortune
7. Occident
8. Beginning of Death
9. God (the part in trine dexter the horizon) Deus (Sun)
10. Mid Heaven (the part in quartile dexter)
11. The Good Daemon (the part in sextile dexter the horizon)
12. Bad Daemon

Palchus

Little is known of Palchus except that he was in Smyrna presumably when he drew up the following chart. He enquires here for the safety of a ship from Alexandria to Smyrna, which was greatly overdue. I reproduce it from *Greek Horoscopes*, by Neugebauer and van Hoesen, with kind permission of the American Philosophical Society. [13]

The chart is for Saturday 14 July A.D. 479 at 7.30 A.M. local time in Smyrna. (Figure 24.3.)

Before you exclaim and say, "That early Ascendant invalidates the chart," I must explain to you that it is computed in a tropical zodiac which uses 3° Aries for its vernal equinox, which moves the Ascendant to about 5° Virgo.

It is not easy to interpret a chart without cusps, yet there is some information to be gleaned from this chart, and we can follow the reasoning of Palchus.

Saturn and Mars rising would be a warning of the negative outcome to the question. Yet he considers it significant that Saturn rules the day and Mars the hour of the chart. He had asked if the ship would arrive safely, and it did not. However, the passengers and crew changed boats. The aspect of the Moon to (or from) dexter sextile Saturn indicates the storm that injured the ship. (Also notice the Ascendant ruler, Mercury, retrograde shows the ship will not go very far.) The ship was saved, according to the reasoning of Palchus, because of the trine between Venus and Jupiter, and because the Moon had been in square to Jupiter--he was, after all, speaking of a matter in the past--and in the past Jupiter had collected the light of the Moon and of Venus. This reminds me of Lilly's chart for the ship that had sunk, where prior to the question, and in the last sign, the Moon had squared Saturn. [14]

Palchus thought the ship would arrive after the seventh day because then the Moon would have passed the position of Jupiter (literally and not by symbolic direction), and also the dodecatamoria of the Moon, in Taurus, was moving away from Jupiter in Aquarius. (!) (In seven days time on 21 July the

Moon is at 17° Aquarius having passed Jupiter at 8° Aquarius).

The Lot of Fortune was in Sagittarius, with which Argo rises (a constellation concerned with shipping), and its ruler, Jupiter, was in the watery sign Aquarius.

Figure 24.3: The Safety of a Ship Travelling from Alexandria to Smyrna, from the Collection of Palchus

14 July A.D. 479
7:30 A.M.
Latitude and Longitude of Smyrna

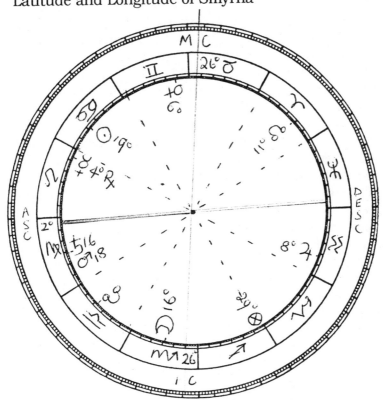

Now we come to the part about changing ships. This was deduced from the fact that the Ascendant (the Horoscopus) was in a bicorporeal sign, Virgo, and Venus on the M.C. was in a bicorporeal sign, Gemini, and the ruler of Fortuna was in a bicorporeal sign, Virgo, and with Mercury retrograde, Palchus thought they would change ships. (Perhaps "bi-corporeal" is synonymous with "mutable," causing something to happen twice.)

The cargo he deduced from the fact that Virgo is a winged sign, and so is Sagittarius, and so the cargo would include feathered things. Because the Moon was in the house of Mars and the terms of Mercury, he thought they would bring books and papyrus and some bronze objects because of Scorpio. He noticed that Asclepius was rising with the Moon, so he decided they would bring medical supplies. As to when the ship would come, he said it would be when the Moon was in Aquarius (or Pisces) the latter because of the motion of Fortuna towards its own house ruler, (sign ruler is meant here.)

They arrived on the eighth day after the question, and they spoke about the rough sea and the rudder that struck a rock and broke. They reached a harbour and transferred to another ship with the cargo, bringing ostrich feathers, plain papyrus (because Mercury was retrograde), cooking implements (because of Scorpio), and a shipload of medical supplies (because of Asclepius and Hygeia).

What Palchus forgot to mention, and which I think he can hardly have overlooked, is that the Moon trines the Sun. That is why he expected them to return at all. The Sun is in Agathos Daimon, the house of harbours, and comfort and relief.

Figure 24.4: The Use of the Dodecatamorie as in the Chart by Palchus

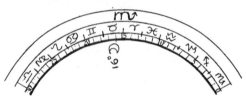

In the chart by Palchus he states that the Moon is in the dodecatamorie of Taurus. Each sign is divided into segments of 2 1/2° starting with the sign concerned. Here you see the first 2 1/2° belong to the dodecatamorie of Scorpio, the next 2 1/2° to Sagittarius, and so on. The Moon, therefore, falls in the segment belonging to Taurus.

In his interpretation he considers that the dodecatamorie of Taurus departs from Jupiter in Aquarius. My understanding of this would be that were Jupiter also to be drawn onto the above diagram, at Aquarius 8° the Moon would be separating from it. But I am unaccustomed to using this technique, and hope there will be investigations into it.

Other Notable Early Astrologers

Thasyllus was astrologer to the Emperors Tiberius and Claudius, and father to Balbillus.

Balbillus was astrologer to Nero and Vespasian. We have his chart for the Coronation of Nero preserved in the writings of Tacitus Annales XII, chapters 68-69. Antigonus gives us the chart of Hadrian. Vettius Valens is well known for his *Anthology* and the number of charts he has left us.

Critodemus is another astrologer of the period. Later, in the fifth century, the great names were Hephaestion, Rhetorius, and Palchus.

Firmicus Maternus, author of *The Mathesis*, lived in the fourth century. Although his astrological theory is interesting, his interpretations are exaggerated in my opinion, and rather fatalistic.

Mention must be made also of Porphry (A.D. 232-304) whose house system is still well known.

Al Biruni

In the fifth century astrology was persecuted and valuable books were burnt. Ptolemy was forgotten in most of Europe, but fortunately his information was rescued by the Arab and

Jewish astrologers, who translated the *Tetrabiblos* and *Almagest* into Arabic.

Some famous names during this period were Stephanus of Alexandria (in the fifth century), who foretold Islam; the Jewish Abu Masha 'Allah (789-886), and the Arabian Al Kindi (born 873). There was also Abraham Ibn Ezra who lived in the eleventh century and who wrote *The Beginning of Wisdom,* [15] a title I so much admire. I would like to have written more about these brilliant men, but their work has been inaccessible to me.

However, I can say something of Al Biruni (born 973) who was a follower of Al Kindi. Abu'l-Rayhan Muhammad Ibn Ahmad Al Biruni wrote *The Book of Instruction in the Elements of the Art of Astrology* in A.D. 1029 at Ghazah. This book is in the British Museum and was translated by Ramsay Wright, M.A., in 1934. It is the only literature of the period I have read, and I found it most interesting to know the attitudes and developments of our art at that date, seven hundred years after *The Mathesis* of Firmicus Maternus.

Al Biruni opens his book with an invocation. Fragments of the older Greek charts show the Greeks also did that. Indeed, Lilly tells us it is well to pray before we try to interpret a chart. Al Biruni writes, "In the Name of God the Merciful, the Compassionate, Him do we ask for aid," and later he adds--and I am fervently with him here--"May God by his grace, and in the fullness of His mercy, favour accuracy of statement in the work." [16]

The early part of his book deals with instruction on geometry, arithmetic, spherical astronomy, the solar system, the fixed stars, the constellations, the epicycles of Ptolemy (yet the Jewish astrologers of the period had rejected this), handwriting, and the geography and peoples of his world. Then he reaches the ultimate: astrology. And it is strangely familiar, for of course, Al Biruni was conversant with Ptolemy's work. However, there seems to be an extra stress on the signs that was missing in classical astrology where the planets were viewed as all powerful. I believe this is because he had travelled in India and Persia and brought back influences which he discusses and compares. He uses the decanates, which I think are Hindu, and the faces of Ptolemy. Like the Greeks he uses the dodecatamorie and equipollent signs (similar to antiscia but counted from 0° Aries to 0° Libra). This is not mentioned by Lilly. Al Biruni also uses conjunction by latitude, reminding me of Ivy Goldstein-Jacobson's methods. He even speaks of besiegement by benefics (trapped between one benefic and another), whereas our seventeenth century astrologers use besiegement between malefics only, as when a town was beseiged.

He lists manners, appearances, vegetation, metals, countries, and diseases, according to signs and according to planets; sometimes the lists vary for nativities or horary. But the most impressive contribution is his information on the lots (or parts), which I have discussed in my chapter on that subject. The technique of using lots was obviously highly developed.

His birth data is as follows: September 4, A.D. 973 5:05 A.M. 41° 40' North at Khwarizm, 8° Virgo ascends, Sun 16° 22' Virgo, Mercury 20° Virgo, Jupiter 7° Libra, Moon 6° Scorpio, and Mars, Venus, and Saturn in Cancer.

Bonatus and Cardan

Guido Bonatus lived in the thirteenth century, but we know nothing about him. Lilly obviously had a high regard for his work, for the *Anima Astrologiae* by Bonatus was edited and published by Lilly in 1676, at the end of his life. Its influence is found in Lilly's writings. Bonatus' book contains 146 Considerations in which he attempts to enumerate all we should consider in judging a chart. It is not an easy book, but as Lilly says, "it contains much excellent matter necessary to be observed by all honest students that practice Art to discover truth and not to vapour with it." [17]

The first Consideration alone is worthy of great thought:

to observe what it is that moves a person to...ask a question of an Astrologer, we must take notice...of the mind, when a man is stirred up in his thoughts and hath an intent to enquire; secondly of the superior and celestial bodies; so that they at that time imprint on the thing inquired after, what shall become of it; and third, of the free will [note that] which disposes him to the very act of enquiring; for although the mind be moved to inquire, 'tis not enough unless the superior bodies sympathize therewith; nor is such motion of the stars enough, unless by the election of his will the person actually does enquire.

Then there is an endearing footnote by Lilly, "for the foolish querent may cause a wise respondent to err, which brings scandal upon the Art amongst inconsiderate people, whereas the astrologer is not blameable, but the ignorant silly querent." [18]

Lilly includes Aphorisms from Cardan's writings in the same book. Cardan was born in 1501 on the first of October. He was physician and professor of medicine to Pope Gregory XIII. He was an extremely eccentric man, sacrificing every other consideration to a desire of being sincere (unusual indeed). "I have been admired by many nations; an almost infinite number of panegyrics in prose and verse have been composed to celebrate my fame," [19] he wrote. He claims to have written a book in seven days. But it wasn't all boasting; he also admits to all his sins.

Cardan differs from Culpeper in assigning the curative medicines to the fifth house and its Lord, rather than the tenth. Again, one recognizes snatches of his information incorporated in Lilly's *Christian Astrology*.

John Dee

While we advocate historical research in astrology, the main purpose for astrologers must surely be to gain insight into the astrological skills and methods of our illustrious predecessors, like John Dee.

We have an excellent opportunity to consider his methods when comparing the charts of Elizabeth I and that of her Coronation. [20] Dee most certainly would have known and studied Elizabeth's natal chart before electing the time of such an event as her Coronation. It is interesting to see why he chose the time he did. The most important factor has been observed by Geoffrey Cornelius who notes that the lights in the Coronation accorded perfectly with the benefics in the nativity of Elizabeth. In that observation lies an invaluable principle for use in electional astrology, that most obscure and difficult branch of our art. It is for the discovery of such facts that we make our study.

Figure 24.5: The Coronation of Elizabeth I, elected by John Dee

Regiomontanus House System

15 January 1558
Noon
Latitude and Longitude of Westminster

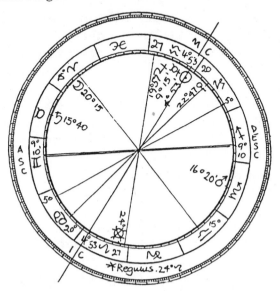

Figure 24.6: Elizabeth I's Birth Chart

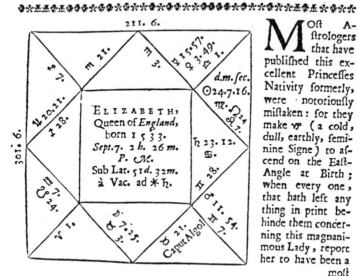

Moſt Aſtrologers that have publiſhed this excellent Princeſſes Nativity formerly, were · notoriouſly miſtaken : for they make ♑ (a cold, dull, earthly, feminine Signe) to aſcend on the Eaſt-Angle at Birth ; when every one, that hath left any thing in print behinde them concerning this magnanimous Lady, report her to have been a moſt

It would have been recognized in those days that upon Dee's skill in his election of the time of the Coronation would depend much of the success of the Monarch's reign. He would have studied the previous Great Conjunctions and Ingresses, and considered some fixed signs necessary, and used the positions of fixed stars. Bonatus points out that fixed stars confer lasting benefits and are used for events such as foundations of buildings [21]...they confer great gifts, and elevate even from poverty to an extreme height of fortune, the seven planets do not. [22] Surely this would be just what was needed for a coronation. It was, therefore, interesting to observe that the final aspect of the Moon was to Fortuna conjunct Regulus, the Royal Star, then at 24° Leo, which confers glory, honor, and fortune. In my opinion that was a configuration of the greatest importance.

The Sun, Mercury (significator of Elizabeth since it is ruler of the Ascendant, and she had Sun in Virgo), and Jupiter are angular in the tenth house of Glory, in a fixed sign. Mercury applies to Jupiter, the greater benefic. It is at least in its own terms. Mercury is conjunct within 1 degree of the place of Mars in the 1066 map of England (Aries rules England).

Mercury applies to Jupiter, lord of the seventh house, with Sagittarius on its cusp. Sagittarius rules Spain, and during Elizabeth's reign Spain was "the other." Implicit in this placement is the possibility of Elizabeth's marriage to the Spanish King, but the two planets are just out of orb.

It is possible that the opposition of Mars and Saturn contributed to a ruthlessness in her reign, for Mars rules her unknown enemies (twelfth house) and Saturn rules the eighth. The Monarch, with Sun on the Midheaven, was strong enough to outshine her enemies, however. Saturn, lord of the twelfth from the tenth, although not strong in Taurus is in mutual reception with Venus, which must have made her many enemies abroad.

However, there must be many points of interest still to be found in this chart.

Elizabeth's nativity as reproduced here is from Gadbury's Collection of Genitures, which, he tells us is proved by several events in her life. However, there is another version by Junctinus, a contemporary of Elizabeth. Junctinus gives 16° Capricorn rising. It is impossible after such a span of years to be sure, yet 16° Capricorn is the Ascendant of her grandfather. From the manner of her death, which showed her power of endurance, and from the pearls and diamonds she so obviously favored, as well as the structure of her face, I incline to the Capricorn Ascendant. Not that it alters any of the above remarks.

Nicholas Culpeper

Nicholas Culpeper was born on 18 October 1616. He was dark complexioned, with dark brown hair, lean, neither tall nor short, with quick piercing eyes. He was full of agility, very active and nimble. Witty and intelligent, his brilliance was well known before the end of his short life. He was a good speaker, but liked to tell jokes, and even his serious articles were peppered with jokes.

He spent his money freely, soon finishing all that had been left to him by his parents. (He had no brothers or sisters.)

He ridiculed the College of Physicians who were angry with him for speaking of medicine in his mother tongue. He thought no good could come of Monarchy, and he hoped the Spaniards would lose their American colonies because they were cruel to the Indians. He also believed the rich should help the poor!

At eighteen he went to University, and at twenty-four began to study "physic." At twenty-seven he fought against Monarchy and was wounded by shot. He married Alice and by her had seven children, only one of whom was still alive at the time he died, at age thirty-eight.

Culpeper himself admitted to having a weak body, and said that was how he knew that health was the greatest thing in life. He died of consumption, from which he had suffered a long time, and it wasted him away until he was as thin as a skeleton.

He wrote some brilliant books, the best known are the *Astrological Judgment of Diseases from the Decumbiture of the Sick*, and *The English Physician*, on which the modern herbals bearing his name are based. *The English Physician Enlarged* contained descriptions of English medicinal herbs that were not published in any impression before this. The book was commented upon by a contemporary, John Gadbury, as "a work of such rarity that never any herbalist before him durst adventure to do." [23] And he wrote a *Directory for Midwives* that was highly praised.

Culpeper believed that the whole world and everything in it is formed of a composition of contrary elements, in which is the wisdom of God. This Creation, though composed of contraries is one united body, and man is the epitome of it. Illnesses are caused naturally, and as the cause is, so is the cure; therefore, to know the workings of the herbs, look up to the stars. [24] His book, he said, showed the harmony of Creation, the influence of the stars upon herbs and the body of man, how one part of Creation is subservient to another, and all for the use of man showing the infinite wisdom of God, who has stamped his image on every creature. Therefore, to abuse the creature is a sin. How much more excellent and wise does God appear when you realize the harmony and creation of every herb? He denounced priests, and stated "all the religion I know is in Jesus Christ and Him crucified, and the indwelling of the spirit in me."

It was the effort of his life to bring reason to the diagnosis of illness and to prescriptions of herbal medicine. He wrote a book explaining which planets ruled disease called *Semeiotica Uranica*, and another explaining which planets ruled English herbs. Every disease was ruled by a particular planet, according to Culpeper, so you cured it by the use of the herb ruled by that planet, or conversely, by the opposite planet. In his instructions about how to use his book on herbs, he suggests we should first consult *Semeiotica Uranica* to ascertain what planet causes the disease. Then we should consider if it is a disease of the flesh, bone, blood, or ventricles.

We then look at the herbal to discover what herb will cure the illness. This can be done by sympathy, as, the brain would be helped by herbs of Mercury, the breast and liver by herbs of Jupiter, the heart by herbs of the Sun etc. Or, it may be done by opposites, as diseases of Jupiter would be cured by herbs of Mercury, and vice versa, or diseases of the Sun and Moon by herbs of Saturn and vice versa, or diseases of Mars by herbs of Venus and vice versa. Every planet cures its own disease. The Sun and Moon by their herbs cure the eyes, Saturn the spleen, Jupiter the liver, Mars the gall, Venus the organs of generation.

Culpeper observed the fluctuation of illness according to the motion of the planets. It was apparent to him that every physician should be an astrologer. In his book *The English Physician Enlarged*, published in 1653, the forerunner of the modern *Herbal*, he includes a chart showing his methods of diagnosis and prescribing herbs.

Figure 24.7: "The Enclosed Scheme" from *The English Physician Enlarged* 1653 by Nicholas Culpeper

Regiomontanus House System

24 July 1651
11:20 A.M. local time

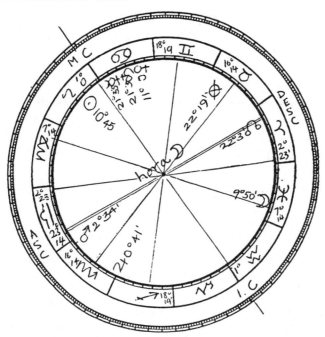

Because Mars is the trouble, the cure was to give cooling medicines of the nature of the Sun and Venus. These Culpeper judges from the tenth house. Arrach, Ros Solis, (which is also under Cancer) would be helpful since Venus is here in Cancer; also lettuce (of the Moon) and tansie (of Venus in Libra) and Orpine (of the Moon).

The chart was sent to Culpeper for his diagnosis and help. It refers to a young woman's illness. In the interpretation that follows the comments and asides in parentheses are my own, for any beginner who may be following the account.

He replied that Venus symbolized the young woman because it rules the sign on the Ascendant, is also ruler of the twelfth (unnamed enemies) and eighth (unfortunate), and that she had therefore been her own worst enemy in regard to health. The position of Venus in the ninth house in Cancer suggested that she might have caught cold (Saturn) while travelling (ninth) or eaten a surfeit of moist fruit. (The Moon in a moist sign pointing to Venus in a moist sign, Cancer, suggests moistness in eating.)

The chill of Saturn, in Cancer (the breast) square the Ascendant (the body) troubled her with phlegm and melancholy.

There is mutual reception between the Moon and Venus from fruitful signs, the Moon in the fifth, showing she may be pregnant.

The ruler of the sixth shows disease, and as Aries is on that cusp, Mars rules the disease. It is here in Scorpio, ascending. This, said Culpeper, connected the disease with her womb, and as Mars is in the first house, near the second, this could well denote the "breakings out" around her face and throat. (The first house is connected with the head and the second with the neck.)

In considering whether the illness was curable and how long it would last, Culpeper said he could see no danger of death, "the Moon being strong in her wain"; and applying to the trine of Venus, with additional mutual reception. He pointed out, however, that because Mars is strong in a fixed sign it would be a long disease. She would be particularly despairing around August 2, when Venus conjuncted Saturn exactly. Culpeper suggested that the disease might go when Mars left the sign it is in and reached Jupiter, (the greater benefic), or at least it might then change to a different disease that was more propitious.

The Sun strong (in Leo) in the tenth shows the curative medicine. The trouble, caused by Mars (heat) in the womb, and a "salt humour in the blood" ought to be removed before dealing with the phlegm and cold of Saturn. The medicine, he advised, must first be cool, secondly strengthen the womb, thirdly repress vapours, and fourthly of the nature of the Sun and Venus.

He therefore suggested and enclosed stinking Arrach, which he explained could be found on dung hills, especially horse dung. It is a cold moist herb of Venus in Scorpio. Also he prescribed Ros Solis, a herb of the Sun in Cancer, which grows in bogs and uncultivated places, with roundish green leaves full of red hairs, full of dew when the Sun is hot. Tansie, which belongs to Venus in Libra, and lettuce, and Orpine, herbs of the Moon, were recommended. "Mars having his fall in Cancer, use them as you please they are all harmless,"[25] (so cooling the fever).

Culpeper, as we've said, could never resist telling a joke, so for readers who might wonder what sort of joke, read on, but don't expect to fall about laughing.

"A woman whose husband had bruised himself, took his water and away to the Doctor trots she; the Doctor takes the water and shakes it about, "How long hath this party been ill (saith he). "Sir," saith the woman, "He hath been ill these two days," "This is a man's water, quoth the Doctor presently, this he learned from the word HE; then looking at the water he spied blood in it, "the man hath a bruise" saith he, "I indeed" saith the woman, "my husband fell down a pair of stairs backward", then the doctor knew well enough that what came first to danger must needs be his back and shoulders, said, the bruise lay there; the woman she admired at the doctor's skill, and told him, that if he could tell her one thing more she would account him the ablest physician in Europe; "Well, what was that?" "How many stairs her husband fell down?" This was a hard question indeed, able to puzzle a stronger brain than Mr. Doctor had, to pumping goes he and having taken the urinell and given it a shake or two, enquires whereabouts she lived, and knowing well the place, and that the houses thereabouts were but low built houses, made an answer (after another view of the urine for fashions sake) that probably he might fall down seven or eight stairs, "Ah", quoth the woman, "now I see you know nothing, my husband fell down thirty"; "Thirty!" quoth the Doctor, and snatching up the urinell, "is here all the water" saith he; "No" saith the woman, "I spilt some of it in putting it in," "Look you there", quoth Mr. Doctor, "there were all the other stairs spilt." [26]

Fig. 24.8: A Modern Decumbiture Showing the Application of Culpeper's Information

In the days when astrologers were doctors illnesses were diagnosed from the time when the patient took to his or her bed because of the illness. This was called the decumbiture, hence the famous book by Nicholas Culpeper called *The Decumbiture of the Sick*. The time was also sometimes taken from the time when the doctor received the urine specimen.

One day a friend telephoned me to say she was very ill and asked me to come and sit with her. She knew the exact time when she first had gone to bed, so I drew up a horary. (See Figure 24.8 on the following page.)

She was very ill, near death, confirmed by the Sun, ruler of the Ascendant representing herself, at the eighth cusp. She was parched with a very high temperature and urine like dark brown varnish. The Moon opposes Mars, planet of fevers. The Moon is in Virgo, a dry sign; also Saturn, ruler of the sixth, indicates dryness.

The sixth house represents illness; the first house is the house of life and health and so represents her recovery. It is a battle

Figure 24.8: A Modern Decumbiture

Regiomontanus House System

19 February 1981
3:30 P.M. G.M.T.
51° 13' N 1° 25" E

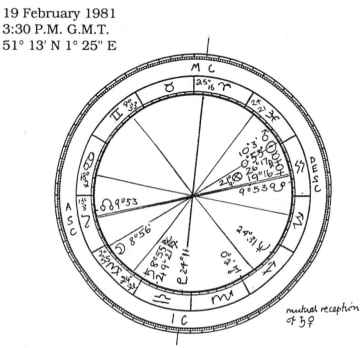

DECUMBITURE

Extract from *Ebertin's Anatomical Degrees*, translated by Mary Z. Vohryzak, from *Anatomische Entsprechungen*, by Elspeth and Reinhold Ebertin.

LIBRA

1--Kidney pelvis	7--Jaundice nervous system
2--Renal cortex	8--of the kidney
3--Adrenals (abscess)	9--and
4--Kidney surfaces goitre	10--renal
5--Malphigi's Pyramid	11--pelvis
6--Pubis	

between the relative strengths of the planets ruling those houses. Saturn ruling the illness is strong by exaltation and conjunction with Jupiter, but weakened by being retrograde. The Sun is weak on the eighth cusp, but in the terms of benefic Venus, which is angular.

"The application of the Moon to a planet in the eighth is always dangerous." [27] The Moon transfers the light of the Sun, the querent, to Mars (fevers). But neither luminary aspects Jupiter, lord of the eighth.

Knowing nothing of medical matters, I looked at my list of *Anatomical Degrees* by Ebertin. I found the ruler of her sixth house of illness at 8° Libra. Below the chart you will see a partial list compiled by Reinhold Ebertin in which every degree is associated with a part of the anatomy. Beside 8 degrees are the words "of the kidney." The doctor called it *Pylonephritis*.

Of course, Culpeper and Lilly did not have the advantage of Ebertin's list, and their methods were no doubt too difficult for those of us who know nothing of medicine. Yet I notice that in the example Culpeper gives of a decumbiture in *The English Physician Enlarged*, Ebertin's diagnosis holds good.

My friend did recover, in about six weeks. After further consideration I reached the conclusion that the mutual reception between Venus and Saturn accounts for the recovery, giving a way out about six weeks later.

In decumbiture charts the seventh house rules the doctor and the tenth the medicine. Although it is now against the law for an astrologer to diagnose illness one can at least see from such a chart if it would be advisable to change one's doctor, and if there is antipathy between the ruler of the first and that of the seventh.

There was formerly much argument about the time of decumbiture, since weak people might go to bed with a headache and strong ones might wait until they were nearly dying. I have always wondered if this was the reason why Queen Elizabeth I would not lie down to die.

Figure 24.9: From the Collection of Gadbury King Charles I

Regiomontanus House System

19 November 1600
10:02 P.M. local time
56° N Scotland

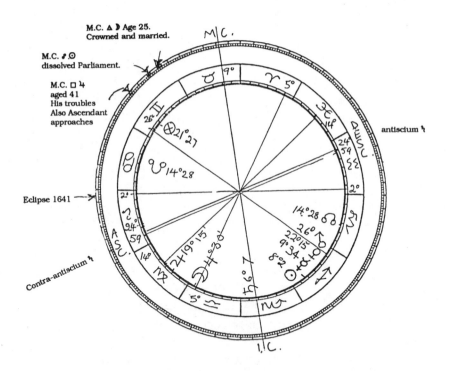

M.C. △ ☽ Age 25.
Crowned and married.

M.C. ☌ ☉
dissolved Parliament.

M.C. □ ♃
aged 41
His troubles
Also Ascendant
approaches

antiscium ♄

Eclipse 1641 →

Contra-antiscium ♄

King Charles I was executed in 1648, when the Ascendant reached the square of Mars. The antiscium of Saturn falls on the Descendant and the contra-antiscium of Saturn on the Ascendant.

It is worthy of note that his Pluto is conjunct England's A.D. 1066 Ascendant.

Figure 24.10: The Nativity of Nero

Regiomontanus House System

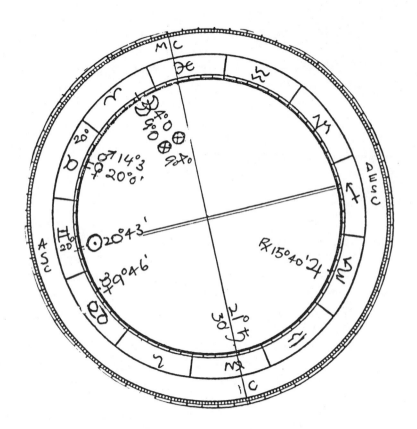

From Gadbury's *Collection of Nativities*, Gadbury having found it in Cardan's collection.

Another version of the chart of Nero, preserved by Vettius Valens, is as follows: Ascendant, sunrise; Sun, 23° Sagittarius; Mars, 27° Sagittarius; Mercury, 1° Sagittarius; Moon, 9° Leo; Saturn, 27° Virgo; Jupiter, 14° Scorpio; and Venus, 24° Capricorn.

Fig. 24.10: The Nativity of Nero

The Moon is illustrated at 4° Aries, but this I believe is a misprint because Gadbury tells us that the Moon is in exact square to Mercury, which is at 9° Cancer. I believe, therefore, that the Moon is at 9° Aries. Moreover if the Moon is at 9 degrees its antiscium would fall on Saturn. That Mercury is correctly placed is suggested by the fact that its antiscium falls on the Ascendant and Sun; the significance of this position will be understood when you read the following extract and notice the emphasis placed on "The Quartile of the Sun and Saturn."

Gadbury comments that "snow doth not more resemble snow than this Nativity the Actions, Manners and Fortunes of this Prince."

He continues:

His harsh Inclinations, Temperament, Manners and Crueltie, are well depointed, and most lively represented in this Figure of his Birth: for it is (indeed) a scheme so cross, that it denotes a person born under it of Disposition so strange and prodigiously mischievous, that the very worst of them cannot be acquainted with greater.

For to signifie that monstrous and horrid Act of his, toward his Mother Agrippina, (for that was her name) here is Mars in Opposition of Jupiter Lord of the tenth House, and Mercury Lord of his Ascendant in exact Quartile to the Moon; (who ever generally hath signification of Mothers,...) and this hateful Aspect happeneth from Angles, and from Cardinal Signes; Arguments most eminent to denote Matricide: Yet I remember to have read one, that terms his murthering his mother an ingenious cruelty in him, his end being to determine the cabinet of his Conception.

The Quartile of the Sun and Saturn from Angles, make him not only hated by those whom he by Prerogative Ruled, but inclined him also to commit things worthy of Hatred and Disdain. In the Black List of his Actions, it is not to be forgotten that he did not only murther his Mother, but first committed incest with her, then he poison'd his Brother, kicked his Sister-in-Law, destroyed his wife Poppea (being great with Childe) by a Kick; burnt Rome, and rejoyced at the sight of the Flames...After all which unheard-of Cruelties, and bloody inhumane Acts, he was by the Senate proclaimed an Enemy of the State; Upon hearing of which he became his own Butcher.

The danger of malefics mid fixed signs is that their antiscium reflects to fixed signs and one has a grand cross in fixed signs. Here, the antiscium of Mars falls mid-Leo, and the antiscium of Jupiter (which granted is a benefic, but is inclined to enlarge all it touches) falls at mid-Aquarius, so that the Mars-Jupiter opposition is repeated, as in a grand cross.

Reader Participation

For those who are interested in studying astrology and not just reading about it, it is worth drawing up the chart of Adolf Hitler, another greatest villain in history. Chronologically the lives of Nero and Hitler may be widely separated, but astrologically they share much in common.

The chart of Hitler never seemed to me to emphasize the outstandingly bad characteristics one might expect. Never, that is, until I read Firmicus and understood about antiscia, and read Ptolemy's comments on Eclipses.

Hitler's data is as follows: 20 April 1889. 6:21 P.M. LMT 48° 12 N 13° 2 E (Data from Rupert Gleadow's *Astrology and Everyday Life*, Faber & Faber, Ltd., London, 1950, p. 26.)

Hitler's M.C. is 2° Leo; Ascendant 25° Libra; Sun 0° 47 Taurus; Moon 6° 31 Capricorn; Mercury 25° 38' Aries; Venus 16° 42' Taurus retrograde; Mars 16° 23' Taurus; Jupiter 8° 15 Capricorn; Saturn 13° 28 Leo; Uranus 19° 8 Libra retrograde, Neptune 0° 30 Gemini; Pluto 4° 35 Gemini.

It is interesting that his Ascendant is conjunct the previous full Moon at 26° 7' Libra and his M.C. near the previous Eclipse at 27° Cancer. (See Ptolemy's *Tetrabiblos*, page 261.) But what is fascinating is the repeated pattern of grand cross in fixed signs as with Nero. To find this draw in the antiscium (solstice) point of the two malefics, Mars and Saturn, and their contraantiscium. (See my previous chapter on Antiscia.)

This will give you a new perspective on Hitler's chart. Notice the involvement of the Ascendant ruler.

William Lilly and His Contemporaries

Now that astrologers are investigating the methods of horary used in the seventeenth century and earlier, many are setting up the old charts to check for accuracy. It should not be forgotten that the date of a day was considered to start at noon. For example, Gadbury tells us that Lilly's birth chart is for 14.08 P.M. on 30 April 1602, because he was counting the hours from noon on the previous day. Today we would call the time 2.08 A.M. on May 1.

The dates given in *Christian Astrology* are for the Julian --not the Gregorian--Calendar, and therefore ten or eleven days should be added, depending on the way Lilly has recorded the time and date.

There was also confusion as to the date of New Year's Day, which began on either January 1 or March 24. In one chart drawn up in March Lilly mentions both years.

Bear in mind, too, that it was extremely difficult to be sure of the exact time. Skies are often overcast in England and clocks at that time were rare. It is truly remarkable how accurate Lilly was. In most charts the Moon is within a degree of it's accurate position; in a few it is 1 or 2 degrees away, and in one chart only it is 3 degrees away. We do not study these charts for their astronomical exactitude, however, but for the principles they demonstrate, and their example of the way in which to make a judgment. Despite the lessons they teach us, it is, in the end, only through our own use of horary in an honest fashion that we can prove it to ourselves.

It is impossible to summarize the life or work of Lilly in such a short space. He was our greatest astrologer; he is to astrology what Shakespeare is to literature. In Lilly's day astrological books were in Latin, and his was the first astrological textbook in the English language, compiled and inspired by his large collection of over three hundred books, which he lists for us. These books were by the astrological authorities of the past, translated directly by Lilly, who incorporated their information, together with his own experience, to produce his 870-page masterpiece in 1647, *Christian Astrology*, now republished.

Lilly was a working astrologer, at one time judging as many as two thousand charts a year. [28] His language is the beautiful language of the seventeenth century, but the content is timeless, as indeed is all great astrology. Its truths are of as much practical value today as when they were written. He was master of his art and famous for it both as a natal and horary astrologer. *Christian Astrology* is a comprehensive and lengthy book, yet Lilly wrote *Englands Prophetical Merline* and several other shorter works, as well as periodical almanacs which preceded modern newspapers.

He wrote a brief biography in the *Introduction to the Reader* in *Christian Astrology*, and if you wonder what he taught, the first part of this book is an abridgment of some of his teachings.

He was born 1602 in Diseworth, a hamlet in Leicestershire, where his parents' large cottage still stands near the church, pretty and timbered and thatched, opposite the Bull Public House. "Lilly's Cottage" it is called. When he had finished school in nearby Ashby, owing to financial difficulties of his family which precluded him from Cambridge, he was procured a job in London "to wait on Gilbert Wright." He was eighteen when he walked the hundred and fifteen miles to London. On the way the weather was cold and wet and windy and the soles of his shoes wore through so that his feet hurt. [29] (Lilly had Pisces ascending). Gilbert Wright lived in the Strand, not far from Waterloo Bridge, in the house Lilly was later to buy. Lilly worked there both menially and in a secretarial capacity, and after Gilbert Wright's death married his widow. Lilly's first wife died after a few years and he was married again, to a very pretty woman. [30] It was at his Saturn return that Lilly was strangely attracted to astrology. He studied very hard, sometimes eighteen hours a day, becoming famous and wealthy, with an estate in Hersham near Walton-on-Thames.

Accounts of his life are written elsewhere (his *Life and Times*, 1715). His escapades on behalf of Parliament and how he helped Charles I escape, and how he foretold the Fire of London and was then blamed for it, are well known. He remained grateful for the friendship of Sir Elias Ashmole, who founded the Ashmolean Museum in Oxford, and whose influence so assisted Lilly in his career. Ashmole was also an astrologer, but not of Lilly's calibre.

But the extent of Lilly's studying had its effect on his eyes, which pained him, and his sight suffered towards the end of his life. Also he grew thin so that his collars became too large for his neck. [31] Before his death he was paralysed in one side of his face. Lilly is buried beside the altar in the Parish Church, St. Mary's, Walton-on-Thames beneath a black marble stone which Sir Elias Ashmole donated. It still can be seen.

One of his most brilliant followers was John Gadbury, but some difference of opinion divided them. Some say it was over

Gadbury's *Collectio Geniturarum*, a book which may contain inaccuracies but which is a masterpiece by today's standards. As Lilly grew older his great helper was Henry Coley, and it was at the instigation of Lilly that Coley translated Bonatus from the Latin, and three hundred aphorisms which he included in his book *Clavis Astrologiae Elimata*. This is a fine book by today's standards, but a paler reflection of his teacher Lilly.

By then Gadbury had turned his attention elsewhere. He wrote *The Doctrine of Nativities* and a *Life of Charles I*. Gadbury was friendly with George Wharton, Lilly's greatest rival, and astrologer to Charles I. George Wharton was bitter in his comments against Lilly, likening his friends to a dog named Jack, that jumped when its master told it to. Lilly was equally vituperative in reply, especially when Wharton treated the conjunction of Mars and Saturn as if it were a major conjunction. He had nothing but scorn for the astrological interpretations of Wharton.

Wharton, however, collected some fine essays in a book called *Gesta Britannorum* which includes "a succinct chronology" of the remarkable events between 1600 and 1667, with preface by John Gadbury. Here is an extract from the Chronology! "January 29th 1648 [Old calendar] King removed to St. James, whither his children came from Sion House and took their leave of him. Jan. 30. King Charles beheaded Hor. 1.52 P.M." Wharton also preserves for us the Cabal of the Twelve Houses from Morinus, translated into seventeenth century English.

Other notable astrologers of the time were John Booker and John Partridge.

But then astrology declined. People ceased to believe it. It no longer fitted into the concepts of a society which required scientific proof of everything, where materialism reigned (and still does).

English astrology books were watered down from Lilly with each successive generation; veering further and further into error. (An exception is Reinhold Ebertin, a giant in this century, an inspiration in Germany). But otherwise astrology has remained dormant until the recent work of the astro-psychologists who have gained some foothold in making us respectable again. This work, under the guidance of Liz Greene and Howard Sasportas, has produced fine results. Of course, everyone is glad psychology has begun to incorporate astrology; this is as it should be, but it has led some to forget that astrology exists independently of psychology.

However, let us remember William Lilly, the greatest real astrologer. It is always better to hear from someone directly than to read of him secondhand, so I leave you with his letter, and when you read the libels against him, his biography and works altered and tampered with, remember the man who wrote these words.

A Letter to the Student of Astrology

My Friend whoever thou art, that with so much ease shalt receive the benefit of my hard Studies, and doth intend to proceed in this heavenly knowledge of the Stars, wherein the great and admirable works of the invisible and alglorious God are so manifestly apparent. In the first place consider and admire thy Creator, and be thankful unto him, be thou humble and let no natural knowledge how profound and transcendant soever it be, elate thy mind to neglect that divine Providence, by whose allseeing order and appointment, all things heavenly and earthly, have their constant motion, but the more thy knowledge is enlarged, the more do thou magnify the power and wisdom of Almighty God, and strive to preserve thyself in his favour; being confident, the more holy thou art, and more near to God, the purer Judgment thou shalt give. Beware of pride and self-conceit and remember how that long ago, no irrational Creature durst offend Man, the Microcosm, but did faithfully serve and obey him, so long as he was master of his own Reason and Passions or until he subjected his Will to the unreasonable part. But alas! when iniquity abounded, and man gave the reins to his own affection, and deferred reason, then every Beast, Creature and outward harmful thing, became rebellious and unserviceable to his command. Stand fast, oh man! to thy God, and assured principles, then consider thy own nobleness, how all created things, both present and to come, were for they sake created; nay, for thy sake God became Man, thou art that Creature, who being conversant with Christ, livest and reignest above the heavens, and sits above all power and authority. How many pre-eminences, priviledges, advantages hath God bestowed on thee? thou rangest above the heavens by contemplation, conceivest the motion and magnitude of the stars, thou talkest with Angels, yea with God himself; thou hast all Creatures within thy dominion, and keepest the Devils in subjection. Do not then, for shame, deface thy nature, or make thyself unworthy of such gifts, or deprive thyself of that great power, glory, and blessedness God hath allotted thee, by casting from thee his fear, for possession of a few imperfect pleasures. Having considered thy God, and what thyself are, during thy being God's servant; now receive instruction how in thy practice I would have thee carry thyself; As thou daily converse with the heavens, so instruct and inform thy minde according to the image of Divinity; learn all the ornaments of vertue, be sufficiently instructed therein, be humane, courteous, familiar to all, easy of access, afflict not the miserable with terror of a harsh judgment; in such cases, let them know their hard fate by degrees; direct them to call on God to divert his judgments impending over them, be modest, conversant with the learned, civil, sober man, covet not an estate, give freely to the poor, both money and judgment, let no worldly wealth procure an erroneous judgment from thee, or such as may dishonour the Art, or this Divine Science: Love good men, cherish those honest men that cordially study this Art, be sparing in delivering Judgment against the Common-wealth thou livest in. Give not judgment of the death of thy Prince; yet I know experimentally that Reges subjacent legibus Stellarum, marry a wife of thy own, rejoyce in the number of thy friends, avoid law and controversie; in thy study, be totus in illis that thou mayest be singular in arte; be not extravagant or desirous to learn every Science, be not aliquat in omnibus; be faithful, tenacious, betray no ones secrets, no, no I charge thee never divulge either friend or enemies trust committed to thy faith. Instruct all men to Live well, be a good example thy self, avoid the fashion of the times, love thy own Native Country; exprobrate no man, no, not an enemy, be not dismaid, if ill spoken of, Conscientia mille testes, God suffers no sin unpunished, no lye unrevenged. [32]

William Lilly

Astronomer Astrologers

Always, since the beginning of history, the astronomers were astrologers and the astrologers were astronomers. But as the Age of Reason and materialism encroached the two separated. Astronomy, the physical reality, thrived, and astrology, the intangible, the invisible law of the Universe, was made into public entertainment and included in the *Breakfast Show*.

Many men whose names we know and associate with a variety of achievements were astrologers: Paracelsus the noted doctor, Copernicus, Mercator, famous for his projection of the world onto a map. Then there was Flamsteed, the

Astronomer Royal, and Newton. Tycho Brahe, Kepler, and Galileo Galilei worked as Court Astrologers.

Kepler has sometimes been misunderstood (he had Neptune ascending natally) because of his well-known reference to astrology as the "foolish daughter" of astronomy. Yet from the excellent translations of his writings by Ken Negus it is obvious that he clearly defended serious astrology, for, he says, "Unfailing experience of mundane events in harmony with the changes occurring in the heavens, has compelled my unwilling belief." [33]

Kepler was born on December 27 1571 at 2.37 P.M. in Weil der Stadt, Germany. His planets were predominantly in Capricorn and Scorpio, with an airy Ascendant and Moon, explaining the fact that he was a deep thinker and philosopher reasoning logically as he searched for the truth of astrology. However, Kepler's chart lacked any fire.

He dismissed predictive astrology as Arabic superstition, reflecting the political and religious prejudices of his times, for the Arabs were infidels. (This may also explain Lilly's dismissal of many of the Arabian Parts). Certainly had Kepler practiced horary he would not have given the world the plethora of minor aspects, which were the result of his intellectualization of astrology rather than the practical use of it, that has confused and bewildered horary astrologers ever since. If you want to practice horary astrology, give priority to the Ptolemaic aspects.

However, Kepler was a great man, famous in the world (with his strong and elevated Jupiter). His observations are enlightening and interesting as he seeks to probe for the truth. He struggled to apply his reason and intelligence to God's acts of Creation, to Fate and Freewill, to Benefics and Malefics. There are not many famous men today who have thought deeply enough to insist that the Earth has a Soul, yet has no nativity to give it the character of its beginning, as human beings have. That is what Kepler thought.

Lilly refers to Kepler in the early pages of Christian Astrology as "a clever man," and so he was.

I illustrate the chart below in which Galileo shows his discovery of Neptune but never realized it, thinking it was a Moon of Jupiter--so typical of Neptune.

Fig. 24.11: The Discovery of Neptune by Galileo Galilei 1612

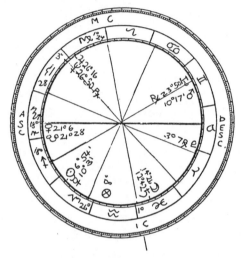

This is the chart reconstructed from Galileo's notes of the time, 3:00 A.M. local time in Florence, 1612, when he thought he had found one of Jupiter's Moons. Really it was the conjunction of Neptune and Jupiter. [34]

This can be considered an event chart. Scorpio rising and Mars its ruler, and the Moon represent Galileo. He was, I hear, red-headed. His significator is in the seventh house, where he rushed to tell of his discoveries. And the others listened to him, for Venus is in the first, but unfortunately with the Nodes. The tenth house of success is ruled by Mercury, here combust (obscured).

Neptune is retrograde, showing that although it was lost then, it would be found again.

I also present the chart for Flamsteed's Founding of Greenwich Observatory (Figure 24.12), the brilliance of which confirms that Flamsteed was a great astrologer.

Figure 24.12: Greenwich Observatory

Regiomontanus House System

10 August 1675
3:14 P.M.
51° 28' N

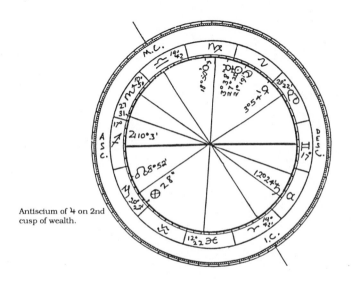

Antiscium of ♃ on 2nd
cusp of wealth.

Astrologers who know the chart of the Greenwich Observatory may have noticed that apart from the interesting planetary configurations the two most benefic fixed stars were
prominent. In Flamsteed's day Spica would have been conjunct the M.C. and Regulus conjunct the Sun. Great matters
like this are usually judged from eclipses and fixed stars,
whereas domestic matters are judged by the planets. I do not
know where the previous eclipse was. Jupiter, ruler of the
chart, is conjunct the second cusp of wealth by its antiscium.
This antiscium and the fixed stars are what make the chart
outstanding.

Chapter 25
The Houses in History

In order to predict events, whether from nativities, horary charts, eclipses, or ingresses, it is necessary to understand the houses. In William Lilly's book *Christian Astrology* is the key to all predictions and to every horary question. Much of his information, derived from his large collection of books, had not been translated into English before. Although he uses the knowledge of many astrologers, he often follows Ptolemy.

Ptolemy is important to us because he has recorded some of the astrological rules of the ancient world. His books are for those who understand something of astrology; they are not elementary text books, and so he has sometimes been misunderstood. It has been said that he uses Equal House, yet this cannot be so because the very name he gives to the tenth house is the Mid-heaven, and to the fourth house the Lower Mid-heaven. Because of the latitude of Alexandria, so near the equator, his houses must necessarily be more equal than ours in the north.

We have easy access to even earlier writings than Ptolemy's in the work of Manilius, who lived about the time of Christ. By reading these early authors we can see that the meanings of the houses has remained constant throughout history, with only one or two occasional deviations.

Figure 25.1 : The Houses in History

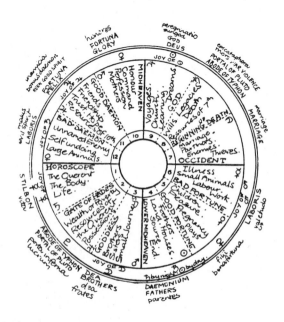

DARK CAPITALS: PTOLEMY
OUTSIDE CAPITAL WORDS: MANILIUS
small print: Lilly
Joys of planets: Lilly and Culpeper
small print outside: Firmicus

In this century there has been an emphasis on signs and Sun signs for the sake of simplicity, psychology, or commercial gain. This was not formerly so, the houses were considered more potent than the signs. Manilius, who called the houses temples (for they were the abode of the gods, or planets), wrote: "In any geniture every sign is affected by the sky's division into temples; position governs the stars, and endows them with power to benefit or harm; each of the signs, as it revolves, receives the influences of heaven and to heaven imparts its own. The nature of the position prevails, exercises jurisdiction within its province, and subjects to its own character the signs as they pass by, which now are enriched with distinction of every kind and now bear the penalty of a barren abode. [1] (The eighth was considered a barren abode, for instance.)

There are astrologers today who wish to ignore houses or events. They have found perhaps, that by using our present methods of natal astrology they cannot predict events. This is because they identify the signs with the houses. This will not do in horary. *From The Houses Can Be Discerned The Nature Of Events.* The signs are helpful adjectives.

During the seventeenth century the rot had begun to set in. Culpeper expresses his disgust by writing, in a passage so relevant to our present times, "some authors hold an opinion that the signs carry the same signification in order that the houses of heaven do, and Aries should signify life, Taurus estate, Gemini bretheren and short journeys, you know the rest. Truly my own opinion is many authors invented whimsies, and when they had done, set them down to posterity for truth." [2]

William Lilly does justice to many authors by quoting their opinions, for he had his ruler, Jupiter, in Libra in his birth chart, but when he does not agree he says so, and gives us the benefit of his experience. He does not agree with Ptolemy, for instance, (and nor does anyone else) in giving children to the eleventh house. Ptolemy's reasoning was that since "the culminating sign" rules mothers, and succedent houses show the possessions or resources of the preceding house, this must be the case.[3] But on the whole our predecessors, knowing they were dealing with the truth, did not seek to change it so much as to understand it. Ptolemy, who was more prosaic than Manilius, calls the houses places or parts. He explains to us that the part in sextile dexter to the horizon is the house of the Good Daemon; the part in quartile, the Midheaven; the part in trine, called the House of God. [4] Of these priority of strength and virtue was given to the Midheaven, the tenth house.

Here is the poetry of Manilius:

> First place goes to the cardinal which holds sway at the summit of the sky and divides heaven in two with imperceptible meridian; enthroned on high this post is occupied by Glory, (truly a fit warden for heaven's supreme station), so that she may claim all that is pre-eminent, arrogate all distinction, and reign by award-ing honours of every kind. Hence comes applause, splendour, and every form of popular favour; hence the power to dispense justice in the courts, to bring the world under the rule of law, to make alliances with foreign nations on one's own terms, and to win fame relative to one's station..."[5] He continues later, "Here does the Cytherean claim her abode among the stars, placing in the very face of heaven, as it were, her beauteous features, wherewith she rules the affairs of men. [6]

We may think it strange he gives marriage to this house as well as to the seventh, yet we also find it by progressions of the M.C.

To this house Lilly gives kings, princes, judges, those in command and authority, the profession or trade. (For profes-sion look at the ruler of the tenth, the Ascendant and its ruler.) Lilly says that either the Sun or Jupiter here is well-placed, but Saturn or the South Node denies honour and promises little joy in profession or trade. I think we have found that Saturn does not so much deny honor, as cause a fall from it, or delay it. Culpeper tells us that Mars rejoices here. [7] It is angular, cardinal, and feminine. Prime Ministers and Presidents belong to this house.

Next in importance is the first house, so beautifully described by Manilius: "Turn now your gaze upon heaven as it climbs up from the first cardinal point, where rising signs commence afresh their wonted course, and a pale Sun swims upward from the icy waves and begins by slow degrees to blaze with golden flame as it attempts the rugged path where the Ram heads the procession of the skies. This temple, Mercury, son of Maia, men say is yours...." [8]

Lilly, too, tells us Mercury joys in this house which rules the head, for Mercury represents the tongue, the fancy, and memory, and produces good orators when placed here natally. [9]

Any planet or fixed star positioned in the first house assists in the description of the body. It rules white and pale things, thus, a significator here shows something white or near white. Mars or Saturn produce some blemish on the face or in that member appropriate to the sign on the cusp.

Firmicus Maternus called it *Vita*. [10] Manilius called it *Stilbon* [11] apparently meaning Mercury. (The ancients called Mercury "Glistener".) Ptolemy called the first house *Horoscope*, [12] as the Greeks did. The first house rules we ourselves, our "home team," the vehicle we move in, whoever takes an initial action. Culpeper says it is the joy of Saturn. [13] It is angular (cardinal) and masculine.

Ptolemy called the seventh house the *Occident*. [14] It rules marriage, lovers, partners and, says Lilly, all manner of love questions, sweethearts, their shape, description, and condition. [15] In war, the seventh shows the opposing party, all quarrels, duels, lawsuits. It is associated with the colour black. In astrology it is the house of the artist, in medicine the physician. It describes thieves and outlaws. In short, it represents 'the other.' Besides marriage, Manilius thought it was connected with death, [16] because here the Sun went down, but Ptolemy moved death up to the eighth cusp. [17] Culpeper says the Moon rejoices here, [18] so that it is interesting that Mrs. Watters mentions public opinion in this connection. [19] Mrs. Watters had read Argolus in the Latin.

The eleventh house, called the House of the Good Daemon, was highly revered. This is how Manilius wrote of it:

> The temple immediately behind the summit of bright heaven, and (not to be outdone by its neighbour) of braver hope, surges ever higher, being ambitious for the prize and triumphant over earlier temples; consummation attends the topmost abode, and no movement save for the worse can it make, nor is aught left for it to aspire to. There is thus small cause for wonder, if the station nearest the zenith, and more secure than it, is blessed with the lot of Happy Fortune...in this temple dwells Jupiter, let its ruler convince you that it is to be reverenced. [20]

The Greeks and Manilius called it Fortuna Felix or Good Spirit. It rules friends and friendship, hope, trust, confidence, praise, and all the favorites, counsellors of the King, e.g., the resources of the tenth house. The eleventh is the house of the Exchequer. Lilly said that in London it rules the Lord Mayor. [21] The Sun is well-placed here, but the house belongs to Jupiter and it is where Jupiter rejoices.

The fourth house, called by Ptolemy the Lower Midheaven, through the centuries has been the House of the Fathers, for it gives judgment, says Lilly, of Fathers in general and ever of the father of who enquires. It rules land, houses, tenements, towns, inheritances, agriculture, treasures hidden, castles, cities, fields, orchards, the quality and nature of the soil. The sign of the fourth shows the town and the ruler of the town is the ruler of the sign. A feminine house, the fourth was called the angle of the Earth or north angle. [22]

Not only does the fourth house represent fathers, but so

does the Sun by day and Saturn by night. This agrees with Ptolemy. [23] Manilius, too, says this is the abode of Saturn, and his descriptive comment on the fourth is beautiful.

> Where at the opposite pole the universe subsides, occupying the foundations, and from the depths of midnight gloom gazes up at the back of the Earth, in that region Saturn exercises the powers that are his own: cast down himself in ages past from empire in the skies and the throne of heaven, he wields as a father power over the fortunes of fathers and the plight of the old. Daemonium is the name the Greeks have given it, denoting influences fitting the name.... [24]

Manilius also says of this house that it controls the foundations of things and governs wealth; "mining of metals and what gain can issue from a hidden source." [25] 'The source' seems to be the great meaning of this house. A modern expression belonging to it is 'real estate.' Firmicus called it *Parentes*, [26] but I am not sure if this means both parents or something else. The word *Daemonium* given by Manilius [27] interests me, reminding me of pandemonium, and making me wonder if Pan, the god of all nature, was connected with festivities at the time of the winter solstice.

The fifth house was called Good Fortune by Ptolemy. [28] Lilly called it the house of Pleasure, Delight, and Merriment, [29] ruling children, ale-houses, banquets, plays, and pregnancy. Whereas the fourth represented a town beseiged, the fifth represented its ammunition. It was ruled by Venus, who joys here also. [30] I am always interested that honey colour [31] belongs to this house, and think that honey, and sweetness and bees and flowers probably do also. Firmicus calls the fifth *Filii*, and *Bona Fortuna*. [32]

The ninth house was called *Deus*, the house of God. In fact, Firmicus, who was not a Christian, called it the house of the Sun God.[32] It is ruled by the Sun. Manilius writes, "the stars that follow mid-day, where the height of heaven first slopes downward and bows from the summit, these Phoebus nourishes with his splendour; and it is by Phoebus's influence that they decree what ill or hap our bodies take beneath his rays." This region is called by the Greek word signifying God. [33]

Lilly says that by this house we give judgment about long journeys or voyages. It rules the Church, clergy, further learning, visions and dreams. [34] Firmicus called it *Peregrinatio.* Lilly confirms it is the joy of the Sun and tells us that Jupiter placed here indicates a religious person.

The second house was called the *Gate of Hades* by Ptolemy,[35] and the *Gate of Hell, Porta Inferna,* by Firmicus. [36] It was known as the *Abode of Typhon* and the *Portal of Pluto* by Manilius. [37] (As Pluto was the God of Hades, I cannot think why this house should not be the abode of Pluto.) It rules possessions, wealth or poverty, all movable goods, money lent, and all the resources of the querent or native. [38] Firmicus calls it *Lucrum.* [39] Jupiter placed here shows wealth; so does Venus. But the Sun and Mars are not well-placed in the second. Culpeper says it is the joy of Jupiter. [40]

The eighth house shares with the second the title *Abode of Typhon* and *Portal of Pluto,* [41] but the name given to it by Ptolemy was "The Beginning of Death." [42] *Mors* Firmicus called it. [43] Manilius associated it with violence and war. [44] Lilly says it concerns the estate of men deceased, as well as death, its quality and nature, wills, legacies, dowry. [45] It shows the resources or substance of the partner or enemy, or the other. Lilly and Culpeper say that Saturn rejoices here. [46]

The sixth house, called *Bad Fortune* [47] by Ptolemy, was also known as *Laboris* by Manilius. [48] It is the joy of Mars. It rules work, workers, labourers, all routine tasks, merchandise, especially grain. It also is concerned with illness, and we look for the description of an illness by the planet ruling the sixth cusp. Lilly says Venus and Mars here show a good physician. Manilius wrote of it "here largely abide the changes in our health and the warfare waged by unseen weapons of disease." [49] It rules small animals up to the size of sheep. [50] It is ironic that while we bewail unemployment, our predecessors called this house of labour, the house of misfortune.

Ptolemy called the twelfth house the *Bad Daemon*, [51] or evil spirit. Manilius likened it to the sixth and called it *Laboris, the Portal of Toil*, "in one you are doomed to climb, and the other to fall." [52] He calls it the temple of ill omen, "the cause of ruin." Lilly says it rules self undoing, unnamed enemies, sorrow, tribulation, and imprisonment. He tells us Saturn rejoices in the house, [53] but both he and Culpeper gave strength to Venus here.

Because of its opposition to the sixth, the twelfth rules large animals. Modern astrologers have found it is connected with hospitals, prisons, and large institutions.

So Manilius concludes, "This is the system by which you must mark the powers of the Temples: through them revolves the entire procession of the zodiac, which draws from them their laws and lends to them its own;..." [54]

Chapter 26

Modern Contributors to Horary Techniques

Reinhold Ebertin: Midpoints

There is no denying the immense contribution Reinhold Ebertin has made. His book *The Combination of Stellar Influences* is apt for far more than astropsychological purposes.

When one planet falls exactly midpoint two others look up his book. Whether you are looking for biological correspondences, or circumstances, such as separation, deception, accident, blackmail, quarrels, surprises, marriage, it's all there. (There is only one instance when Lilly almost used a midpoint: the Moon's sextile fell at a degree midpoint a Sun/ Mercury opposition, and saved the ship).

Barbara Watters: The Nodes

Barbara Watters has discovered that any planet in the same degree as the Nodes, regardless of sign or aspect, is unfortunate.

Ivy Goldstein Jacobson: Arabian Parts

Mrs. Jacobson uses "the planet the Moon last passed over and the one it will next pass over" very effectively. This is an extension of the idea of besiegement. Perhaps one of her greatest contributions lies in her use and instruction of the Arabian Parts. These are very valuable and should certainly be used on every relevant chart. Lilly did not use many of these parts. See her *Simplified Horary* and *Here and There in Astrology*.

Gibert Navarro: Progression of a Horary Ascendant

Mr. Navarro has contributed to finding accurate timing by progressing the Ascendant in certain charts. He has also found a wider use for the Part of Death, the Part of Marriage, and other Arabian Parts.

* * * * * * * * * * * *

Calculators and computers have contributed mathematical accuracy, but will never contribute to horary judgment or interpretation. We should be wary of those who try to 'invent' Astrology, because it is God-made, not man-made. It has to be discovered not invented. The over attention to minutely accurate calculation may make us forget that the purpose of a chart is its interpretation.

Notes

Preface

[1] Hermes Trismegistus, *Hermetica*, Vol. 1, ed. with English translation by Walter Scott (Boston: Shambhala Publications, Inc. 1985), p. 271.
[2] *Ibid.*, p. 325.

Introduction

[1] *Speculum Astronomiae*, by Roger Bacon or Albert Magnus is mentioned in *Astrology in the Renaissance: The Zodiac of Life*, by Eugenio Garin, published by Routledge and Kegan Paul, 1983, page 38.
[2] George Noonan, *Classical Scientific Astrology* (Tempe, AZ: The American Federation of Astrologers, Inc., 1983), p. 3.
[3] Neugebauer and van Hoesen, *Greek Horoscopes* (Philadelphia: The American Philosophical Society, 1959).
[4] Manilius, *The Astronomica*, translated by G.P. Goold. Published by Loeb. Harvard University Press and William Heinemann Ltd.

Chapter 2: The Planets

Most of the information in this chapter is from *Christian Astrology*, but comments on the outer planets are helped by *Horary Astrology and the Judgments of Events*, by Barbara H. Watters.

[1] Nicholas Kollerstrom, *Astrochemistry: A Study of Metal-Planet Affinities* (London: Emergence Press, 1984).

[2] Barbara H. Watters, *Horary Astrology and the Judgment of Events* (Washington, DC: Valhalla Paperbacks, Ltd., 1973), p.52

Recommended reading to widen thoughts of planets:

For plants, *Culpeper's Herbal*, any edition gives planetary rulerships. For minerals, *Astrochemistry*, by Nick Kollerstrom, London: Emergence Press, 1984). For beasts and fishes, *Christian Astrology*, by William Lilly, (originally written 1647, reprinted by Regulus Publishing Co., 1985).

Chapter 3: The Houses

[1] William Lilly, *Christian Astrology* (London: Regulus Publishing Co., Ltd., reprinted 1985), p.50. Originally written 1647.

[2] Ivy Goldstein-Jacobson, *Simplified Horary Astrology* (Pasadena, CA: Pasadena Press, 1960), p. 91.

[3] Lilly, p. 157.

[4] *Ibid.*, p. 51.

[5] Manilius, *Astronomica*, ed. Loeb, trans. G.P. Goold, (London: William Heinemann, Ltd., and Cambridge, MA: Harvard University Press, reprinted 1977), Book 2.936.

[6] *Ibid.*, Book 2.918, p. 155.

[7] *Ibid.*, Book 2.938, p. 157.

[8] Nicholas Culpeper, *The Astrological Judgment of Diseases from the Decumbiture of the Sick* (Tempe, Ariz.: The American Federation of Astrologers, reprinted 1959.).

[9] Firmicus Maternus, *The Mathesis*, trans. Jean Rhys Bram (Noyes Press, reprinted 1976), p. 50.

[10] Manilius, Book 2.815, p. 147.

[11] Barbara H. Watters, *Horary Astrology and the Judgment of Events* (Washington, DC: Valhalla Press, 1973), p. 15.

[12] John Gadbury, *Collectio Geniturarum* (Printed James Cottrel, 1662; reprinted Balantrae Reprints, Brampton, Ontario), p. 4.

[13] Ptolemy, *Tetrabiblos*, ed. Loeb, trans. F.E. Robbins (London: William Heinemann, Ltd. and Cambridge, MA: Harvard University Press, reprinted 1980), pp. 241, 251.

[14] Lilly, p. 570.

[15] Maternus, pp. 49, 51. Also Al Biruni, *The Book of Instruction in the Elements of the Art of Astrology*, trans. Ramsay Wright (London: Luzac and Co., reprinted 1934), p. 275.

[16] Lilly, p. 558.

[17] *Ibid.*, p. 95.

[18] *Ibid.*, p. 89.

[19] *Ibid.*, p. 603.

[20] *Ibid.*, p. 52.

[21] Culpeper, p. 54. *Astrological Judgment of Diseases from the Decumbiture of the Sick*

[22] Lilly, p. 157. Also Manilius, Book 2.935.

[23] Lilly, p. 53.

[24] *Ibid.*, p. 569.

[25] Manilius, p. 147.

[26] *Ibid.*, Book 2.930-938, p. 157.

[27] *Ibid.*, Book 2.825-830, p. 147.

[28] *Ibid.*, Book 2.938, p. 157.

[29] Neugebauer and van Hoesen, *Greek Horoscopes* (Philadelphia: The American Philosophical Society, 1959), p. 81.

[30] Manilius, Book 2.880-295, p. 158.

[31] Lilly, p. 56.

[32] *Ibid.*, p. 54.

[33] Ptolemy, Book 3.10, p. 273. Loeb edition.

[34] Neugebauer and van Hoesen, p. 83.

[35] *Star Tech*, Vol. 1, No. 3, March 20, 1987, ed. Richard Nolle. With permission.
[36] Manilius, Book 2.920, p. 155.
[37] Maternus, p. 49. Also Manilius, pp. 153-155. Also Lilly, p. 53.
[38] Ptolemy, p. 273. Also Maternus, p. 51. Also Neugebauer and van Hoesen, p. 8.

Chapter 4: The Satellite

[1] William Lilly, *Christian Astrology*, (London: Regulus Publishing Co., Ltd., 1985), p. 154.
[2] *Ibid.*, p. 158.

Chapter 5: Terminology and Aspects

[1] Nicholas de Vore, *Encyclopedia of Astrology* (Littlefield Adams & Co. 1977) p. 5.
[2] William Lilly, *Christian Astrology* (London: Regulus Publishing Co. Ltd., 1985), p. 110.
[3] *Ibid.*, pp. 111, 126.
[4] The finest description of orientality and occidentality is in *Classical Scientific Astrology* by George C. Noonan (Tempe, AZ: American Federation of Astrologers, Inc., 1984), p. 116.
[5] Guido Bonatus, *Anima Astrologiae*, (Washington, DC: American Federation of Astrologers, reprinted 1970). Footnote by Lilly on the 74th Consideration.
[6] *Ibid.*, 74th Consideration.
[7] Al Biruni, *The Book of Instruction in the Elements of the Art of Astrology*, written A.D. 1029. Trans. by R. Ramsay Wright, (United Kingdom: British Museum, 1934), p. 299.
[8] Edward W. Whitman, FFBA, CIA Astro-kinetics, Volume 3 "Aspects and Their Meaning" (London: L.N. Fowler & Co., Ltd., 1970), p. 6.
[9] *Ibid.*, p. 53.

Chapter 6: The Dignities and Evaluations
of the Planets

[1] William Lilly, *Christian Astrology* (London: Regulus Publishing Co., Ltd., reprinted 1985) p. 400.
[2] John Gadbury, *A Collection of Choice Nativities*, or *Collectio Geniturarum* printed James Cottrel, 1658 (available through Balantrae Reprints), p. 1.
[3] Hazrat Iayat Khan, *The Guyan.*
[4] Claudius Ptolemy, *Tetrabiblos*, translated by F.E. Robbins (Loeb edition) (London: William Heinemann, Ltd., and Cambridge, MA: Harvard University Press, reprinted 1980), Book 2.8, p. 189.
[5] Lilly, p. 112.
[6] Al Biruni, *The Book of Instruction in the Elements of the Art of Astrology*, translated by Ramsay Wright (London: Luzac & Co., 1934) paragraph 453.
[7] For the extent of the terms, read *Christian Astrology*, p. 510, and *The Speculum* on p. 509.
[8] Lilly, p. 173.
[9] *Ibid.*, p. 1 of "To The Reader."

Chapter 7: Planetary Hours

[1] William Lilly, *Christian Astrology.* (London: Regulus Publishing Co., Ltd., 1985), p. 298.
[2] Zadkiel, *An Introduction to Astrology by William Lilly.* (Hollywood: Newcastle Publishing Co., Inc., 1972), p. 186.

Chapter 8: Divisions of the Ecliptic

[1] Morin de Villefranche, *Astrosynthesis*, trans. by Lucy Little (Zoltan Mason Emerald Books, 1973), p. 40. Originally titled *The Rational System of Horoscope Interpretation.*
[2] William Lilly, *Christian Astrology* (London: Regulus Publish-

316 Horary Astrology Rediscovered

ing Co., Ltd., 1985), p. 100. Originally published in 1647.

[3] *Ibid.*, p. 154.

[4] *Ibid.*, p. 347.

[5] Nicholas Campion, *The Book of World Horoscopes* (U.K.: The Aquarian Press, 1988).

[6] Lilly, p. 224.

[7] *Ibid.*, p. 48.

[8] *Ibid.*, p. 138.

[9] Manilius, *Astronomica*, ed. Loeb, trans. Goold (London and Cambridge, MA: William Heinemann, Ltd. and Harvard University Press, 1977), p. 149.

[10] Claudius Ptolemy, *Tetrabiblos* IV. 10, ed. Loeb, trans. Robbins (London: William Heinemann, Ltd., and Cambridge, MA: Harvard University Press, reprinted 1980), p. 443.

[11] Lilly, p. 133.

[12] *Ibid.*, p. 347.

[13] For use of the Dodecatamoria see chapter on History, Palchus, in Part 5. Also, Manilius Introduction, p. iii, and Book 2. 700, Loeb edition, p. 137.

[14] Nicholas de Vore, *Encyclopedia of Astrology* (NJ: Littlefield Adams, 1977), obtainable from Balantrae Reprints, Brampton, Ontario. Also Charles Carter, *An Encyclopedia of Psychological Astrology* (Wheaton, IL: Theosophical Publishing House, 1924), last page.

[15] David Anrias, *Man and the Zodiac* (London: George Routledge & Sons Ltd., 1938).

Chapter 9: Cautions and Strictures

[1] Barbara Watters, *Horary Astrology and the Judgment of Events* (Washington, D.C.: Valhalla Paperbacks, Ltd., 1973), p. 15.

Chapter 10: Collection

[1] William Lilly, *Christian Astrology*, (London: Regulus Publish-

ing Co. Ltd., reprinted 1985). pg 401. Originally published 1647.

[2] Barbara H. Watters, *Horary Astrology and the Judgment of Events* (Washington, DC: Valhalla Paperbacks, Ltd., 1973), p. 73.

Chapter 12: Perfecting the Matter

[1] William Lilly, *Christian Astrology*, (London: Regulus Publishing Co. Ltd., reprinted 1985), pp. 23, 444. Originally published 1647.

[2] Guido Bonatus, *Anima Astrologiae*, 18th Consideration (Washington, DC: American Federation of Astrologers, reprinted 1970).

[3] Lilly, p. 112.

[4] *Ibid.*, p. 176.

[5] *Ibid.*, p. 172.

[6] *Ibid.*, p. 125.

Chapter 13: Antiscia

[1] Firmicus Maternus, *The Mathesis*, trans. Jean Rhys Bram (Park Ridge, N.J.: Noyes Press, reprinted 1976), pp. 60-68.

Chapter 14: Fixed Stars

[1] William Lilly, *Christian Astrology* (London: Regulus Publishing Co., Ltd., reprinted 1985), p. 621. Originally published 1647.

[2] Guido Bonatus, *Anima Astrologiae*, trans. Henry Coley, 1675 (Washington, DC: The American Federation of Astrologers, reprinted 1970), 9th Consideration.

[3] Claudius Ptolemy, *Tetrabiblos*, Loeb ed., trans. F.E. Robbins, Ph.D. (London: William Heinemann, Ltd., and Cambridge, MA: Harvard University Press, reprinted 1980), Book 2.7.

[4] *Ibid.*, p. 47.

[5] George C. Noonan, *Fixed Stars and Judicial Astrology*.
[6] Vivian E. Robson, *Fixed Stars and Constellations in Astrology* (York Beach, ME: Samuel Weiser, Inc., 1984), p. 13.
[7] Ebertin Hoffman, *Fixed Stars and their Interpretation*, trans. Irmgard Banks (Tempe, AZ: The American Federation of Astrologers, 1971), p. 11. Note: I use this book.

Chapter 15: The Part of Fortune

[1] Claudius Ptolemy, *Tetrabiblos*, III. 10, trans. F.E. Robbins, ed. Loeb (London and Cambridge, MA: William Heinemann & Co., Ltd. and Harvard University Press, 1980), p. 275.
[2] William Lilly, *Christian Astrology* (London: Regulus Publishing Co., Ltd., 1985) p. 143. Originally published 1647.
[3] Ptolemy, *Tetrabiblos*, Book 4.2, pp. 373, 375.
[4] Lilly, pp. 508, 656.
[5] *Ibid.*, p. 703.
[6] Robert Hurtz Granite, *The Fortunes of Astrology* (San Diego: A.C.S. Publications Inc. 1985), p. 17.
[7] Neugebauer and Van Hoesen, *Greek Horoscopes* (Philadelphia: The American Philosophical Society, 1959), p. 112.
[8] Manilius, *Astronomica*, trans. Goold, ed. Loeb (London: William Heinemann & Co., Ltd., and Cambridge, MA: Harvard University Press, reprinted 1978), Introduction, p. lxiii.
[9] Ivy Goldstein Jacobson, *Simplified Horary Astrology* (Pasadena, CA: Pasadena Press, 1961).
[10] Al Biruni, *The Book of Instruction in the Elements of the Art of Astrology*, A.D. 1029, p. 283.
[11] *Ibid.*, p. 291.

Chapter 16: Regiomontanus and House Systems

[1] J.D. North, *Horoscopes and History* (London: Warburg Institute, 1987), pp. 33, 44.
[2] Nicholas de Vore, *Encyclopedia of Astrology* (Littlefield, Adams and Co., 1977), p. 413. (Obtainable from Balantrae Reprints, Brampton, Ontario)

[3] John Gadbury, *Collectio Geniturarum* (printed by James Cottrel, 1662), p. 176.

[4] North, p. 21.

[5] Nicholas Culpeper, *Astrological Judgment of Diseases from the Decumbiture of the Sick* (Obtainable from Balantrae Reprints, Brampton, Ontario), p. 68. Originally written in 1655.

[6] William Lilly, *Christian Astrology* (London: Regulus Publications Ltd., reprinted 1985), p. 137. Originally written in 1647.

[7] *Ibid.*, p. 197.

[8] Dona Marie Lorenz, *Tools of Astrology* (Topanga, CA: Oemega Press, 1973).

[9] George C. Noonan, *Classical Scientific Astrology* (Tempe, AZ: American Federation of Astrologers, 1984), p. 143.

Chapter 17: Specific Questions

[1] Dennis Elwell, *The Cosmic Loom* (Great Britain: Unwin, 1987). Also, Dr. Theodor Landscheidt in his talk at the "Conference on Astrology and Science," 1987.

Chapter 18: Partnership Questions

[1] William Lilly, *Christian Astrology* (London: Regulus Publishing Co., Ltd., 1985), first published 1647, p. 54.

[2] Zadkiel, *Introduction to Astrology* (London and New York: George Bell, 1893), p. 190.

[3] This is a paraphrase of a rather long quote by Lilly. Those who want more details are advised to read Lilly themselves.

[4] Barbara H. Watters, *Horary Astrology and the Judgment of Events* (Washington, D.C.: Valhalla Paperbacks, Ltd., 1973), p. 15.

Chapter 19: Questions Concerning Things Lost or Mislaid

[1] William Lilly, *Christian Astrology*, (London: Regulus Publishing Co., Ltd., reprinted 1985), p. 154.

[2] *Ibid.*, p. 96.

[3] *Ibid.*, pp. 323-325.

[4] The place where he is can be judged from the significator's sign. In this case, Virgo, indicating south and on the ground or floor. See *Christian Astrology*, p. 154.

[5] Claudius Ptolemy, *Tetrabiblos*, Loeb ed., trans. F.E. Robbins (London: William Heinemann, Ltd., and Cambridge, MA: Harvard University Press, reprinted 1980), p. 309.

[6] Lilly, p. 54.

[7] *Ibid.*, 327.

[8] Lilly, pp. 406, 468.

[9] *Ibid,* pp. 198, 211, 406.

[10] *Ibid.*, pp. 419, 462.

[11] *Ibid.*, p. 349.

[12] *Ibid.*, p. 353.

[13] *Ibid.*, p. 355.

Chapter 20: Miscellaneous Questions

[1] Manilius, *The Astronomica*, trans. G.P. Goold, Loeb ed. (London: William Heinemann, Ltd., and Cambridge, MA: Harvard University Press, reprinted 1977), Book 2.890, p. 147.

[2] This method was shown to me by Derek Appleby.

[3] Ebertin Hoffman, *Fixed Stars and their Interpretation*, trans. Irmgard Banks (Aalen, Germany: Ebertin-Verlag, 1971), p. 43.

[4] Reinhold Ebertin, *Combination of Stellar Influences*, trans. Dr. Alfred G. Roosedale (Aalen, Germany: Ebertin-Verlag, 1969), p. 153.

[5] William Lilly, *Christian Astrology*, (London: Regulus Publishing Co., Ltd., reprinted 1985), p. 151.

[6] *Ibid.*, p. 197.

[7] Lilly, pp. 157, 158.

[8] *Ibid.*, p. 162. See also charts on pp. 162, 165.

[9] *Ibid.*, p. 703.

[10] Hoffman, pp. 32-33, 74.

[11] Lilly, p. 158.

[12] Claudius Ptolemy, *Tetrabiblos*, ed. Loeb, trans. F.E. Robbins (London: William Heinemann, Ltd., and Cambridge, MA: Harvard University Press, reprinted 1980), Book 4.5, p. 397.

[13] Nicholas Culpeper, *Astrological Judgment of Diseases from the Decumbiture of the Sick* (Tempe, AZ: The American Federation of Astrologers, reprinted 1959), p. 6.

Chapter 21: Mundane Astrology

[1] Claudius Ptolemy, *Tetrabiblos*, ed. Loeb, trans. F.E. Robbins (London: William Heinemann, Ltd., and Cambridge, MA: Harvard University Press, reprinted 1980), p. 161.

[2] Charles Carter, *Encyclopedia of Psychological Astrology* (Wheaton, IL: Theosophical Publishing House, 1972), see "Sight," p. 198.

[3] Nicholas de Vore, *Encyclopedia of Astrology* (Totowa, NJ: Littlefield, Adams & Co., 1976), p. 95.

[4] Ivy Goldstein-Jacobson, *Here and There in Astrology* (Pasadena, CA: Pasadena Press, 1964), p. 11.

[5] Reinhold Ebertin, *Combination of Stellar Influences*, trans. Dr. A.G. Roosedale, (Aalen, Germany: Ebertin-Verlag, 1969), pp. 200-210, 196-197.

[6] de Vore, p. 105.

[7] Hoffman, p. 67.

[8] *Ibid.*, p. 19.

[9] William Lilly, *Christian Astrology* (London: Regulus Publishing Co., Ltd., reprinted 1985), p. 703.

[10] de Vore, p. 105.

Chapter 22: Eclipses and Syzygys

[1] Claudius Ptolemy, *Tetrabiblos*, trans. Robbins, ed. Loeb, (London and Cambridge, MA: William Heinemann, Ltd., and Harvard University Press, reprinted 1980), p. 161.

[2] William Lilly, *Christian Astrology* (London: Regulus Publishing Co., Ltd., reprinted 1985), p. 50.

[3] Robert Carl Jansky, *Interpreting the Eclipses* (San Diego, CA: ACS Publications, Inc., 1979).
[4] Ptolemy, Book 3.7, p. 261.

Chapter 23: Egypt

[1] Cyril Fagan, *Zodiacs Old and New* (London: Robert Anscombe and Co., Ltd., 1951). Much of Fagan's work has been discredited because it was based on a misreading of cuneiform by the archaeologist Schnabel. Fagan also believed we should use a sidereal zodiac, but that should not detract from some of his other historical research, none of us is right all the time.
[2] Sir Norman Lockyer, *The Dawn of Astronomy*
[3] John Michell, *Astro-archaeology* (Thames and Hudson, 1977), p. 28.
[4] *Ibid.*
[5] John Michell, *View Over Atlantis* (Garnstone Press, 1969). Also, Alfred Watkins, *The Old Straight Track* (London: Methmen & Co., Ltd., 1925).
[6] Neugebauer and van Hoesen, *Greek Horoscopes* (Philadelphia, PA: American Philosophical Society, 1959), No.L.80, p. 92.
[7] Fagan, p. 21

Chapter 24: Early Astrologers

[1] Manilius, *Astronomica*, ed. Loeb, trans. G.P. Goold (London: William Heinemann, Ltd., and Cambridge, MA: Harvard University Press, reprinted 1977), Book 1.204, p. 21.
[2] *Ibid.*, Book 1.235, p. 23.
[3] *Ibid.*, Book 1.265, p. 25.
[4] *Ibid.*, Book 1.485, p. 45.
[5] *Ibid.*, pp. 87-88.
[6] *Ibid.*, pp. 147-158.
[7] *Ibid.*, p. 95.
[8] *Ibid.*, pp. 151, 153, 157, 159.
[9] Neugebauer and van Hoesen, *Greek Horoscopes*, (Philadel-

phia: American Philosophical Society, 1959). p. 112.

[10] Claudius Ptolemy, *Tetrabiblos*, ed. Loeb, trans. F.E. Robbins (London: William Heinemann, Ltd., and Cambridge, MA: Harvard University Press, reprinted 1980), Book 3, Introduction, p. xv.

[11] George C. Noonan, *Classical Scientific Astrology* (Tempe, AZ: American Federation of Astrologers, 1984). This book is a brilliant account of classical astrology written almost from the viewpoint of Ptolemy himself.

[12] Ptolemy, p. 273.

[13] Neugebauer and van Hoesen, p. 144.

[14] William Lilly, *Christian Astrology*, (London: Regulus Publishing Co., Ltd., reprinted 1985), p. 165.

[15] Abraham Ibn Ezra, whom I mentioned in the chapter on Regio Montanus' house system, had a synagogue named after him. It is the oldest synagogue in the city of Cairo. A heavy tax had been imposed and the Jews were afraid they would have to close the synagogue, but Abraham Ibn Ezra paid their tax and saved them. He was married there.

[16] Abu'l Muhammad Ibn Ahmad al Biruni, *The Book of Instruction in the Elements of the Art of Astrology*, trans. Ramsay Wright (London: Luzac and Co., reprinted 1934), p. 1. Originally written 1029.

[17] Bonatus Guido, *Anima Astrologiae*, ed. William Lilly, 1675 (Washington, DC: American Federation of Astrologers, reprinted 1970). Address by Lilly to the Ingenious Lovers of Art.

[18] *Ibid.*, 1st Consideration, p. 1.

[19] *Ibid.*, Introduction, p. iii.

[20] Data for Coronation from the Astrological Lodge of London History Seminar, 1985.

[21] Bonatus, 141st Consideration, p. 49.

[22] Lilly, p. 621.

[23] John Gadbury, *Collectio Geniturarum*, printed by James Cottrel, 1661, p. 14. (Obtainable from Balantrae Reprints, Brampton, Ontario)

[24] Nicholas Culpeper, *The English Physician Enlarged*, printed

by Peter Cole, 1653, "To the Reader", p. 1.

I know well enough the whole world, and everything in it, was formed of a Composition of contrary Elements, and in such a Harmony as must needs show the wisdom and Power of a great God; I know as well, this Creation, though thus composed of contraries, was one united Body, and Man Epitome of it; I knew those various affections in Man in respect of Sickness and Health were caused Naturally (though God may have other ends best known to himself) by the various operations of the Microcosm; that as the Cause is, so must the Cure be; and therefore he that would know the Reason of the operation of Herbs, must look up as high as the Stars; I alwaies found the Disease vary according to the various motions of the Stars; and this is enough one would think to teach a man by the Effect where the Cause lay....

The Admirable Harmony of the Creation is herein seen, as the influence of Stars upon Herbs, and the Body of Man, how one part of the Creation is subservient to another, and all for the use of Man, whereby the infinite Power and wisdom of God in the Creation appears....

God hath stamped his Image upon every Creature, and therefore the abuse of the Creature is a great sin, but how much more doth the Wisdom and Excellency of God appear if we consider the Harmony of the Creation in the Vertue and Operation of every Herb.

[25] *Ibid.*, p. 396.
[26] *Ibid.*, p. 398.
[27] Lilly, p. 256.
[28] Derek Parker *Familiar to All*, (London: Jonathan Cape, 1975), p. 119.

[29] Jane Lawrence, an incredible clairvoyant. I would like to mention here that I never mix information received from a clairvoyant with information derived from astrology. Nor have I ever consulted a clairvoyant for help with a horary question. Jane Lawrence saw my original 1647 edition of *Christian Astrology* and told me about William Lilly. I asked him, "How many planets are there?" and he said, "Five, and two are different." (e.g., the Luminaries). It's just what he would have said!

[30] *Ibid.*

[31] *Ibid.*

[32] Lilly, first page (unnumbered) after the Index.

[33] Ken Negus, *Kepler's Astrology Excerpts* (Princeton, NJ: Eucopia, 1988), p. 7. This is a quotation from Fred Gettings *Book of the Zodiac* (London: London Tribute Press, 1971), p. 115.

[34] *Transit Magazine*. August 1983 (published by The Astrological Association of Great Britain).

Chapter 25: The Houses in History-A Summary

[1] Manilius, *Astronomica*, trans. G.P. Goold (Cambridge, MA and London: Harvard University Press and William Heinemann, reprinted 1977), p. 151.

[2] Nicholas Culpeper, *Astrological Judgment of Disease from the Decumbiture of the Sick* (Tempe, AZ: American Federation of Astrologers, reprinted 1959), p. 54.

[3] William Lilly, *Christian Astrology* (London: Regulus Publishing Co., Ltd.), p. 606.

[4] Claudius Ptolemy, *Tetrabiblos*, trans. F.E. Robbins (Cambridge, MA: Harvard University Press, and London: William Heinemann, reprinted 1980) Book 3.10, p. 273.

[5] Manilius, Book 2.810, p. 147.

[6] *Ibid.*, p. 155.

[7] Lilly, p. 57. Also Culpeper, p. 47.

[8] Manilius, p. 157.

[9] Lilly, p. 51.

[10] Firmicus Maternus, *The Mathesis*, trans. by Jean Rhys Bram, (Park Ridge, NJ: Noyes Press, reprinted 1975). p. 49.
[11] Manilius, p. 157. Introduction lix.
[12] Ptolemy, p. 273.
[13] Culpeper, p. 47.
[14] Ptolemy, p. 273.
[15] Lilly, p. 54.
[16] Manilius, p. 155.
[17] Ptolemy, p. 273.
[18] Culpeper, p. 47.
[19] Barbara H. Watters, *Horary Astrology and the Judgment of Events* (Washington, DC: Valhalla Press, 1973), p. 65.
[20] Manilius, p. 153.
[21] Lilly, p. 56.
[22] *Ibid.*, p. 52.
[23] Ptolemy, p. 241.
[24] Manilius, p. 157.
[25] *Ibid.*, p. 147.
[26] Firmicus, pp. 49-51.
[27] Manilius, p. 157.
[28] Ptolemy, p. 273.
[29] Lilly, p. 53.
[30] Culpeper, p. 47. Also Lilly, p. 53.
[31] Lilly, p. 53.
[32] Firmicus, p. 49.
[33] Manilius, p. 155.
[34] Lilly, p. 55.
[35] Ptolemy, p. 273.
[36] Firmicus, pp. 49-51.
[37] Manilius, pp. Introduction lviii., 151.
[38] Lilly, p. 51.
[39] Firmicus, p. 49.
[40] Culpeper, p. 47.
[41] Manilius, p. 151.
[42] Ptolemy, p. 273.
[43] Firmicus, p. 49.
[44] Manilius, p. 153.

[45] Lilly, p. 54.
[46] Culpeper, p. 47. Also Lilly, p. 54.
[47] Ptolemy, p. 273.
[48] Manilius, p. 153.
[49] Manilius, p. 153.
[50] Lilly, p. 53.
[51] Ptolemy, p. 273.
[52] Manilius, p. 151.
[53] Lilly, p. 56.
[54] Manilius, p. 159.

Glossary

AIR SIGNS--Gemini, Libra, Aquarius.

ALGOL--A Fixed Star in the constellation Perseus that affects the throat of humans. It is sometimes called Medusa's Head.

ANGLE--The Midheaven, Ascendant, and their opposite points on a chart. The houses that commence at those points, the tenth, first, fourth, or seventh are angular, and planets posited in those houses are angular planets.

ANTISCIA--Called solstice points in America. A line is drawn from 0° Cancer to 0° Capricorn and planets are reflected across that line to the degree corresponding on the other side.

APPLYING ASPECT--The faster planet approaches the slower.

ASCENDANT--The eastern horizon, and the cusp of the first house which commences there.

ASPECTS--Fractional divisions of the circle measured between planets.

ASTROLOGY--The comparison of events on Earth with the position of heavenly bodies.

BENEFICS--Helpful planets. Jupiter and Venus naturally.

BESIEGED--A planet bound on either side by an unhelpful planet, limiting its scope.

CADENT--A house farthest from an angle.

CARDINAL SIGNS--Aries, Libra, Cancer and Capricorn.

CAZIMI--Planets within 17 minutes of the center of the Sun.

CHALDEAN ORDER-- Saturn, Jupiter, Mars, Sun, Venus, Mercury, Moon.

CIRCLE OF ATHLA--An antique technique counting the houses every 30 degrees starting from Fortuna.

COLLECTION--When two planets that do not aspect one another do both aspect a slower planet, who collects their light and brings the matter to perfection. The collecting planet should best be received by the faster in some one of their dignities.

COMBUST--A planet within 8 degrees of the Sun, and in the same sign.

CONJUNCTION--The joining of the two planets.

CONSTELLATIONS--The many groupings of fixed stars, twelve of which lie along the Ecliptic, the path of the Sun, and are called zodiacal signs.

CONTRA ANTISCIA--The degree opposite the antiscia.

CUSP--The division between one house and another. Yet a planet within 5 degrees of a house cusp is in the following house.

DAY--In previous centuries a day started at dawn.

DEBILITY--A weakly placed planet.

DECANATE--A 10-degree subdivision of a sign, into signs of the same triplicity, as Aries divided into Aries, Leo, and Sagittarius, or Leo divided into Leo, Sagittarius, and Aries. (The sign being subdivided rules the first 10 degrees). This emphasis on signs seems to be of Indian origin.

DECLINATION--Distance north or south from the Celestial Equator.

DECUMBITURE--The moment in an illness when the patient takes to his or her bed. This is an Event.

DEGREE--The circle is divided into 360 degrees, thirty to each sign.

DETRIMENT--A planet weakly placed in a particular sign.

DEXTER--A planet applied to by a faster planet that is further forward in the direction of the flow of the signs.

DIGNITIES--*Essential dignities* are those positions of planets in signs in which they are always strong, and which belong to them. Ptolemy left us a Table showing such positions. As well as planets ruling the whole sign, there are sub-divisions of signs belonging to planets in various ways such as exaltation, triplicity, term, and face. *Accidental dignities* are planets in positions of strength in individual charts, as for instance, a planet angular, or conjunct a benefic.

DISPOSITOR--A planet in a section of the zodiac in which it has essential dignity then disposits any other planet in that section, like a landlord and tenant.

DODECATAMORIA--A division of a sign into twelve sections of 2 1/2 degrees each, representing the twelve signs of the zodiac and starting with the sign being divided.

EARTH SIGNS--Taurus, Virgo, Capricorn.

ECLIPTIC--Path of the Sun.

ELEMENT--Earth, Air, Fire, Water.

EPHEMERIS--Almanac listing planetary positions.

EXALTATION--An Essential Dignity--a particular sign position in which a planet functions well, as Jupiter in Cancer, Venus in Pisces. This shows someone who holds himself or herself in esteem.

FACE--A position of weak dignity. The signs are subdivided into sections of 10 degrees ruled by planets. Lilly uses the word as if synonymous with decanates, but we now associate decanates with sub-rulership by signs, and faces with sub-rulership by planets.

FIRE SIGNS--Aries, Leo, Sagittarius.

FIXED SIGNS--Taurus, Leo, Scorpio, and Aquarius.

FIXED STARS--Stars beyond our solar system.

FORTUNA--The Part of Fortune. The place where your fortune is. The place of the Moon is to the Sun the same as the place of Fortuna to the Ascendant in a daytime chart, and the place of the Sun is to the Moon the same as the place of Fortuna to the Ascendant in a nighttime chart.

FORTUNES--Jupiter and Venus.

FRUSTRATION--One planet speeds towards a second, but before the conjunction is accomplished the second planet joins with another, and the matter cannot be accomplished.

HELIACAL--Near the Sun. When a planet is too near the Sun it is obscured, but reappears later, at dawn or sunset.

HERMES--Mercury. Hermes Trismegistos, the Egyptian Thoth, who wrote philosophically and religiously in the ancient world.

HORARY--Of the hour.

HOROSCOPE--The eastern horizon, the Ascendant.

HOURS--Daylight divided into twelve sections of equal length, each ruled by a planet. Also nighttime divided into twelve sections of equal length, each ruled by a planet.

HOUSES--12 sections of the sky that do not rotate. A division tabled by Regiomontanus is effective in horary astrology.

HYLEG--Giver of Life. The strongest planet, from which duration of life was judged in antique nativities.

HYLEGICAL PLACES--The principle places in a chart such as the M.C. Ascendant, the luminaries, and Fortuna.

INCONJUNCT--Planets in signs semi-sextile or quincunx were not considered to be in aspect.

INTERPRETATION--Astrological meaning of a planetary configuration.

JOY--House positions of planets which are their joy the place in which they can function best, as Mercury in the first. There are also signs in which planets work best, as Saturn in Aquarius.

LATITUDE--Celestial latitude is the distance north or south of the Ecliptic, (which is measured in celestial longitude).

LIGHT OF TIME--"Sun by day and in the morning twilight. The Moon by night when she is above the Earth and in her morning rising, so that sometimes there may be two Lights of Time and sometimes it so happens there is none." (Cardan)

LIGHTER PLANETS--Faster-moving planets.

LONGITUDE--Celestial longitude is measured along the Ecliptic.

LUMINARIES--Sun and Moon.

MALEFIC--Mars and Saturn. South Node.

MIDPOINT--A degree exactly between two others.

MINUTE--A unit of measurement. There are sixty minutes in a degree.

MUTUAL RECEPTION--Planets in each others' essential dignities can exchange places and are thereby offered a way out of difficulties. They exchange degree as well as sign.

MUTABLE SIGNS--Gemini, Virgo, Sagittarius, Pisces. These signs were considered to have a dual quality.

NODES--The places where the Moon or planets intersect the Ecliptic. We more usually refer to the Nodes of the Moon. Both north and south, and any planet in the same degree as the Moon's mean Node seems to be unfortunate.

OCCIDENTAL AND ORIENTAL--A planet is oriental of the Sun when it rises and sets before the Sun. It is occidental of the Sun when it rises and sets after the Sun. A planet is placed in oriental houses on the eastern side of the chart, and occidental on the west, but this latter definition has varied and some authorities say the quadrant above the Ascendant and below the Descendant are oriental.

ORB--A halo around a planet in which it is effective. Half an orb is a planet's moiety. Thus, although Ptolemy gave the luminaries orbs of 12 to 15 degrees the moiety is similar to allowances given today.

PARTILE--An exact aspect.

PEREGRINE--A planet having no essential dignity, (see Ptolemy's Table of Essential Dignities) and not in mutual reception, (for then it would exchange back into its dignity).

PERFECTION--When two planets come to a perfect aspect, then the matter desired occurs.

PLANETS--For the purpose of horary judgment we include the luminaries and planets within our solar system. The planets rule, both signs and houses. In horary the planets become symbols for the people or things asked about.

PLATICK--An inexact aspect.

PROHIBITION--One planet approaches a second, but before it can conjunct, another faster planet overtakes it and prevents the hoped-for perfection.

QUADRANT--The chart is divided into four quarters by the cusps of the four angular houses.

QUERENT--Whoever asks the question.

QUESITED--Whoever or whatever is asked about in a question.

RECEPTION--A planet disposited by another, by any essential dignity. But when two planets are in each others' essential dignity that is mutual reception. This may be by sign, exaltation, triplicity, term, or face.

RETROGRADE--The apparent backward movement of a planet which infers that an object or person will return, that there is delay, or when the Moon aspects a retrograde planet that the matter will happen suddenly. It can also denote detriment.

REFRANATION--An aspect that never completes, as for instance, a planet may approach another but turn retrograde before the aspect is perfected.

SEPARATION--Two planets separating from an aspect, even by six minutes.

SIGNIFICATOR--"Symbol of."

SINISTER--Aspects made forward in the same order as the signs, as from Aries to Leo.

SOLSTICE--Midsummer or 0° Cancer, and midwinter when the Sun is at 0° Capricorn.

STARS, OR FIXED STARS--In horary we consider only the most prominent, about forty.

STATIONARY--A planet changing from forward movement to

retrograde and vice versa is stationary, or at its station. This can deepen its effect. Planets from forward to retrograde greatly slow down matters, but those turning again forward are like a cat waiting to pounce.

SUCCEDENT--Houses in the middle section of a quadrant, following from angular. These houses provide the resources of the angular houses.

SWIFT--The Moon or planets travelling at more than their average speed.

SYZYGY--A configuration of the luminaries as eclipses, full Moons, new Moons.

TERMS--Subsections of a sign allocated to a particular planet.

TRANSLATION OF LIGHT--Two planets may not be in aspect, and perfection may not be achieved between them, except that a faster planet moves between them, translating the light from the more backward planet to the more forward one and thereby achieving a desired result. The translating planet should be received by the planet from which it translates.

UNDER THE SUN-BEAMS--Within 17 degrees of the Sun. A weak disability.

VIA COMBUSTA-- 15° ♎ to 15 ° ♏. The Moon here renders the chart unreadable--a precarious area.

VOID OF COURSE--The Moon or any planet making no aspect before it leaves the sign it is in. In interpretation the Moon so placed shows there is nothing that can be done.

WATER SIGNS--Cancer, Scorpio, Pisces.

ZODIAC--The 12 sections of sky that comprise the Ecliptic.

Bibliography

Al Biruni, Abu'l Rayhan Muhammed Ibn. *The Book of Instruction in the Elements of the Art of Astrology*, trans. R. Ramsay Wright. M.A. Edin. L.L.D. Toronto and Edin. Luzac and Co. London 1934

Anrias, D. *Man and the Zodiac*, George Routledge & Sons Ltd. London E.C. 1938.

Appleby, Derek. *Eclipses. The Powerpoints of Astrology*. Thorsons, Wellingborough. U.K. Aquarian Press. 1989.

Bonatus, Guido. *Anima Astrologiae*, ed. William Lilly. Trans. Henry Coley 1675. The American Federation of Astrologers, Washington, DC. 1970.

Campion, Nicholas. *An Introduction to the History of Astrology*, Institute for the Study of Cycles in World Affairs. London 1982.

The Book of World Horoscopes, The Aquarian Press. 1988.

Capp, Bernard. *Astrology and the Popular Press*, Faber &

Faber. London and Boston. 1979.

Carter, Charles. *Encyclopedia of Psychological Astrology*, The Theosophical Publishing House, London. 1972.

Introduction to Political Astrology, The Theosophical Publishing House, London. 1951.

Astrology of Accidents, The Theosophical Publishing House, London. 1977.

Coley, Henry. *Clavis Astrologiae Elimata*, or *A Key to the Whole Art of Astrology*, foreword by William Lilly 1676. Reprinted by Balantrae Reprints, Canada. 1988.

Carelli, Adriano. *The 360 Degrees of the Zodiac*. The American Federation of Astrologers, Arizona. 1977.

Culpeper, Nicholas. *The Astrological Judgment of Diseases from the Decumbiture of the Sick*, The American Federation of Astrologers, Arizona. 1959.

The English Physician Enlarged. Printed by Peter Cole. 1653.

Ebertin, Reinhold. *The Combination of Stellar Influences*, trans. Dr. Alfred G. Roosedale, Ebertin Verlag, Germany. 1969.

Directions, Co-Determinants of Fate, trans. Linda Kratzsch. Ebertin Verlag, Germany. 1976.

Ebertin-Hoffmann. *Fixed Stars and their Interpretation*, trans. Irmgard Banks, Australia. Ebertin Verlag. 1971. The American Federation of Astrologers Inc.

Elwell, Dennis. *The Cosmic Loom*, Unwin Hyman. London. Sydney. 1987.

Fagan, Cyril. *Zodiacs Old and New*. Robert Anscombe and Co., Ltd., London. 1951.

Firmicus Maternus, Julius. *The Mathesis*, trans. Jean Rhys Bram, Noyes Press, New Jersey. 1976.

Gauquelin, Michel. *Cosmic Clocks*. Peter Owen, London. 1969.

The Spheres of Destiny J.M. Dent and Sons Ltd., London, Melbourne and Toronto. 1980.

Gadbury, John. *The Doctrine of Nativities*. 1658.

Collectio Genitorarum. Printed by James Cottrel. 1662.

The Life of Charles I. Printed by James Cottrel. 1659.

Garin, Eugenio. *Astrology of the Renaissance*, trans. Carolyn Jackson and June Allen. Translation revised in conjunction with the author by Clare Robertson. Routledge and Kegan Paul. London, Boston, and Melbourne. 1983.

Gleadow, Rupert. *Astrology and Everyday Life*. Jonathan Cape, London. 1940.

Origins of the Zodiac. Jonathan Cape, London. 1968.

Goldstein-Jacobson, Ivy. *Simplified Horary Astrology*. Pasadena Press, California. 1961.

Goldstein-Jacobsen, Ivy. *Here and There in Astrology*. Pasadena Press, California. 1961.

Granite, Robert Hurtz. *The Fortunes of Astrology*. Astro-Computing Service Publications, San Diego.

Hermes Trismegistos. *Hermetica*. Edited with English translation and notes by Walter Scott. Volume 1. Shambala Publications Inc., Boston. 1985.

Jansky, Robert Carl. *Interpreting the Eclipses.* Astro-Computing Services. 1977.

Jones, Marc Edmund. *Horary Astrology.* Shambala Publications, Berkeley, Calif. and London. 1975.

Kepler, Johann. *Concerning the More Certain Fundamentals of Astrology.* 1602. Clancy Publications, New York. 1942.

Kollerstrom, Nicholas M.A. Cantab. *Astrochemistry, A Study of Metal Planet Affinities.* Emergency Press Chiswick, London. 1984. Shortly to be republished by Element Books.

Lilly, William. *Christian Astrology,* 1647. Republished by Regulus Publishing, London. 1985.

Lindsay, Jack. *Origins of Astrology* Frederick Muller Ltd., London. 1971.

Lorenz, Donna Maria. *Tools of Astrology.* Omega Press, Topanga, California. 1973

de Luce, Robert. *Horary Astrology* Llewellyn Publications, Los Angeles. 1942.

Manilius. *Astronomica,* trans. G.P. Goold William Heinemann Ltd., London and Harvard Univ. Press, Massachusetts for Loeb Classical Library. 1977.

Michell, John. *Astro-archaeology.* Thames and Hudson. 1977.

Morin de Villefranche. *Astrosynthesis,* trans. Lucy Little. Zoltan Mason Emerald Books, New York. 1973.

Neugebauer and van Hoesen. *Greek Horoscopes*. The American Philosophical Society Independence Square, Philadelphia. 1959.

Noonan, George C. *Classical Scientific Astrology*. American Federation of Astrologers, AZ. 1984.

North, J.D. *Horoscopes and History*. The Warburg Institute, Univ. of London, 1986.

Parker, Derek. *Familiar to All*. Jonathan Cape, London. 1975.

Ptolemy, Claudius. *Tetrabiblos*, trans. F. E. Robbins Ph.D. University of Michigan, William Heinemann Ltd., London and Harvard University Press, Cambridge, MA, for Loeb Classical Library. 1980.

de Vore, Nicholas. *Encyclopedia of Astrology*, Littlefield Adams and Co. by arrangement with the Philosophical Library Inc. 1977.

Watters, Barbara. *Horary Astrology and the Judgment of Events*. Valhalla Paperbacks Ltd., Washington, D.C. 1973.

Wharton, Geo. *Gesta Britannorum*. Collections of the Works of Sir George Wharton, Baronet. London. 1657. 2nd edition with preface by John Gadbury. 1682.

Whitman, Edward W. F.F.B.A., C.I.A., *Astro-Kinetics*. L.N. Fowler & Co. Ltd., London. 1970.

Wigglesworth, Harold. *Astrology of Towns and Cities*. Astrological Association of Great Britain. 1973.

(Unknown) *The Desatir or Sacred Writings of Ancient Persian Prophets* with Commentary translated by Mulla Firuz Bin Kaus. Courier Press Bombay. 1818. Photographic copy of the 1888 Edition Wizards Bookshop Savage. Minnesota.

Index